complimants of

*f*P

BEING *S*INGLE
IN A COUPLES' WORLD

HOW TO BE
HAPPILY SINGLE
WHILE LOOKING
FOR LOVE

XAVIER AMADOR

◄o►

JUDITH KIERSKY

THE FREE PRESS
New York   London   Toronto   Sydney   Singapore

THE FREE PRESS
A Division of Simon & Schuster Inc.
1230 Avenue of the Americas
New York, NY 10020

THE FREE PRESS and colophon are trademarks
of Simon & Schuster Inc.

Designed by Jenny Dossin

Manufactured in the United States of America

10   9   8   7   6   5   4   3   2   1

Library of Congress Cataloging-in-Publication Data

Amador, Xavier Francisco.
    Being single in a couples' world : how to be happily single while looking for
love / Xavier Amador, Judith Kiersky.
      p.   cm.
    ISBN 0-684-84349-8 (hc)
    1. Single people—United States—Psychology. 2. Single people—United
States—Attitudes. 3. Interpersonal relations—United States. I. Kiersky, Judith. II. Title.
HQ800.4.U6A63   1998
646.7'0086'52—dc21   97-44090
                                                                 CIP

ISBN 0-684-84349-8

Page 61: "Better Days" by Bruce Springsteen. Copyright © by Bruce Springsteen.
Reprinted by Permission.

Pages 62, 63: By James Henke from *Rolling Stone*, August 6, 1992. By Straight Ar-
row Publishers, Inc. 1992. All Rights Reserved. Reprinted by Permission.

To Susan Arellano, with gratitude

Contents

Preface by Dr. Amador   ix
Preface by Dr. Kiersky   xiii

BEING SINGLE

1. It's a Couples' World   3
2. Being Single Today   12
3. Where Do You Fit In?   26
4. Taking Charge   45

WHY ARE YOU SINGLE?

5. Stuck on the Ideal   69
6. The Grass Is Always Greener   89
7. Afraid to Make the Wrong Choice   107
8. Hasn't Left Home Yet   121
9. Never Goes All the Way   145

HOLDING YOUR OWN IN A COUPLES' WORLD

10. Avoiding Friendly Fire   165
11. Competition Among Friends   182
12. Feeling Invisible   201

Afterword   223

Preface

by Dr. Amador

◄o►

The idea to write this book came to me during a time in my life when I was single. I have to admit that for a couple of years I was very unhappy about being single. I was in my early thirties and never married. I felt like a failure. I felt out of place with my married friends and relatives and increasingly worried, with each disappointing blind date, that I would "end up all alone." Sometimes, I was certain that the problem lay with the women I was meeting. But most of the time I thought something must be wrong with me. I felt abnormal.

Despite feeling this way, I knew for a fact that I was not unique. Most of the single people I knew had been plagued by similar doubts and feelings of alienation at one time or another. No, I was not so unusual. This point was driven home in my experience conducting psychotherapy with single patients who had many of the same feelings, often in spades. I started a journey of personal discovery back then and I must admit that I learned much from my patients that I could apply to my own life. I hope that my honesty is reassuring to you rather than unsettling. Like a cardiologist who is vulnerable to the same heart disease that his patients suffer, I learned from my patients' success how best to preserve my own happiness.

By the end of this period of self-examination, I had learned why I was unhappy, the truth about why I was single, and in the process I became much happier and more open to love. It was at this point that the idea to write *Being Single in a Couples' World* first came to me.

Excited by the prospect of writing a book for and about single people, I bounced the idea off several friends. But to my surprise, I got two very different types of responses. For example, one friend responded, "But there's a million books about single people. Hasn't it all been done before?" She was referring to the overabundance of books that focus on telling single people what they're doing wrong in an effort to help them "cure" themselves of being single. These books are not about being single. They are about getting married. The books my friend was referring to actually worsen the same problems I planned to help solve in my book because they focus on marriage as the only means by which you can feel better about yourself. In doing so, they help to make the experience of being single an unhappy one and promote marriage for all the wrong reasons. Another friend, who is also a psychotherapist, understood my idea immediately, saying, "I know so many people who will feel relieved just to know that one other person understands how it feels to be single and living in a world of couples!" That friend is my coauthor, Judith Kiersky.

Although it's true that *Being Single in a Couples' World* will help in your quest to find a partner in life, it is at its core a book about being single. Whether it's for a month, a year, or decades, being single can be a wonderful and fulfilling time in your life. But only if you understand and counter the forces at work that can make you feel bad about it. I know I can speak for Judith too when I say that this book was a labor of love. Too often, we have seen people feel bad about themselves, pessimistic about their prospects for love, and out of step with the culture because they didn't really understand the reason they were single. To make the problem worse, they were subscribing to outdated notions about what it means to be a single man or woman today. In this book, you will learn that you are in very good company. Whether you have never before been married, or find yourself single again after a divorce or death of a spouse, you are not alone. And, more important, you are not abnormal! But more than likely, you have never questioned some ideas you have held your entire life that are now causing you to feel bad about being single. Being clear about why you are single and more at peace with who you are will not only make you happier, but also more open to love. Our message is one of hope, not resignation.

There are many people whom I want to thank for their help with the researching and writing of this book. I interviewed over forty single people over the past two years who gave not only of their time, but also of their hearts. Without their stories this book could not have been written. My patients whose courage to be curious about themselves, to question beliefs they have held for a lifetime, also provided much of the material for many of the stories in this book. Their willingness to take risks in order to better themselves is a constant source of inspiration. Thus, you will read about many of the people I have worked with in therapy over the past fifteen years; the names have been changed and the stories altered to protect their privacy. You will learn much from them that you can use in your own life.

I wanted to write this book with Judith because she knows the territory from both a professional and a personal perspective. She is as passionate about addressing the problems that single people face as I am. Over the course of our friendship she has taught me much about myself for which I am very grateful. We had several debates while writing this book, not the least of which was what the title should be. In fact, there were so many different discussions of what this book should be called that we could have written a second book on the interpersonal dynamics between coauthors and their editor, publisher, friends, and family. Everyone had an opinion. We didn't know the answer until the book was nearly finished. Our collaboration has worked in exactly that way. I want to thank her for her perseverance, empathy, and insights.

Several people commented on earlier versions of the manuscript and provided other kinds of feedback. I want to especially thank Christine Leonhardt, Hilda Speicher, Annette Zygmunt, Paul Rudin, Regine Seckinger, Ivan Amodt, Michelle Friedman, Gail Friedman, Jody Williams, and Raina Korman and her friends Jenny, Dylan, Sara, and Julia. Their insights and challenges made this a much better book than it would have been otherwise. Special thanks to Diane Demarfino for her friendship and faith in my ability to "say something smart." And to Scott Yale for making me laugh and for our daily "bouts." I am proud to have him as a colleague and lucky to have him as a friend.

Others have provided moral support and help during the time this book was being researched and written. Katie Amador, Carmen Chenal, and, of course, Robert, Suli, Christina, Michael, and Grace. Thanks again to my mother, Maria Cristina—your willingness to change and to open your heart is truly inspiring.

Thanks to Lew Korman for his guidance and faith in me and to Sharon Korman for her enthusiasm and warmth. I want to take this opportunity not only to thank Bubie (a.k.a. Sylvia Weiss), but also to let her know that I am *her* biggest fan. Thanks to my new family for making me feel so welcome and loved.

Thanks to Jim, Yvette, Gary, Harriet, Michael, Impy, Bob, and Shirley for making me dinner, being supportive in other ways, and being the kind of neighbors that help to make our neighborhood a home.

Susan Arellano, our editor, understood the purpose of this book and fought hard for it. Her enthusiasm kept me going during periods when my own resolve wavered. She is an exceptional editor who, once again, understood what it was I wanted to say—sometimes better than I did—and helped me to say it. Many thanks.

Finally, I want to thank Stacie. She has blessed my life in so many ways. Her sense of self is astounding and that is what first attracted me to her, although Pancho, Luke, and Sophie played a critical role. When we met I was just beginning to work on this book. I was very content being single. I was at peace with myself. So was she. But she had a vision of the two of us together and more courage than I did when it came to love. I am grateful for her courage and for my heart being open to it. I have never before felt so loved and supported as I have with her. She is a beautiful, intelligent, passionate woman. I am a very lucky man.

Preface

by Dr. Kiersky

-◄◦►-

T he urgency for me to write this book arose during an especially poignant moment in a psychotherapy session with a lovely, bright, and accomplished young single woman named Suzanna.* Suzanna was from a large family with several brothers and sisters, most of whom were married with children. Although they were all close, it was clear that Suzanna was her mother's, and even her father's, favorite. In the last year, the family had been coping with the impact of their mother's newly diagnosed heart trouble. It was a congenital problem that was being well-managed by an excellent team of specialists. One particularly bleak and wintry evening, Suzanna and I sat together trying to understand her current distress, despite her seemingly charmed life. She had just taken her "dream job," moved to a beautiful new apartment, and successfully put on a major fundraiser for her favorite charity. Although she was not in a relationship, there were a couple of "prospects" on the horizon. But Suzanna was nearly despondent. She seemed tortured by one lone concern that she explained this way.

"If I thought I'd never get married, I couldn't go on." With that, she began to cry, softly at first and then inconsolably. I listened to her pain and wondered how this wonderful young woman could reach such depths of despair. Her next statement made it all too clear.

"You know, I am sure that I am killing my mother with all this."

"With all what?" I asked.

"If I don't get married before she dies, it will be my fault."

"What will be your fault?"

"That's all she wants, and I can't seem to give it to her. My whole

---

*Name and details have been changed for confidentiality purposes.

family says the same thing, that I'm killing her because I'm not married. If she dies, it will be my fault. And I agree."

I was stunned. And then I was outraged. How could such a good and thoughtful human being—productive, loving, and giving—be tormented by this one uncontrollable fact of her existence? How could a family of intelligent and sophisticated people justify placing this burden on their favorite family member? None of it made sense. I think it was at that moment that I became convinced that this book had to be written. And if it ultimately has a positive effect on just one or two single people, that is, if it reduces in some small measure the pain of being single in a couples' world, not only for single persons but also for their loved ones, then we will have done our job.

If it is not clear already, this book was written for the millions of single men and women who struggle everyday not to feel alone, stigmatized and afraid, just because they are single—in short, not to feel the way Suzanna did. As part of that group for much of my adult life, my interest in writing this book is naturally very personal. In addition, as a psychotherapist who experiences on a daily basis the joys and anguish of the many single clients I have come to know so well, I feel that this book is of great professional importance to me. And as a longtime friend to my coauthor, who has been at my side while we battled many of the same demons of singlehood, I believe this book represents the restorative power of caring connections. In a way, *Being Single in a Couples' World* is the synthesis of these three perspectives: the personal, the professional, and the close friend or compatriot.

From a personal standpoint, being a single woman living in a world of couples has, at times, been profoundly lonely, awkward, and filled with fear and dread. Paradoxically, it has also included many supportive affiliations and healing connections, culminating in a wealth of self-revelations, not the least of which has been the awareness of singlehood as a potentially rich and important time in one's life, for however long it lasts.

What has it been like professionally to explore the inner worlds of so many different single clients and their loved ones? Sometimes astonishing. The fear and self-loathing that has been articulated by the collective voice of my clients has, as you saw with Suzanna, stunned me. Even more stunning has been the tenacious capacity each one has exhibited in confronting his or her unique difficulties while being single. It is each person's willingness to understand and then to change that has provided the real backbone of this endeavor.

The role of friend, and at times surrogate family, during the years when both my coauthor and I were living single in what seemed like an alienating world of couples was as complex and difficult as it was lifesaving. Our friendship has been the springboard from which our ideas could be thought through, our feelings identified and labeled, and our actions analyzed. We both have been hurt by, as well as restored by, our friendship. But in the end, I have come to believe in the extraordinary benefit of strong connections. Connections protect, heal, and motivate as nothing else can. Ultimately, it is the enriched capacity to be open to the possibilities of the connections available to each of us, single and married alike, that constitutes the true goal of this book.

Is it fitting, then, to acknowledge a number of important connections that have made this book possible. Although it would be a breach of privacy to name them, I want to again thank my single clients for sharing their personal journeys with me. Their journeys have shaped my thinking from the very beginning.

Special thanks as well as gratitude go to my wise and steadfast single friends—especially Sybil Kaufman, Patty Pontecorvo, and Susan Freeman. They encouraged me, challenged me, and cheered me all along the way. In addition, there are a number of loved ones who are in couples, who also never wavered in their support and insights: a special thanks to Oksana Lyubarsky, Linda Fitzsimons, Marita and David Glodt, Mimi and Al Hernandez, Jane Blackstein and Max Varon, and The MSKCC Alumnae Group, which is made up of all kinds of people at all stages of single- and couplehood! (And, for those of you who know me well, a special thanks to my main man Max, who's always there for me whenever he's needed!)

I would like to "formally" thank my coauthor, Xavier Amador, who has held this project close to his heart for many years. Without his extraordinarily hard work and characteristic perseverance, this book would still be but a glimmer in our eyes.

Finally, I want to thank my sister, Sandra, to whom I am forever indebted, both personally and professionally. It is through our relationship that I have learned, and continue to relearn, the power of loving ties that seek to liberate, and never to bind. She has done a superb job of fulfilling the true and best meaning of family.

BEING SINGLE

1

IT'S A COUPLES' WORLD

All my friends are getting married. If I have to go to one more wedding single I am going to scream! I feel so out of place with my friends and family because everyone is either married or in a serious relationship. I am starting to hate getting together with them because I leave feeling like a failure.

Ellen, a thirty-four-year-old school teacher

—◦—

I wish my family would understand that I would much rather be single and happy than married and miserable. Even my friends don't seem to get it. I am open to marriage but I am not hurting for it. I am basically happy and fulfilled. Why can't they see that and stop focusing on why I haven't yet remarried?

Sally, a forty-one-year-old medical technician

—◦—

Being single isn't nearly as much fun for me as everyone thinks it is. At least not for me. I want to share my life with someone and I want to have kids. My sister and other women I know tell me "at least you don't have to worry about a biological clock!" But I do, especially if I want to be a father. Who wants to be in their sixties with teenagers? Not me. And anyway, it's beside the point. I am lonely and I want to be in a serious relationship. I sometimes think that if I died in my sleep no one would know for days! But I can't figure out what I am doing wrong. I don't understand why I am still single.

Mark, a thirty-eight-year-old money manager

—◦—

I know it's irrational because I'm still relatively young, but my biggest fear about being single is that I'll end up alone. I feel like I am going to get left behind somehow.

Patti, a twenty-three-year-old student

Whether or not you are longing to be married at this moment, you picked this book up because you are dealing with the problems that come with being single in a couples' world. If you are anything like the people we quoted above, being single leaves you feeling a little alienated from your married friends and family, anxious about your future, and somewhat self-conscious. Or perhaps you are like many people we have come to know who feel miserable and lousy about themselves simply because they are single. Regardless of whether you are a little unhappy and anxious or you loathe the experience, our book will help you to learn why you are single.

It's true that marriage can be a wonderful experience and can make you happy in a number of ways. At its best, marriage promises intimacy, companionship, love, and a sense of belonging. But so can being single. And contrary to what many people think, finding happiness as a single person does not require that you give up on marriage!

What is required is that you uncover the reasons you are currently single. Because once you know, you'll find that you're more accepting of yourself, confident, and ultimately more open to love. Whether or not you then go on to marry is up to you. If that is what you want, it will come easier. If marriage is not high on your list of priorities, or is missing from it altogether, knowing why you are single will clarify how you fit into a world of couples. This book will help you to connect with friends, family, and lovers with confidence and self-respect. Although there are many valuable lessons to be learned in the pages that follow, few will be as important as coming to a more complete understanding of why you are single.

You may feel that you already know the answer. Perhaps you think you are single because you haven't found the "right one." Or maybe you worry that you don't know how to compromise; or that you jump ship when relationships get too close for comfort. On the other hand, maybe you think the opposite sex is to blame for your single status. There is often a kernel of truth in such theories, but they merely describe a small aspect of what is going on rather than explain why it is happening. They miss the forest for the trees, and in doing so they leave the single people who hold such beliefs feeling bad about themselves and the opposite sex.

The real problem is that you are confusing your past with the present. If you take a moment to reflect on it, you will find that you hold a number of expectations about what it will mean for you personally to be married. For example, some people feel they will never be complete as a person or satisfied with life until they are married. Others feel that marriage is a sign of maturity, or respectability: "He's a respectable guy; he's married." Still others fear that marriage will somehow swallow them whole and destroy their independence. Although expectations such as these have developed over a lifetime, they are mostly formed in childhood.

Your outlook on marriage and singlehood comes from a script you learned growing up. Like a script for a play or a movie, you know what to expect at every turn, provided you've committed the parts to memory. You know what motivates each character in the story, what they are supposed to be feeling, their relative importance to the other characters, and whether they are "good guys" or "bad guys." It is vital to your happiness as a single person that you uncover the marriage script you penned for yourself growing up. Because, among other things, your personal marriage script directs you to act, feel, perceive, and think in ways that can make being single either a joy or a misery. If it is making you miserable and keeping you from the things you want, including a good relationship, then it needs updating. But you can't revise your script until you are clear about what it contains.

PERSONAL MARRIAGE SCRIPT

C lose your eyes and imagine the home you will live in when you are married. Will it be in a city, a suburb, or the countryside? What will the furniture and decor look like? Will there be a yard with a lawn and trees? Children? Pets? Do it now.

What did you see? Even if there is no one in your life that you want to marry, even if marriage is currently low on your list of priorities, you had an image. Where did it come from? If you examine it closely you will find that, more than likely, the image you projected had more to do with your past than your present. Matt, for example, a thirty-four-year-old never-married lawyer, said, "I see a two-story house with a big yard, a white picket fence, and a couple of kids and a dog wrestling together on the lawn." Matt had been living in New York City for the past sixteen years. The only time he had ever lived in a house like the one he imagined was when he lived at home with his parents. When he talked more about his image he had to admit that he couldn't see himself moving to the suburbs because he loved city life so much.

This picture of the home he might live in when he married is but one scene in the personal marriage script that he had unconsciously written down while he was growing up. Because it had been written a long time ago and then locked away in the vault of unconscious expectations we all hold about marriage, it had never been revised. It didn't take into account the life Matt had been living since moving from the home in which he was raised.

But this scene from Matt's personal marriage script is fairly benign. When Matt realized he held it he laughed and said, "I am addicted to this city. I would die if you tried to transplant me to the suburbs!" He easily revised his script so that when he thought about where he might live with a family of his own, he now imagined a large and sunny co-op in the city. But your marriage script describes much more than the kind of home you will live in when you marry. As such, it has a huge impact on your desire to tie the knot—or not. For example, if your marriage script leaves you fearful of losing yourself when you marry, you'll act in ways to defend yourself from this fate: perhaps you'll shy away from making long-term commitments. If you had a father who was emotionally distant you may have learned to give him your undivided attention to win his love. It worked in that you felt loved, but it left you little if any room in the relationship to voice your own feelings. Or perhaps your mother was depressed while you were growing up and you felt you had to walk on eggshells around her and cater to her moods, just to keep her functioning. The details of each script will vary from person to person, but confusion and heartache caused by following the script's outdated lessons on intimacy and marriage are the common outcomes.

Because the script was written and memorized long ago and is now locked away in the vault of unconscious expectations about marriage and intimacy, it is acted upon reflexively without any conscious effort or thought. It's like driving a car. When you first learn to drive you think about every move of your foot, when and how to turn the wheel, which mirror to look in when changing lanes, and how much gas and brake pressure to apply. In time you stop thinking about the numerous details and steps involved. You just get in your car and go.

Single people who have memorized their personal scripts act on them in exactly the same way.

This is how we learn most things. The more experience we have with a given task the less we have to think about how we do it. The problem arises when you try to drive your new stick-shift like the automatic you learned on years before. Much of what you learned before is applicable, but the lessons that aren't lead to shaky starts, jarring stops, and unexpected stalls. The world has changed dramatically in the past twenty years. Your marriage script—the childhood lessons you learned about intimacy and marriage—will result in shaky starts, jarring stops, and unexpected stalls if you apply them reflexively. The good news is that you can fix the mismatch between the past and the present by opening the vault and rereading your outdated script. Once you make it conscious, you can revise it to make it more relevant to the world in which you now live.

THE CULTURAL MARRIAGE SCRIPT

All of us also learn a cultural marriage script. Our culture's expectations about marriage invariably translate into a kind of prejudice against singles. For example, if marriage is a sign of maturity, respectability, and success, then being single suggests you are immature, reckless, and a failure. The outdated cultural script makes singlehood unappealing in exactly the way that your personal marriage script may be making it difficult to "tie the knot."

The cultural script was first penned in a historical, even genetic, quest for self-preservation. In this case, however, it was physical rather than emotional self-preservation that was at stake. The cultural marriage script that lingers today evolved because it helped to preserve our ancestors physically. Just about everyone has a natural desire to mate. But the very strong social pressures to marry that have evolved have more to do with an outdated script than any natural drive for connection. Indeed, some conservative politicians argue that marriage is a moral imperative. Being single is all right, so long as you are well on your way toward marriage and "family values." We never hear much about "single values" unless it is in the context of warnings: "Careful—he's a wolf on the prowl," or "When are you going to settle down and get serious?"

Such warnings are sounded by those who have never questioned the present-day relevance of the now ancient cultural script. Although they are not blameless for promoting "single stigma," they are in fact following a tradition of blind adherence to a script that is literally thousands of years old. The dogma of most religions declares that it is your responsibility to get married and that if you remain single you are irresponsible and should feel ashamed. Your part in the play is clear: God wants you to get married. For both men and women the alternative to marriage is disgrace. Consider the following advice found in the book of Isaiah (4:1): "And seven women shall take hold of one man in that day saying 'We will eat our own bread, and wear our own clothes, only *let us be called by your name; take away our reproach*'" (emphasis added). This one passage overstates a common theme that can be found in the holy books of all major religions: singlehood is shameful and marriage is something to feel proud about. When these books were written, marriage was equated with being mature and responsible; it was an economic necessity and essential to survival. A women who did not marry made life much more difficult for her father and mother—she was a disappointment, a burden, and a failure.

Women today have avenues other than marriage to enable them to move from their parents' home. This is one of many obvious examples of how the cultural marriage script has become antiquated. Just as there are many religions and cultures in the world, there are many variations to the cultural marriage script. The scripts also vary depending on whether you are a man or a woman. But the common theme to nearly all cultural scripts is the same: marriage is good, being single is bad.

When you combine your personal script with the cultural script, it's a recipe for misery. On the one hand, you have a personal script that makes tying the knot more difficult than you might like. On the other hand, the cultural script leads you to conclude that you are a "loser" for being single. Friends and family who have memorized the same cultural script reinforce such thoughts, and abet you in your self-flagellation, sometimes enthusiastically, but almost always unintentionally. Because they also have memorized the lines of the culture's script so well, they follow the dogma with little thought as to the pain they might cause their single loved ones. The concerned mother may say, "But you're so pretty, I don't understand why no one has snapped you up!" Or friends will advise you that "If you really tried, you'd meet someone," or "You'll find someone when you're not looking," or "You're too focused on your career, that's why you're alone." These are but a few examples of what we refer to as friendly fire. This problem is so pervasive, yet so easily remedied, that we have devoted chapters 10, 11, and 12 to showing you and your loved ones how to avoid acting out this particularly painful aspect of the cultural marriage script.

BEING SINGLE IN THE PRESENT

The problems created by both the cultural and personal marriage scripts are worsened by living in a culture with a rapidly changing marriage landscape. You no longer have to be married to move from your parent's home, or to have economic security, a sex life, or even children. The gap between the outdated scripts and real life is wider now than at any other time in history. Knowing the antiquated cultural script that you have been following is vital to protecting yourself from the stigma and prejudice that it creates for single people like yourself. Meanwhile, if you can uncover your personal script and learn the reasons why you are single, you will then be able to choose whether or not to stay single with confidence. In this book, we pay special attention to showing you how to unlock the vault so that you can get your hands on your personal script. Because when you do this, you'll find that you can easily revise it. You can stop looking at yourself and your relationships through the distorted lens provided by it and start living your life in the present.

To live in the present means that you are not worrying about who you would like to be or preoccupied by sadness over who you once were. You have learned to accept yourself for who you are now. There is no shame or feeling of being a second-class citizen because you are single. Self-acceptance is the cornerstone to becoming happier and to changing yourself in ways you'd like to. It is not the same as resignation. You do not have to give up on your desire for marriage to live in the present. Indeed, the irony is that the more confident you feel about your place in the world, and the more self-accepting you are, the more attractive you will be to others.

Our basic strategy is "show and tell." Throughout this book we will show you what other single people have come up against in their quest to live in the present and to feel less alienated from friends, family, and lovers. We will also tell you how to discover for yourself why you are single and what it is you expect from being married.

In the next chapter, you will read about Ellen and Sarah, who were feeling bad about being single and were stalled in their attempts to move from the position they found themselves in. Today, single people are up against two opposing forces that spring from the gap between an outdated cultural script and the reality of how our culture has evolved. We focus on women in this chapter because the cultural changes that have widened the gap between the old script and modern reality are easier to see in the case of women. But as you will discover, the gap between what we were raised to believe about singlehood and marriage and the reality of our experience is just as wide for men. In chapter 2 we begin to unravel the confusion these singles and others like them face when trying to figure out why they are unmarried and how to fit into the world in which they live.

In chapter 3 we tell you about the four stages of being single in a couples' world that describe the common experience of single people like yourself. You enter the first stage when you begin to feel alienated from friends, family, lovers, and even yourself. If you find that you are suddenly single because of a divorce, a breakup, or the death of your partner, this experience is all too familiar. It can be like a cold hard slap in the face. In places and with people you once felt you belonged, you now feel like an outsider. If you have never been married, the feeling creeps up on you as you near, then surpass, your marriage milestone: that is the age at which, as a child, you imagined you would be married. In either case you feel alienated from the world in which you live. Not everyone graduates from one stage to the next. It takes effort and knowledge. But the journey is well worth the effort. Because, as you will see, the last stage describes people who are truly comfortable being single, knowledgeable about their marriage scripts, and living their lives in the present.

In the fourth chapter we give you specific steps that show you how to be single in the present. These steps will help you to uncover your personal marriage script and protect yourself from becoming a pawn in the culture's script which casts singles in only secondary roles, and show you how to take your life off hold. Our belief is that after reading this book you will be better equipped to live your life in the present, rather than succumbing to the stigma that springs from the old-fashioned cultural script and the outdated fears that stem from your personal script.

In chapters 5 through 9, we show you how other single men and women were able to accomplish these goals. Each chapter focuses on a common type of personal marriage script that we have seen in our work with single people. In the last three chapters we focus our attention on some specific problems created by the cultural marriage script. We show you how to avoid friendly fire from your married loved ones in chapter 10, and how to deal with the competition and jealousy that this script promotes between single friends and relatives in chapter 11. How to make your needs count with coupled loved ones who sometimes make you feel like a third wheel or even invisible is the topic of our final chapter. Throughout this book, we will teach you the skills you need to live in the present, to find a place for yourself in this couples' world, and to stop putting your life on hold. Turn this page to learn what you can do to start moving forward with confidence.

BEING SINGLE TODAY

When I was a little girl, I always thought that I'd be married by now. But here I am in my mid-thirties and single. I don't know why, because I want to get married. It's not like I am trying to avoid it or anything! I must be doing something wrong. . . . I was married once, for a couple of years, when I was in my twenties. But that was a disaster and I've been single ever since. It seems like everyone's married but me. I feel like such a failure.

Ellen, a thirty-four-year-old school teacher

—◦—

I feel like I keep getting drawn back to this fork in the road: to the right is marriage, respectability, and boredom, on the left is my career, travel, and excitement. I am in no hurry to get married. I usually take the path on the left. But somehow I keep getting drawn back to that fork. I feel like I should be heading toward marriage, or at least my parents do. . . . It makes me feel flawed, like I am a loser and I don't know what I am doing. I feel kind of like a kid who needs to grow up.

Sarah, a twenty-eight-year-old travel agent

Our culture's marriage script dictates, first and foremost, that everyone is supposed to be married. Despite the numerous single role models today working in entertainment, sports, politics, business, and other high-profile fields, people still feel tremendous internal pressure to marry. We are not talking here about the natural desire to mate or to fall in love. We are referring to an outdated cultural mandate to marry. The expectation is so ingrained that when we are single and unhappy in any way, we assume it is our unmarried status that is to blame. And we jump to the conclusion that something is terribly wrong—either with us or with the opposite sex—because we are unmarried.

Ellen had some vague ideas about why she was unhappy, but she was so caught up in looking for a scapegoat that she was not getting any closer to uncovering the real reason. Because she was involved in blaming, she also was blinded to the fact that she was playing the part demanded by the culture's script. That part demanded she feel like a failure and generally miserable about herself for no other reason than because she was single. But actually she was not nearly as unhappy about being currently unattached as she was miserable about the pressure created by the culture's marriage script.

ELLEN

"I've never been to therapy before. It feels really strange, but I am starting to feel desperate," explained Ellen, a thirty-four-year-old school teacher who came to see me at the advice of a friend of hers.*

"What's the problem?" I asked.

"The problem is that I am in my mid-thirties and still single. I was married once, for a couple of years, when I was in my twenties. But that was a disaster and I've been single ever since. It seems like everyone's married but me. I feel like such a failure."

"A failure at what?" I countered, thinking that Ellen might have fallen into the cycle of blame that I have encountered so many times working with single people in therapy. The cycle, which feeds on itself, involves alternating back and forth between blaming the opposite sex and blaming oneself, whenever unhappy about being single.

"I don't know exactly, I guess a failure at life. I thought that I would be happily married by now. I am really starting to worry that something is wrong with me. I used to think it was the fault of the guys I was dating. But now, I can't help but think that it's me. It's got to be my fault. I've got to be doing something wrong."

"Like what?" I asked.

"I don't know exactly, I mean I have some ideas, but I'm not certain. I guess that's the reason that I am here . . . to figure out what it is I am doing wrong. Can you help me with that? Do you have experience with this sort of thing? I mean, is this a legitimate reason to come to therapy?"

---

*Some of the dialogue in this book is drawn from our conversations with patients and research subjects. Whenever a conversation was with only one of us, we identify which one of us was involved. In this instance it was X.A.

"At the risk of sounding self-serving, I think there are very few bad reasons and yours is not one of them. Can I help you with what you want to accomplish? I suppose I have to say yes and no." Inwardly I cringed a little at my answer to her last question. This was our first meeting and Ellen's first time seeing a psychologist. One of the most popular preconceptions about psychotherapy is that a therapist will never answer your question directly. "Yes and no" would do little to disabuse Ellen of that bias if she held it.

"I will need to hear more before I can answer that question. You sound like you want to get married. But the fact is that for some reason—or reasons—you haven't."

"Right. That's my problem," Ellen interrupted. "To be perfectly honest, if I was married, or in a good relationship right now, I wouldn't be here talking to you."

"I understand that this is the reason you're here, but it sounds like you might have other reasons. You said that you feel like a failure?"

"I guess I did say that. . . . I do feel like a failure. When I was a little girl, I wrote in my dairy the age at which I wanted to get married. I wrote 'twenty-five years old.' Well I was married at twenty-five but it didn't last. I always thought I'd be happily married with a couple of kids by the time I was thirty. Now look at me, I'm thirty-four, a failed marriage, and I'm *still* single."

Ellen had asked if I had experience with her type of problem, and I had. I wanted to reassure her at the outset that the fact that she was single was not unusual, and that she wasn't a failure at anything other than perhaps not understanding herself and the situation she was in as clearly as she should. So I asked her, "This may sound like an odd question, but what percentage of women in your age group do you think have never before been married?"

"I don't know, I never thought about it really."

"Take a guess," I encouraged.

"Maybe around ten percent. Never married? Not counting divorced? Probably less, maybe eight percent," she ventured.

"Actually, around thirty percent—that's nearly one out of every three. And it's not just women. The number of men in your age group who have never been married has also more than doubled in the past twenty years. So although you feel that everyone is married by the time they're your age, the fact is they're not. And I don't believe it's because they are all failures."

"Then what are we all waiting for?" she shot back. "Look, you're a therapist, you're supposed to say reassuring things. What else are you going to say? 'I agree with you Ellen, you're such a loser!'" She laughed out loud and then added wryly, "Actually, now that I think about it, you've made me feel worse! You've convinced me that there's a mess of us out there that are losers!"

As you read what Ellen had to say, we hope you're smiling, as she did when she proclaimed that tens of millions of single women and men were all losers. She smiled because she knew that one out of three women in her age group could not all be "failures." Although it may seem counterintuitive at first glance, this information helped her to feel less alienated and less like a failure. It did make her feel a little pessimistic initially because, as she puts it, "If that many women are not yet married then the odds are definitely against me." But like medicine that tastes bad when you first put it in your mouth, this knowledge helped put Ellen on the road to recovery from her misery about being single. The cultural script she followed told her "Everyone is married by your age," but the reality she lived in, which she had been blinded to by her adherence to the script, told a very different story.

And the reality of how the culture has changed is not nearly as depressing as the script Ellen had been following. The fact is, *people are staying single longer.* According to the U.S. census the average age at which people marry has risen dramatically since the 1970s. The facts do not indicate that people who want to marry are unable to do so, as Ellen first thought. If you want to get married the odds are decidedly in your favor, although it may take you longer to walk down the aisle than you imagined it would as a child. But this trend begs the question that Ellen asked: "What are we all waiting for?"

Ellen's question is an important first step toward solving the problems she is having. Up until that moment, she was generalizing from her personal experience and blaming herself. From the perspective of the cultural script, she saw herself as an old maid, a spinster, a statistical aberration rather than what she really was: part of a growing trend in this country and around the world.

So why are people waiting longer to get married? Why do some people never marry? And why do people leave marriages so often? The cultural script tells us that Ellen and people like her must be to blame. She probably hasn't grown up. She hasn't yet learned how to compromise or to share. Equating marriage with maturity is not a terrible idea on the face of it. Oftentimes, the characteristics one should ideally have to be married are mature ones: the ability to compromise, to share, to consider other people's needs, and to take on responsibilities. But this aspect of the cultural script doesn't quite fly in the face of the reality single people face today. Clearly marriage is irrelevant to the task of becoming a mature, successful, and responsible adult. Are the Matt Lauers, Jerry Seinfelds, Sandra Bullocks, George Stephanopouloses, and Oprah Winfreys of the world immature, irresponsible, and unsuccessful? If you accept the argument that maturity has little if anything to do with the fact that tens of millions of Americans are single, then we are still left with Ellen's question.

Could the problem be one of character rather than maturity? People are just too selfish nowadays—yes, that must be it—that's the problem. Or, they're too lazy, they're just not trying hard enough. If these explanations sound all too familiar and even a little appealing, it's because they spring from an ancient, unquestioned mandate to marry. This mandate is so deeply imbedded in the cultural script that people like Ellen often confuse it with their natural desire for connection and love. And the stigma that singles often experience comes from being raised to comply with this mandate at all cost.

THE CULTURAL MANDATE TO MARRY

Why do people marry? There are many good reasons, not the least of which is love. But as we have discussed above, there is also a cultural script that exerts tremendous pressure on people to marry. The script demands marriage from its actors. Over and above all the good reasons out there to tie the knot, the cultural script promotes an outdated, senseless mandate to marry.

In the last chapter we touched on how the holy books of nearly all religions contain obvious expressions of the cultural script and its mandate to marry. As children, many of us read or listened to passages such as the one we cited from Isaiah and they helped to shape our view of what it takes to be a respected man or woman. According to these writings married men and women with children had reason to feel proud. Single men and women were considered with disdain and pity if they were considered at all. Even if you are not a Christian, a Muslim, or a Jew you have grown up in a culture that was shaped by one or more of these belief systems. Religion provides, among other things, rules for moral living. In subtle and not so subtle ways, these three major religions have equated marriage with morality and maturity and in doing so, have added an unneeded mandate to marry to our natural inclination for intimacy.

In particular, the need to marry in order to have economic security is now largely irrelevant. Nevertheless, the mandate continues to wield tremendous power over one's sense of self. One reason for this is that the mandate is reinforced by a mythology of marriage we learned as children. All of us are born into a family. Most of us have parents who are, or were, married to one another. Although it sounds odd to think of it this way, when you were a child you were a single person and your parents were married people. Now, think about how you viewed your mother and father back then. They were more powerful than you were. Your parents' desires ruled nearly every aspect of your life. You lived where they wanted to live and in the home they chose. You went to the school they wanted you to attend and ate the food they prepared. They ruled the roost and you did not.

Your parents' seemingly unlimited importance and status, especially until you were about ten years old, seemed even greater whenever you overheard their conversations about their single friends and relatives. Mention of these pitiful souls was often prefaced with expressions of sympathy. For example, "Poor uncle Larry, is he seeing anyone?" Their worried expressions when talking about their unmarried loved ones and the fact that you never went over to your single aunt's house for the holidays, but she always attended the festivities your parents planned, conspired to add to the image of single people as having less status.

With childhood lessons such as these, it is not difficult to see why the needs of married individuals are frequently valued more highly than those of single people, nor is it hard to imagine why many of us never recognize the inequities that exist between the married and the unmarried. This particular circumstance is so common that we have devoted chapters 10, 11, and 12 to teaching you how to recognize such inequalities in your own life and showing you ways to balance the scales. Whether you have realized it before or not, you were raised to equate marriage with maturity, power, social status, and living happily ever after.

Before we examine how the mandate and the cultural marriage script it comes from have become outdated, we will tell you a little of

Sarah's story. Like Ellen, Sarah had also surpassed her marriage milestone (i.e., the age at which as a child she always imagined she would be married) without getting married.

SARAH

Sarah is a travel agent who founded her own agency with two partners. She is a vivacious, infectiously enthusiastic woman who has been largely responsible for the rapid growth of the business. By single-handedly luring several large corporate accounts over the past two years, she more than tripled the income of the agency she helped found. She loves to travel and does so whenever she has the opportunity.

Recently, she broke off a five-month relationship with her boyfriend as she felt it was "going nowhere and there had to be someone better out there." He was a musician and traveled a good deal of the time. Her parents never really warmed up to him. They didn't understand how she could tolerate his frequent absences. As her mother put it, "I think you can do better. You should find someone more like your father. At least we spend the weekends together." The irony is that Sarah rather enjoyed that her boyfriend was so independent because she was as well. That was not the reason she broke up with him. Nonetheless, Sarah is starting to worry that maybe her mother was right because the truth of the matter was that she wasn't finding anyone she wanted to marry. Maybe she was too independent and should date more traditional men. Although she thinks her father is a great guy, Sarah does not feel drawn to the kind of relationship her parents have.

"I feel like I keep getting drawn back to this fork in the road: to the right is marriage, respectability, and boredom, on the left is my career, travel, and excitement. I am in no hurry to get married. I usually take the path on the left. I love being independent and besides, there's so many cute guys and so little time!" she added, laughing. "But somehow I keep getting drawn back to that fork. I feel like I should be heading toward marriage, or at least my parents do."

"How does it make you feel about yourself when you don't?" I asked.*

---

*X.A.

"It makes me feel flawed. I wish that I was attracted to the kind of man my mother believes would make a good husband. But I am not."

"How do you feel flawed?" I asked, thinking that if we could gain some clarity on how Sarah experienced herself we might find the reason she was drawn back to this place where she felt that either choice was a mistake.

"Like I don't know what I am doing . . . kind of like a kid who needs to grow up. I think my problem is that I don't always give the men I date much of a chance. It's hot and heavy at first, then I sort of get disinterested. I like change and the excitement of the chase. The confusing thing is that I do enjoy being in a relationship most of the time I'm in one. More times than not it's better than being alone. And if I ever find the right one, I would like to get married. But I worry that maybe I won't know when it's the right one and I'll dump him before I really give it a chance. I feel like maybe I don't want it enough, like my priorities are screwed up."

"What are your priorities?"

"Growing up, my mom and dad always told me that I should have a career. And that a woman could do anything a man could do—only better, you know, like that bumper sticker? I think that some women, and my mother was once one of them, were raised to feel that only a man could make them complete. I don't feel that way. Self-reliance has always been a priority. That's how I was raised and that's what I believe in. But I feel like I got a double message. Not just from my parents, but from everyone. You're supposed to get married. Everyone is supposed to grow up and get married like their parents did. I also learned that. It's such a double message and it's so annoying. Sometimes the pressure is so strong that it makes me lose sight of the reasons I would want to get married! I feel like I don't know what I am doing when it comes to having a serious relationship."

There is much we could say about Sarah's predicament and we will in chapter 6, "The Grass Is Always Greener," where you will learn how she uncovered her personal marriage script and the role it played in keeping her stalled. But for now we will focus on the ways in which the cultural marriage script helped to keep her at the fork in the road she described. Like Ellen, Sarah revealed that she too had a marriage milestone. It was not as precise as Ellen's but the effect was the same. Sarah revealed that as a little girl she always imagined that "I would be happily married by my early twenties." At twenty-eight, she had surpassed her marriage milestone without ever having had the inclination to tie the knot with anyone.

You might wonder why, if she had never met anyone she wanted to marry and she was generally happy with her life, she was worried about being single. If you are older than Sarah you may even be shaking your head as you read this because you're thinking something like "she's still young, she's got nothing to feel anxious about!" But in fact she does feel anxious about being single as do a lot of women and men in their twenties, thirties, forties, and fifties.

No one *decides* to feel anxious, it's a feeling that comes unbidden. There are several sources for this type of anxiety. Her personal script that we will discuss in chapter 6 has made it more difficult for Sarah to pursue her natural inclination to be intimate with a man. But this in and of itself would not be problematic for her if she did not also have to deal with pressure to marry from the cultural script. Whenever you try to comply with this script while living in a modern world full of new opportunities for single people, you risk getting stuck in the same fork in the road that Sarah described. If you are like most people, any natural ambivalence you have about marriage is greatly intensified.

You will never feel entirely comfortable with your choice—to marry or to remain single for now—until you understand the ambivalence you have inside. It is a choice after all, even if it doesn't feel that way. Think about it, if you didn't care who it was you married, you could be married. *You want something specific, not just marriage in general.* Until you know all of your reasons for staying single and what it is you realistically want out of a marriage, you will never be able to choose with confidence. Until you understand both the cultural and personal scripts you are following, you will remain stuck at the crossroad Sarah described, stalled between the past and the present. It is a place that is no place. That is why so many single people often feel alienated from family and friends, as if they don't belong.

Today, single people are up against two opposing forces that spring from the gap between an outdated cultural script and the reality of how our culture has evolved. On the one hand, being single is stigmatizing; on the other, it is something to be cherished and protected. To complete our analysis of the mixed messages that single people today have to contend with, we turn to a brief discussion of "single stigma" followed by an examination of the dramatic changes in women's roles that have occurred over the past two decades. These changes have far outstripped the minor revisions to the cultural script that most people have made. For example, most people agree that there's no such thing as an "old maid" anymore. But when you read about the extent to which single people are still stigmatized and even discriminated against, we think you will agree that the cultural script is badly in need of some major revision.

STIGMATIZING SINGLEHOOD

Whenever you are aware of the negative messages you get about being single, you inoculate yourself from the insidious infection such prejudicial beliefs spread to your self-esteem. That is why it so important to be aware of the various ways in which you are exposed to negative messages about singlehood that are promoted by the cultural marriage script. The stigma we have been describing is so intricately woven into the fabric of our culture that single people are discriminated against systematically and yet few complain. The axiom "it's a couples' world" is codified in our legal system, marketing practices, and politics. For example, estate and tax laws favor married people and penalize singles. Everything from health insurance to air fare is cheaper if you have a spouse. Two for one specials were not intended for use by singles. And can you think of a U.S. president who didn't have a first lady on the day he was sworn in? There's a reason for that. Most people would think twice about electing a "bachelor president."

We are not arguing that single people need emancipation, but we are encouraging you to take note of how such practices affect your sense of self-worth. When you keep your eyes peeled for this aspect of the culture's script you can protect yourself from getting hurt by it. To help you to become better at detecting these negative messages we turn to how the news media typically portray single people. Singlehood is frequently vilified in the news. We wouldn't blame you if you're thinking "now they've gone too far." But bear with us for a moment longer because if you look closely at how the popular media describe criminals and psychopaths, you'll find many examples of what we are saying. For example, *Time* magazine reported that Thomas Hamilton, the "monster" that shot and killed sixteen children in Scotland, left his "shabby bachelor apartment" to head to the school where he committed the murders. In the writer's mind, the fact that Hamilton was a bachelor was somehow relevant to his report of the crime. At a press conference following the guilty verdict in the O. J. Simpson civil trial, the Los Angeles chief of police defended his rank and file saying that the men and women of the L.A. police force are "decent and respectable people, they're husbands and wives." Similarly, a friend of the "Unabomber" suspect, Ted Kaczynski, told *Newsweek* magazine ". . . I would tell [Ted] what I always told his [married] brother . . . a man alone isn't worth anything." The article goes on to describe how Mr. Kaczynski was never able to develop, much less sustain, an intimate relationship with a woman. This kind of coverage repeats the same mistake that has been made countless times before: it suggests that being single is somehow equivalent to arrested emotional development. Take a look at today's newspaper and see if you can't find examples such as these.

Although it is true that someone with a paranoid or psychopathic personality is more likely to be single, it does not follow that a single person is more likely to be paranoid or a psychopath! Illogical and unsubstantiated generalizations like these add to the sense of alienation that many single people experience while living in a couples' world. The fact is, as you will learn in the next section, there are many good reasons to delay or avoid marriage other than because you are an aspiring serial killer!

MARRIAGE AS THE NEW BALL AND CHAIN

Up until the 1970s, men had the market cornered on ambivalence about marriage. Over the ages, men have had much more independence and power than women. Free to roam wherever and with whomever they wished, men understandably felt their wives were the "old ball and chain." Marriage signified a loss of freedom; it meant having to account for your whereabouts to someone else and taking on financial burdens for another person and ultimately for children.

Tending to the needs of her parents and family, a woman had to wait for a husband before she could live outside her parent's home. She had to wait to be "picked," or if she was cunning she would hunt for a man herself, but with smoke and mirrors lest she give the impression that she was the one doing the choosing.

With women's newfound autonomy and power, marriage has taken on a whole new meaning for them today. Like Sarah and Ellen, more and more women find themselves deeply ambivalent, not necessarily about marriage in principle, but about marriage in practice. In other words, marriage may seem appealing in the abstract, but when it gets down to the reality of actually marrying someone it can sometimes feel like a bad idea.

Both women and men have far fewer reasons to marry than their parents did. The most important reasons to marry have obviously not changed: for love and companionship. But many of the other reasons have become less compelling: to have economic security, independence from our parents, a sex life, and even children. Ellen, Sarah, and the men they are dating have many more options than their parents had. They do not have to marry for economic security, to have a full sex life, or even to raise children.

You can't really blame a woman for being more ambivalent about marriage than her mother or grandmother had reason to be. The traditional reasons for her to wed simply don't hold much currency anymore. In fact, the potential risks can outweigh the imagined benefits. Women today generally support themselves; they have autonomy, freedom, and a seemingly unlimited array of options. In other words, they can now enjoy a lifestyle previously reserved solely for men. In this context, it's no wonder that many women have grown as reluctant as men to walk down the aisle.

If you are like most single people, you are caught between the antiquated cultural marriage script and the new ball and chain. Sometimes this conflict between the past and the present is obvious, as in Sarah's case. Sarah feels caught in a bind where on the one hand she is fulfilling her childhood dream of self-reliance and career accomplishments, while on the other hand she is failing in the cultural script's mandate to marry. She can't help but feel that somehow these goals are incompatible, as if the paths can't lead to the same place. In most cases, like that of Ellen, the conflict is much less obvious. But Ellen is stuck at a similar fork in the road, although she is less aware of it than Sarah. And she is equally involved in the self-blame that Sarah subscribes to.

Sarah and Ellen revealed that they had adopted many elements of the cultural script when each said she felt like a "failure" and a "loser" because she was single. But they were not referring to failing at getting married, to not reaching that goal. Sarah wasn't even trying to get married. She was generally happy with being single. Rather, both of them felt as if they were failures as people in general. Whenever you experience yourself as a failure or a loser, it understandably worsens the fear that you will always be alone. And, if like Ellen you are striving to be married, this kind of experience can lead to a self-fulfilling prophecy. If you feel like a failure you won't be very attractive to people and you won't be confident in who you are. You will be less likely to marry, and regardless of your prospects for marriage you will feel self-conscious and alienated from your coupled friends and family. It's no small wonder then that people who never challenge the negative messages they get every day about being single end up worried that they will always be alone.

This fear is universal. It cuts across gender and age. We interviewed several groups of men and women when writing this book. You may be surprised to learn that a group of twenty-three-year-old women and a separate group of men in their late twenties had uniformly adopted many of the same negative beliefs and anxieties about being single as had the singles in their thirties, forties, and fifties that we spoke with. When asked whether there was anything about being single that worried them, nearly all of them said that their worst fear was "that I will end up alone." It doesn't matter how old you are, whether you are a man or a woman, or whether you have previously been married or not, challenging your negative biases about singlehood is critical to feeling confident about yourself and your ability to connect with other people.

Perhaps you have adopted aspects of these outdated definitions of singlehood and marriage provided by the culture's script? You probably hold some bias, or expectation, about who you will become and the kind of person you will be when you are married. Like your biases about singlehood, the biases you hold about marriage can also affect how you feel about yourself when you are single. For example, if you have never questioned remarks like that made by L.A. police chief Willie Williams, who essentially said that if you are married you are more likely to be respectable, then you probably hold the bias that if you're single you are less than respectable. You have images and expectations locked away in that vault of unconscious expectations we all have about different categories of people. They are locked up only in the sense that they are generally hidden from your conscious awareness. But they affect how you feel about different types of people and about yourself. If your personal marriage script describes married people as "responsible, mature, powerful, and capable of love," then it probably tells you that single people are more likely to be "irresponsible, immature, weak, and incapable of truly loving and being loved by anyone."

But because the world has changed so much in recent decades, your inherited notions about marriage and singlehood can conflict with what you've learned over the course of your lifetime. And hence, a significant source of confusion exists for most single people. If you asked people forty years ago to describe their image of a single woman in her thirties you would have gotten a very different answer than you would today. Back then you would have heard associations like "a school teacher," "a librarian," "still a virgin," and "probably homely looking." Today, millions of unmarried women in their thirties are working at everything from construction to running major corporations. Understanding the culture's script is an important first step toward lessening the confusion and beginning to move ahead at the fork in the road you find yourself in.

The next step involves figuring out where you are in the various stages to being single in a couples' world and how to make yourself aware of the personal marriage script that you are following. Illuminating both types of marriage script is key to becoming more happy as a single person. It is also essential to countering the negative impact of the outdated stereotypes. In the pages that follow you will learn from the experience of Sarah, Ellen, and several other single men and women who, like you, were dealing with being single in a couples' world. In the next chapter we introduce you to four stages of being single. Awareness of these stages will help you to identify the tasks you need to complete to unlock the vault and revise your personal marriage script. Our experience as therapists has taught us that once you have understood the script that you wrote down in your past, you will be able to accept yourself more completely and enjoy your life more fully. You will also protect yourself from the stigma that comes with being single today. And even more important, you will also become more open to love.

3

WHERE DO YOU FIT IN?

I never thought I'd feel like a third wheel with Rick but I do. Ever since he got married we don't hang out as much—and when we do, I feel out of place. It's really awkward. I feel like the pitiful lonely relation who's come to visit. It makes me feel pathetic. I know I wouldn't feel so bad about it if I didn't care about the fact that I'm not married. But I do. I wish I didn't so I could stop feeling so rotten about being single.

Adam, a forty-one-year-old manager of a sporting goods store

◄◦►

No, I guess I am not that happy about being single. Why should I be happy about it? All my friends are getting married and I feel like I don't fit in any-more. If I am ever happy about being single it will be because I've given up on ever getting married.

Susan, a twenty-nine-year-old graduate student

◄◦►

My daughter has not gone to see her cousin's baby once since he was born! She doesn't want to go because she'll feel bad about herself—she's the only one in the family still single. She feels really guilty about not going, but she feels so down about being single that she's just not up to it yet. . . . It sounds terrible to say this, but I'm kind of glad she feels that way. It motivates her to keep on trying. I worry that she's going to end up all alone. . . . Where is she going to go for the holidays after her father and I are gone?

Bernice worrying about her thirty-two-year-old daughter Jane

There are many ways in which single people can come to feel that they no longer fit in. Adam, Susan, and Jane are decades apart in age and have remarkably different backgrounds, yet all three share a feeling of being alienated from friends and family because they are single. The ways in which they are reacting to the experience are typical of singles who feel out of place. Adam wanted to turn off his desire for connection. He wanted to stop feeling any longing to find someone to share his life with. In contrast, Susan saw marriage as the only solution to her feelings of alienation. Worse yet, she was convinced that she needed to feel miserable to be motivated to find someone to marry. And Jane tried to avoid the people and places where she felt most out of place as a single person. In this chapter, you will learn that there are other paths you can take to cope with the feelings of alienation that come with being single in a couples' world. You don't need to suppress your natural desire to mate, rush into a marriage at any cost, or spend your time solely with other single people to feel more like you fit in.

Marriage is the most common remedy that people seek out to feel better about themselves in this regard. But even marriage won't help your self-image unless you've addressed the underlying cause of your discomfort as a single person: your personal marriage script and its impact on your sense of self. Not to mention that the task of finding someone you'd like to marry is more difficult when you haven't dealt with the ways in which your personal script is making you shy away from marriage. We are not suggesting that there is anything wrong with marriage! It can be a wonderful experience and it can make you happy in a number of ways. A good marriage can be one of the sweetest things in life. Everybody wants what the promise of marriage holds out: love, intimacy, companionship, and a sense of belonging. But if by circumstance or choice you are currently single, then why not enjoy it? This is a goal many single people do not strive for as much as they should. You don't have to be married to have intimacy, companionship, love, and a sense of belonging. Finding your place in the world as a single person does not require that you give up on finding someone to share the rest of your life with.

The common misconception, voiced by Susan and Bernice above, is that you need to be miserable and alienated to be motivated to marry. They are confusing *self-acceptance* with *resignation*. Self-acceptance is the key to becoming happier and to changing yourself in ways you'd like to. The irony is that the more confident you feel about your place in the world, the more self-accepting you are, the more likely you are to marry if that is what you want. Whether you'd rather be married or feel certain that staying single is a better choice, understanding and accepting yourself more fully is a win-win endeavor. It is the cornerstone to finding your place in a couples' world.

The first two chapters have shown you that you are not alone or unusual because you are single. You are more aware now of how the cultural script can make you feel unhappy about being single and exert pressure on you to marry at all cost. Staying alert to the ways in which this script can tear down your self-esteem is important for building the foundation from which to begin the process of self-acceptance and "desegregation." In this chapter, we will give you our guidelines for being single in the present and begin to show you how others have used them. We give particular emphasis to showing you how to make the ground fertile for uncovering your personal marriage script and the outdated, but influential, reasons you have for avoiding marriage. What you do with this knowledge is up to you.

ASSIMILATION TO A COUPLES' WORLD

P rior to describing our guidelines for being single in the present, we need to talk about the stages single people go through when they try to "fit in" to a world of couples. Whether you have never been married or are recently widowed or divorced, you have undoubtedly experienced one or more of the stages of assimilation to a couples' world that we describe here.

Like any immigrant to a new country or culture, you find yourself feeling somehow out of step with the world in which you live. Over the past two centuries the Irish, Italian, African, Hispanic, Asian, and Russian immigrants to America all had one thing in common when they first landed in this country: the experience of being an outsider. It's ironic and a little sad that they felt this way, since every race, religion, and culture that exists in America today was transplanted from somewhere else.

The American marriage icon persists despite the fact that the divorce rate hovers steadily around 50 percent and people are getting married much later in life than ever before. Even today, marriage continues to enjoy the most-favored-cultural-myth status among the mass media. Whether you spend most of your time with other single people or not, you are living in a culture that insists that this is still a couples' world. Over time, if the trend toward spending more of our adult lives single continues to grow, this myth too may crumble. But for now, the cultural script holds fast to the idea that this world belongs to, and was made for, couples. The process of assimilating, or fitting in, without giving up your personal identity (in this case being single) involves stages very similar to what immigrants to a new country have to go through. We refer to the four typical stages as the four A's: *Alienation, Assessment, Acceptance,* and finally *Assimilation.* Let's have a look at how the four A's apply to being single.

STAGES OF BEING SINGLE IN A COUPLES' WORLD

Alienation

If you find yourself suddenly single due to divorce, a breakup, or the death of your partner, this stage is more obvious and easy to identify. In places and with people you once felt you belonged, you now feel like an outsider. If you have never been married, the feeling creeps up on you as you near, then surpass your marriage milestone, the age at which, as a child, you always imagined you'd be married. It is at that point that you become a stranger in a well-known land. You feel that you don't belong in the sense that your marital status makes you feel out of place. This is in contrast to your teens and early twenties when being unmarried was the expected norm. The alienation stage understandably results in a good deal of self-doubt and frustration. It is during this stage that the cycle of blame we described in chapter 1 usually begins. Remember how Ellen would alternate between blaming herself for being miserable about being single and blaming the men she was dating? This is a common reaction to feelings of alienation, but one that leads nowhere but round and round.

Single people in the alienation stage stay there until they have broken the cycle of blame. They know with certainty what the problem is so they don't bother looking elsewhere for answers. Blame can sometimes help them deal with the feelings of alienation in the short term (e.g., "All men are dogs," or "The women I've been dating all want to have babies, they don't want me") but never in a lasting way. Until the cycle is broken, the blinders stay on.

Assessment

W hen an immigrant lands in a new country, her senses become heightened as she assesses the lay of the land. She tries to make her way with confidence but without stepping on anybody's toes. Typically, the best way to do that is to follow the ancient axiom "When in Rome do as the Romans do." She looks for ways to fit in. Single people do the same thing in a couples' world. The culture's marriage script posts its dogma in the mass media and in nearly every other facet of day-to-day life, so figuring out the customs and expectations is very easy. Like most immigrants, the alienated single learns the status quo of her new land and in the process discovers she is now a second-class citizen. Only it is not her culture of - origin that accounts for newly lowered status. It is because she is single: now in the minority, worthy of some suspicion ("Why is she still single?"), and a failure for not fitting in with the mainstream culture.

The assessment stage can be terribly frustrating and even demoralizing. The value of who she is uniquely can be lost—even to herself. Attempts at reinventing herself to fit in are common during these periods, as are crusades to change the opposite sex. For example, many singles dive into bad marriages during this stage because they become convinced that the "solution" proffered by the cultural script is the best one available. Those that make this mistake never truly assimilate to the couples' world because when the marriage fails, evidenced either by divorce or marital misery, they find themselves back in the alienation stage feeling more like a failure than ever before.

On the other hand, single people who successfully negotiate this stage do so by uncovering their personal marriage script. They understand their motivations and feelings in relationships in a brand-new light. They are clear about why they are single, making them feel less alienated and anxious. Importantly, they have also become adept at distinguishing feelings and thoughts that come from their past from those that have to do with the reality they face day-to-day.

Acceptance

The start of the acceptance stage is marked by an openness of thought and a new curiosity about what it is the single person can, and cannot, change about his situation. It involves a healthy suspicion about the culture's marriage script and a realistic understanding of how the world has changed in recent decades. Like new immigrants to America, singles in the acceptance stage know that they are in fact a very large "minority." And, as such, they do not have to reinvent themselves to fit in. They have power, influence, and value all their own. They are now free to pursue what it is they want personally, whether an intimate relationship or a happier single life, without being burdened by pressure to become someone they are not.

The stage is complete when the single person learns to accept the feelings created by his personal marriage script. He no longer feels the need to react to them, to protect himself from the fear, anxiety, or dread that his script creates. He understands that these feelings which are aroused whenever he gets "too close" to a potential partner are only memories from childhood. They do not need to be acted upon. They only need to be understood and accepted.

Assimilation

The final stage begins when the single individual has completely shed any feelings of alienation, embarrassment, or failure because she is single. She is impervious to any stigma because she no longer subscribes to it herself. The cultural marriage script holds no power over her sense of self. She is open to the opportunities available to her, is unburdened by pressure to conform, has both single and coupled friends in her life, and is no longer putting her life on hold. She is open to marriage, perhaps even striving for it, but does not need to be married to feel successful, mature, and a sense of belonging.

No longer succumbing to knee-jerk reactions to the feelings created by her personal marriage script, she can see more clearly what she realistically needs to be happy in a relationship. This knowledge frees her to connect when she finds someone worthy of her interest and to feel comfortable with staying single when it's clear that no one currently fits the bill. Because she is crystal clear on what is truly important to her in a relationship, she can choose with confidence which way to go. She is rarely stuck at the fork in the road that Sarah described so well. As such, she is living in the present, unencumbered by antiquated dogma from the cultural script or remembered feelings from her personal script.

STEPS TO BECOMING SINGLE IN THE PRESENT

From our clinical practices, and out of our personal experiences as single people, we have identified four steps that you can take to become happier, more connected to your friends and family, and more able to live in the present. By living in the present we mean that you are no longer responding to the outdated cultural and personal scripts that you had followed. The steps we give here correspond to the four stages of being single that we just described. The techniques we will show you are rooted in the practice of both relational psychology and cognitive behavioral therapy. But be assured that these techniques were chosen not only because they have a strong theoretical basis in the practice of psychology, but because we found them to be effective.

If you consider the forces that negatively influence the happiness of single people—the cultural script and its byproducts stigma, discrimination, and alienation—some of what we are about to say may already be obvious. Nonetheless, there are many subtleties involved in both the problem and the remedy. In summary, the process requires that you take the following steps: (1) Break the cycle of blame, (2) Examine the facts, (3) Take responsibility, and (4) Don't put your life on hold. These guidelines involve a combination of becoming curious about yourself and developing a healthy suspicion of anyone who offers a *simple* solution (e.g., "become a 'rules' girl," "all men are dogs," "I'm a loser," etc.). They also entail learning about the growing gap between the cultural script and the reality single people face today and about your own personal script and how it may be making it more difficult for you to tie the knot. Most important, the entire process will require you to challenge some of your self-perceptions, to keep an open mind and heart, and to take some risks emotionally.

There are rarely simple and easy solutions to problems such as those we are dealing with here. If there were, everyone would know the answers and the problems would disappear. Learning how to apply the principles and techniques integral to each of these guidelines will require patience and practice. To help you, below and in the chapters ahead we provide illustrations of how other single people were able to use these steps and the techniques attached to each of them. Although some of the people you will read about entered fulfilling relationships by the time we lost contact with them and others remained single, the end result was the same for each of them: they felt much happier about themselves, closer to their family and friends, and more open to love. They were living in the present and had stopped putting their lives on hold.

Patrick

P atrick is a twenty-seven-year-old police officer. He is handsome, fit, personable, and prides himself on his courtesy at work. As he explained it, "Cops get such a bad rap—I've never had a civilian complaint against me and I am proud of that." When he called to make his first psychotherapy appointment he explained that he was very anxious and thought that perhaps he had panic disorder. However, during his first session he focused on what he described as his "*inability* to have *real* relationships." Although he had had several relationships in the past, the longest lasting over a year, he felt that they never went anywhere. The fact that he hadn't yet met anyone that he wanted to marry left him feeling alienated and embarrassed. Making him feel worse about himself were the last words his ex-girlfriend spoke to him the night they broke up: "Something's seriously wrong with you, Patrick—no one's ever going to be good enough for you!" These words hit a nerve, because deep down inside Patrick harbored a fear that something was indeed seriously wrong with him.

After this breakup, his feelings of alienation and embarrassment had evolved to the point that he had not been on a single date for over six months and he found himself lying to his family about this. Nobody in Patrick's life was aware of the extent to which he felt humiliated by his single status or realized that this was the reason he wasn't coming around as much as he used to. Indeed, his feelings of humiliation and alienation were so pervasive that nearing the end of his first session he said, "I feel stupid talking about this. Maybe this wasn't such a good idea—it makes me feel weak and ridiculous. You must think I am a real whiner."

Sarah

Sarah, the twenty-eight-year-old travel agency owner we told you about earlier, has generally been much happier about being single than Patrick has. However, she is starting to feel anxious about the fact that she has never dated anyone that she wanted to marry. She is increasingly worried that perhaps her mother is right and she doesn't ever give anyone a chance. Maybe she is too independent and should date more traditional men. Although she loves her father, she does not feel drawn to the kind of relationship that he and Sarah's mother have.

"My mom has some very strong opinions about the kind of guys I should date. So do my friends, for that matter! I am very independent and I like men who are too. But worse than that, everyone says I never give anyone a real chance. One of my friends says that the reason I jump from one relationship to another is because I don't ever want to get too close. She thinks I am scared of commitment. It doesn't feel that way to me, but who knows? Maybe I am. I never used to second guess myself like this, but the fact is that I am getting older and I have not had a relationship last more than six months. I generally feel good about the relationships I've been in. But the fact that I'm where I am today makes me wonder if maybe if they weren't so good after all. Maybe I've been deluding myself. I feel like I need a manual for choosing 'Mr. Right.'

"Listen to the way I sound! If my partners at work could hear me now they wouldn't believe it was me. The last thing they would ever expect me to do is use a manual for anything—I am that sure of myself. I am a different person in the office than what you're seeing now."

Sarah is confident at work but not confident to choose in love. Her love life has become a lightning rod for her insecurities. She never used to feel this way, but as she grew older and passed her marriage milestone, both internal and external pressure to be married increased. Now her unmarried status was eating away at her self-confidence.

It was also making her feel that she no longer fit in: "It's gotten to the point that I am steering clear of my mother and married friends. Whenever I am around them I feel the conversation veering back to who I am dating, how's it going, and am I serious about him. It makes me feel like the rest of my life doesn't count. Until I'm one of them, until I'm married, everything else about who I am doesn't matter."

Ellen

Ellen, whom we introduced in chapter 1, is an attractive thirty-four-year-old teacher who dates frequently. In fact, because she has let her friends know that she is "looking," she is often set up on blind dates. She plays tennis, volunteers at a local community center, and has an active social life. Although her friends and family have expressed some worry because she is "still single" more than seven years after her divorce, they would be surprised to know how bad Ellen feels about this. She fluctuates between believing that something is seriously wrong with her because she's in her mid-thirties and "still not married" and thinking that the blame lies with the single men she is dating.

As she describes it, "I feel like such a loser. I keep going out with men who are scared of commitment. They never want to get married. It makes me feel like an idiot. Why do I keep picking these guys? Either I'm choosing the bad ones or all the good ones are taken." These beliefs about herself—that she is a failure because she's "still" single and that she is drawn to men who are bad for her—lead her to suspect that she is abnormal and to feel demoralized about men in general.

What Patrick, Sarah, and Ellen have in common is that they are all unhappily single. They feel they no longer fit in with friends and family. And to varying degrees, they each feel like failures at life. Patrick's embarrassment about his "inability" to marry results in his shying away from romantic involvements and leads him to avoid spending time with his family. This avoidance adds to his experience of humiliation and sense of alienation from his family and peers. Sarah worries that maybe she is overly afraid of commitment, causing her to be impatient with whomever she's dating and unable to choose well. She is pessimistic about the success of future relationships because she is worried that perhaps she is too independent and her priorities are misplaced. She, too, finds it difficult to enjoy time with friends and family. Ellen feels "abnormal" and pessimistic about the men available to her, the ones she not so affectionately refers to as "the leftovers."

Patrick, Sarah, and Ellen tell different stories, but share several things in common. One of the more noteworthy similarities is their involvement in the cycle of blame. Many single people who are unhappy alternate between blaming their unhappiness on the opposite sex and on themselves. The fact that friends and relatives enthusiastically participate in perpetuating this cycle makes matters worse.

What most people don't realize is that self-blame and blaming others are opposite sides of the same coin. Like the snake oil touted by salesmen who promised a cure for everything from baldness to aging, blame is an easy answer to your problems that offers nothing but a false sense of control and security. Blame has the same appeal that buying a bottle of the elixir from the pitchman had. With a "remedy" for your woes in hand, you could feel more hopeful about your future and have some sense of control over what was happening to you. This is how a placebo, or sugar pill, works and it is why blame is so appealing to so many of us.

However, like the snake oil salesman's elixir, or the doctor's placebo, blame will only get you so far. And there is a very real danger associated with this approach when real treatment is needed. Like a placebo, blame can keep you from addressing the real underlying problem. Taking a sugar pill can help with many things, but if you have an infection you need antibiotics, not a placebo. The cycle of blame is no different than a lifetime supply of snake oil.

BREAK THE CYCLE OF BLAME. Blame involves fault finding and implies that whoever is to blame is guilty and should be punished. Ironically, blame often keeps you from taking responsibility for the things you can change about yourself. In particular, blame eclipses important feelings you need to be aware of if you want to enjoy your life in the present and choose which fork to take with confidence. Blame keeps you from having an open mind and leads to the ambivalence about marriage we described earlier. For these reasons, breaking the cycle of blame is an essential first step in moving from the alienation stage toward beginning to discover the details of your personal marriage script. And the first step in breaking the cycle is to identify the ways in which you are blaming yourself and/or the opposite sex.

Self-blame not only keeps you from taking real responsibility for your problems, but it also breeds self-loathing. For example, Ellen's belief that the men she dated were "leftovers" insidiously ate away at her self-esteem because, even though she was not consciously aware of it, this bias dictated that she must also be second rate since she too had never married. Single people often blame each other (e.g., "Men are afraid of commitment; all they want is sex," or "Women don't know how to compromise; they want it all"), or themselves ("I am too picky; I never give anyone a chance," "No man is going to want me at this age—I might as well throw in the towel"), in a misguided attempt to feel better about their singlehood and to gain an experience of control. Unfortunately, blame rarely leads to understanding the reasons you are single and unhappy about it. And ultimately, blame keeps you from taking responsibility for the feelings your personal marriage script creates. When you break the cycle of blame, you will have laid the cornerstone for building a new positive sense of self and hopefulness about love.

EXAMINE THE FACTS. Catalogue your negative thoughts about yourself and the opposite sex and begin to test their validity. Single people hold many negative views about themselves that will crumble when they are challenged by the objective facts of who they actually are. We have seen this countless times when individuals make the effort to keep track of the things they say to themselves about the kind of person they are. The problem is that many of these beliefs are rarely voiced out loud. They work their damage silently, in the stray thoughts that linger in the back of your mind.

These thoughts are just out of your awareness. It takes no conscious effort to think them just as it doesn't take any conscious effort to be sitting in a chair or lying in a bed as you read these words. But holding this book up so that you can see it requires some part of your mind to be working to apply sufficient pressure to your grasp so the book does not fall. Take a moment and turn your attention to the sensations in your arms, hands, and fingers. You can feel them now, can't you? You are conscious of the pressure on your fingertips and the subtle strain of muscle in your forearms that holds your hands and this book upright. The stray thoughts about yourself that we are referring to exist in the same place as the physical experiences you just became conscious of. They are just out of awareness because they are so common, so well learned, that they happen with no effort on your part. But they can be brought into consciousness as easily as you discovered the sensations involved in holding this book up.

For example, Ellen was talking about a recent conversation with her mother, who had been trying to arrange a blind date for her. As she described her strong reluctance to being fixed up she said, "I don't know what she was thinking. She gave this guy's mother a picture of me, for God's sake! Can you believe the nerve! I know she was just trying to be helpful, but I don't know that I trust her judgment enough to meet this guy."

"Her judgment about what exactly?" I asked.*

"That I would find him attractive. That he would be someone I'd be interested in."

"Does she know what he looks like? What does she know about him?"

"I don't know," she answered, mulling it over for a moment. "Actually, come to think of it—no. She made a point of saying that her friend was going to give her a picture next week so I could see what he looked like. And she didn't say anything about him except that he was divorced and had a little girl."

When she took a moment to reflect further on her comment about her mother's judgment, Ellen realized that she had been thinking "I've got to look desperate to this guy to have my-mother-ask-his-mother-to-ask-him-for-a-date!" Even though Ellen had let her loved ones know that she wanted to meet men, she harbored an undercurrent of humiliation about the fact that she was being proactive. This one stray thought, "I must look desperate to this guy," led her to uncover many similar thoughts. As it turned out, she had been feeling demeaned by her desire to be set up on dates. As you can imagine, when she went on dates feeling this way, it created an undercurrent of defensiveness on her part not unlike her overt thought about her

*X.A.

mother's judgment: "I probably won't be attracted to him." By not being consciously aware of this disparaging thought about herself, she let it tear not only at her self-esteem, but also at her ability to be open to someone new.

But when she examined the facts, she realized that she had not acted desperate in any way. In fact, she had never asked her mother to go to the lengths that she did. Her mother did that all on her own. If Ellen had not been asked to explain what she meant about not trusting her mother's judgment, she would have skated right over the comment and the underlying message she was giving to herself: "I feel humiliated. What man in his right mind is going to go out with a desperate woman?" In reality Ellen was not acting in a desperate fashion and she didn't feel desperate, at least not consciously.

Because you rarely express thoughts like Ellen's out loud, they remain an undercurrent in your internal dialogue and their validity may never be tested against the evidence. When you let such thoughts fester by not bringing them out into the open, you remain blind to important facts that can change the way you see yourself and the degree to which you are open to love.

In addition to examining your personal circumstance and actions, it is vital to keep the bigger picture in view as well. For example, many sociocultural facts, described in chapter 1, fly in the face of thoughts such as "Everyone is getting married but me" and "I am a failure because I am single." As you become more knowledgeable about the world of single people today, you will be better able to stay on your toes with respect to the negative messages you get from the cultural marriage script.

Remember our examples of how the news media sometimes vilify single people? This aspect of the cultural script is so pervasive that some single people, men in particular, see themselves as extremely deviant for no other reason than because they are single. If you never take a step back and look at how ludicrous such culturally based messages are, you remain vulnerable to the infection they can cause to your feelings of self-worth. For example, as he became more open in therapy, Patrick sheepishly revealed that he worried that he was becoming another Joel Rifkin, the serial murderer. The reason? Because like Joel Rifkin, Patrick had never been married! Merely acknowledging this thought out loud was immensely relieving to him because he could hear how illogical and absurd it sounded. It didn't fit with the facts of who Patrick was. He knew himself to be a responsible, law-abiding citizen. Indeed, he enforced the law for a living and believed that everyone deserved to be treated with respect! He was no Joel Rifkin. You may think such thoughts are unusual, but if you take a moment to listen carefully to the things you say to yourself about being single you may be surprised at what you find. Such thoughts are more common than you might think.

It is also important to examine how you *feel*. Most people fail to make a distinction between feelings and thoughts and this gets them into all kinds of trouble. The biggest problem comes from believing you should be able to control what you feel and that feelings should make sense. We discuss this problem at length in chapter 5 where we also teach you how to be more effective at making the distinction between thoughts and feelings. You will learn that feelings do not have to make sense. When you say to yourself "I couldn't feel that way—it wouldn't make sense" you are confusing feelings with thoughts. That is why many people fail to recognize the ways in which they feel ambivalent about marriage. When you think to yourself "I want to get married, so I can't be feeling revulsion at the idea of it!" you are prematurely closing the door to your heart in the sense that you are "deciding" what you feel rather than "feeling" what you feel. Maybe the revulsion you feel does have something to do with marriage and maybe it doesn't. But if you decide ahead of time that your feelings have to make sense, you'll never find out what you really feel, much less why. And more important, you will never uncover the marriage script that these feelings stem from.

TAKE RESPONSIBILITY. Like Patrick, Sarah, and Ellen, you are probably adding to your unhappiness as a single person. Undoubtedly, this knowledge is one of the reasons you are reading this book. But what should you take responsibility for? Isn't taking responsibility the same as blaming yourself? Not at all. Remember, blame involves fault finding and criticism, while taking responsibility simply involves holding yourself accountable for the things you can do to better your situation.

Patrick wasn't taking responsibility for the fact that he was deeply afraid of abandonment. Unbeknownst to Patrick, his personal marriage script led him to equate intimacy with loss. Patrick's mother had died when he was three years old. His father remarried several years later and during the interim Patrick was taken care of by a number of different women. It is beyond the scope of this discussion to tell you exactly how this childhood experience led to fearing abandonment whenever he got close to someone. But it is not difficult for you to imagine the ways in which this early experience had left a big mark on Patrick's personal marriage script. For him, marriage meant risking significant loss. He learned this in two ways as a child: his own experience of losing the person he was closest to in the world and his observations of his father losing the woman he had married and loved.

As we said earlier, the details of the histories often differ, but the fear that marriage will result in excessive loss is shared by all singles who adhere to the script that Patrick follows. We discuss this script at length in chapter 8. For now, we focus on the ways in which Patrick responded to his script and the fear it created. His knee-jerk response to the fear of abandonment was an overly critical and judgmental approach to women. No one was ever good enough for him so he never had to risk abandonment.

When his last girlfriend cut through his defense and forced him to look at the pattern, he turned his critical and judgmental eye on himself ("I think that something is seriously wrong with me") with the common result: he felt alienated and abnormal. This was self-blame, it was not taking responsibility for his outdated script and the ambivalence it caused.

When he committed himself to the task of uncovering the reasons he was so critical, he began to take responsibility. He completed this task when he identified his underlying marriage script and the feelings it created. We will show you how to do this for yourself throughout this book, mainly by the "show and tell" method we described earlier, but also with some specific techniques that are attached to our second guideline: examine the facts. We will explain these techniques in the next chapter where we discuss all four guidelines in greater detail. But for now, the main point is that Patrick took responsibility when he stopped himself from acting on the feelings his script created rather than attempting to stop himself from feeling.

Sarah blamed herself for being independent and for not giving anyone a chance. This blame led to pessimism about her ability to be intimate with a man. The blame also resulted in self-criticism and a general dissatisfaction with the men she got close to, and it did not help her to take responsibility for the fact that she was conflicted about what she wanted in a relationship. When she began to examine the facts, and saw both that she wanted a lasting relationship and that this was the last thing she wanted, she started taking responsibility. As you will learn in chapter 5, she was able to recognize the source of her ambivalence and to move forward with confidence.

Ellen, the thirty-four-year-old school teacher we told you about, also needed to take responsibility for her feelings. When we first met her she was simply reacting to them by attacking herself and the men she was dating. She was particularly vulnerable to succumbing to single stigma because of this blame. She started taking responsibility when she began to keep track of the things she said to herself such as "I am such a loser" and "I guess I am also one of the leftovers." This led her naturally to uncover her personal marriage script.

Unlike Patrick's script, Ellen's marriage script, which was positive on the face of it, was closer to the cultural script in its emphasis on marriage as a panacea for everything from immaturity to feelings of inadequacy. But because her script kept her focused on how a marriage should look outwardly, it created significant barriers to her quest to tie the knot with someone. As you will learn in the next chapter, Ellen's marriage script made her focus so much on the external qualities of the men she dated that it never allowed her to get truly intimate. For example, she would get extremely anxious about the way her boyfriends dressed, their table manners, and other external, ultimately changeable aspects of their persona.

When Ellen realized the ways in which this script was keeping her at the fork in the road that Sarah described, and stopped having knee-jerk reactions to her anxiety, she too started taking responsibility. Like Patrick and Sarah, she accepted the fact that she could not control the feelings her marriage script created, but realized she could learn how to stop acting on those feelings.

DON'T PUT YOUR LIFE ON HOLD. Many single people delay going on vacations, buying homes, and simply living in the present because they have put their lives on hold while waiting for an intimate relationship or marriage.

For example, Sarah was putting her life on hold by not making a home for herself. She was doing well financially and her accountant had advised her repeatedly to buy a home rather than rent. Sarah resisted this suggestion because she felt that if she bought a home and then got involved with a man who already owned a home, or who didn't like hers, she would have to get rid of it. This pattern extended to the way she lived currently: her apartment was small and the furniture and decor were more like a hotel room than a home. Whenever she got together with her best friend, who was married, they almost always did so at her friend's house, which was more comfortable than Sarah's apartment and felt "warm." Despite acknowledging this, Sarah couldn't help feeling less important in the relationship because her friend never wanted to spend an evening at Sarah's place. This left her feeling alienated and that her life did not have the same value as that of her friends.

Not putting your life on hold also involves "getting back up on the horse" after suffering a disappointment. Patrick found himself avoiding dates because he feared being disappointed yet again. He felt frustrated and pessimistic about the whole endeavor and so he avoided it. But putting his life on hold in this way only worsened his feelings of alienation.

You will naturally begin to stop putting your life on hold after you have identified your personal marriage script and taken responsibility for the feelings it creates. But it is also something you can do proactively. If you change your actions, if you start doing the things that you have been putting off because you are waiting to marry, it will help to change the way you feel about yourself and your singlehood. By not recognizing the ways in which they were putting their lives on hold, Patrick, Ellen, and Sarah were unwittingly adding to their experience of stigma and alienation. Once each of them began to recognize these patterns, and started taking chances (e.g., "I guess I can go away for one week and see if I have a good time," "One date won't kill me," and "If I buy a house and don't want it later on I can always sell it"), they began to lead more satisfying, less stigmatizing lives. They also stopped feeling as if they were viewing life from the sidelines.

In the chapters that follow we show you step by step, in concrete terms, how single people like yourself were able to use these steps to start living in the present, neither waiting for the future nor ruled by the past. The result for each of them was that they once again felt that they fit in, they were more content with their lives and more open to connecting with others. In the next chapter, we show you specific techniques that will help you to utilize these steps in your own life.

4

TAKING CHARGE

What do I think about today being Valentine's Day? Today's the day all the coupled people thank God they're not me.

Doug, a thirty-three-year-old doctor

—◦—

What's the point in trying anymore? The only single men out there are gay or leftovers.

Ellen, a thirty-four-year-old school teacher

B eing single can be alienating and sometimes even demoralizing. But that doesn't absolve you from taking responsibility for your own happiness and peace of mind. Some single people like Doug and Ellen, quoted above, rely so heavily on blame that they are slow to take responsibility for their predicament and slow to graduate from the alienation stage of being single in a couples' world. We met Doug, a thirty-three-year-old doctor, while doing a television broadcast. The focus of the program was on helping single people cope with being single on Valentine's Day. During the broadcast Doug said that what he would find most helpful would be to "stomp all over a box of chocolate hearts." Although he hadn't read this book, he probably would have agreed with much of what we have said up to this point. He recognized the ways in which he felt like a second-class citizen and understood the social pressures that come with being single. However, if he were to stop at that point, angry and bitter about his circumstances, he would be doing nothing to better his situation.

Being angry about the inequalities that exist between single and married people is a good thing. But if the anger never evolves into understanding, forgiveness, and action, the result is bitterness. Being better will not help you to feel happier single. The goal is to understand your marriage script and how it makes you feel so that you can take control of how you react to it. The first step toward reaching this goal is to break the cycle of blame. Even if you don't think you're involved in this cycle, we encourage you to read about it anyway so that you can stay alert to its insidious appeal.

Breaking the Cycle of Blame

If you are like many single people today, you have firsthand experience with the *alienation stage* of being single in a couples' world. And you have probably turned to blame to feel better about yourself. Before you can break the cycle of blame you have to be able to see it. In the stories told above you were able to see how others subscribed to the remedy of blame for the unhappiness they felt.

Seeing how you use blame yourself is not always easy. Blameful thoughts can be subtle, but no less damaging for their elusiveness. These thoughts are rarely obvious, as they are woven into the fabric of our language and culture. A common example is the accusation that all men really want is sex. Although it may be true that men generally have a very active sex drive and will sometimes go to great lengths to have sex, when you conclude that you aren't finding anyone you can get close to because "the only thing men are interested in is sex" you are using blame to try to make sense of the situation you find yourself in.

Below are three questionnaires that can help you to identify the extent to which you are relying on blame excessively to resolve the difficulties you encounter as a single person. Blame breeds stigma, and these questionnaires will help you to identify the ways in which you are using blame to add to the stigma that single people encounter. The first is for single women, the next is for single men, and the last is for the friends and relatives of single people. You may want to give the last survey to a loved one who you feel is unwittingly making singlehood more difficult for you.

Completing the survey that applies to you is the first step toward breaking the cycle of blame. The next step is to start a diary of the blameful and stigmatizing things you think about yourself and about the opposite sex. Every day, identify and write down just one blameful thought you had. It's vital that you do this diligently to become more mindful of this type of thinking and the effect it has on you. Start the diary immediately after completing a survey. You won't have to keep it for long because once you learn to identify the unique ways in which you assign blame, it becomes very hard to persist in doing it.

Blame and Stigma Survey for Women

DIRECTIONS

Circle "T" for true, if the statement describes you or the beliefs that you hold. Circle "F" for false, if it does not. In some instances, the statements that appear below may seem unrelated to blaming and instead reflect what you feel is the essential truth of the matter. Even if you feel that a particular scenario or belief has little to do with blaming, try to answer the question posed directly without censoring your response.

T or F   When thinking about a date or relationship that has gone poorly you say to yourself "Men are dogs," "They're all afraid of commitment," or some other negative generalization.

T or F   You often question the motives of the men you date, suspecting that their main interest is in sex rather than in you.

T or F   You commonly question the motives of the men you date, suspecting that their main interest is in finding a wife rather than in getting to know you.

T or F   When thinking back on a date or relationship that ended poorly you find yourself thinking things like "I am a loser," "I'll never find someone again," or "No one will ever want me."

T or F   When thinking back on a date or relationship that ended poorly you find yourself thinking things like "All the good ones are taken."

T or F   You feel like a failure, or a little embarrassed, when you attend a couples-oriented event such as a wedding without a date.

T or F   Placing or answering a singles ad is a little pathetic.

T or F   Most single women over the age of 35 are desperate to get married.

T or F   Most single men over the age of 35 are afraid of commitment.

T or F   People who choose to remain single are less mature than those who marry.

T or F   Most people who divorce do so frivolously. They do not appreciate the responsibilities that come with marriage.

Blame and Stigma Survey for Men

DIRECTIONS

Circle "T" for true, if the statement describes you or the beliefs that you hold. Circle "F" for false, if it does not. In some instances, the statements that appear below may seem unrelated to blaming and instead reflect what you feel is the essential truth of the matter. Even if you feel that a particular scenario or belief has little to do with blaming, try to answer the question posed directly without censoring your response.

T or F   When thinking about a date or relationship that has gone poorly you say to yourself "Women are too emotional," "They're all screwed up," or some other negative generalization.

T or F   You often question the motives of the women you date, suspecting that their main interest is in a husband rather than in you.

T or F   You commonly question the motives of the women you date, suspecting that their main interest is in a father for their baby rather than in you.

T or F   When thinking back on a date or relationship that ended poorly you find yourself thinking things like "I am a loser,"

"I'll never find someone again," or "No one will ever want me."

T or F   When thinking back on a date or relationship that ended poorly you sometimes think, "All the good ones are taken."

T or F   You feel like a failure, or a little embarrassed, when you attend a couples-oriented event such as a wedding without a date.

T or F   Placing or answering a singles ad is a little pathetic.

T or F   Most single women over the age of 35 are desperate to get married.

T or F   Most single men over the age of 35 are afraid of commitment.

T or F   People who choose to remain single are less mature than those who marry.

T or F   Most people who divorce do so frivolously. They do not appreciate the responsibilities that come with marriage.

SCORING KEY FOR SINGLES
Add up the total number of true statements and find your score in the left-hand column below.

Score	Tendency to rely on blame
8–11	*Excessive blaming.* You are relying almost exclusively on blame to help you to feel good about yourself and/or to experience some control over your difficulties. Your use of blame is unhealthy and keeps you from identifying the true source of your troubles.
6–7	*Moderately high blaming.* You frequently rely on blame to help you to feel good about yourself and/or to experience some control over your difficulties. Your use of blame is unhealthy and oftentimes keeps you from identifying the true source of your troubles.
4–5	*Moderate blaming.* You sometimes rely on blame to help you to feel good about yourself and/or to experience some

control over your difficulties. Your use of blame is sometimes unhealthy and occasionally keeps you from identifying the true source of your troubles.

0–3   *Little or no blaming.* You tend to rely on blame minimally
to make you feel good about yourself. Your use of blame is
probably healthy and does not keep you from identifying
the true source of your troubles.

Blame Survey for Loved Ones

DIRECTIONS

Circle "T" for true, if the statement describes you or the beliefs that
you hold. Circle "F" for false, if it does not. In some instances, the
statements that appear below may seem unrelated to blaming and instead reflect what you feel is the essential truth of the matter. Even if
you feel that a particular scenario or belief has little to do with blaming, try to answer the question posed directly without censoring your
response.

T or F   When thinking about why your loved one is single you
have thoughts such as "She should be more realistic,"
"She's aiming too high," or "He's too picky."

T or F   When thinking about why your loved one is single you
have thoughts such as "She's too selfish to share her life
with someone else," or "She doesn't know how to share."

T or F   You commonly begin conversations with questions such as
"So are you seeing anyone?" or "Are you still seeing . . . ?"

T or F   You try to fix your loved one up despite the fact that she or
he has asked you not to.

T or F   You believe that your single loved one would be married if
he or she tried harder.

T or F   When thinking about why your loved one is single you
have thoughts such as "She just needs to grow up," or "He
thinks he has forever."

T or F   Most single women over the age of 35 are desperate to get married.

T or F   Most single men over the age of 35 are afraid of commitment.

T or F   People who choose to remain single are less mature than those who marry.

T or F   Most people who divorce do so frivolously. They do not appreciate the responsibilities that come with marriage.

SCORING KEY FOR LOVED ONES
Add up the total number of true statements and find your score in the left-hand column below.

Score	Tendency to rely on blame
8–10	*Excessive blaming.* You are relying almost exclusively on blame to understand the difficulties your single loved one is experiencing. Your use of blame is definitely adding to the problems and stigma that single people encounter.
6–7	*Moderately high blaming.* You frequently rely on blame to help you to understand the difficulties your single loved one is experiencing. Your use of blame is likely adding to the problems and stigma that single people encounter.
4–5	*Moderate blaming.* You sometimes rely on blame to help you to understand the difficulties your single loved one is experiencing. Your use of blame is probably adding to the problems and stigma that single people encounter.
0–3	*Little or no blaming.* You tend to rely on blame minimally to understand the difficulties your single loved one is experiencing. Your use of blame is likely not adding to the problems and stigma that single people encounter.

After taking the survey that pertains to you, read through the other two so you can see the many ways in which blame is levied against single people. If you take a closer look at the questions that might seem out of place for a questionnaire on blame you will see not only how each item is relevant, but also how subtle blame can be.

In the questionnaire for loved ones, for example, we ask whether you try to fix your loved one up despite the fact that she or he has asked you not to. A "true" answer to this question implies that you know better than your single loved one and that he or she is not trying hard enough. If only they would try harder, they wouldn't be single. In other words, they're probably too shy or lazy. But isn't it true that sometimes people *are* shy or unmotivated to date? Yes. However, by the time you finish reading this book, we think you will be convinced that such shyness and lack of motivation are symptoms of the problem and not the problem itself. By focusing on the symptoms, you miss the underlying cause. Worse than that, these particular symptoms can be confused with personality characteristics. They are frequently talked about in such a way as to become synonymous with a person's character (e.g., "He's too lazy"). In that regard, such beliefs are the embodiment of blame. Finally, in other cases, the single person is actually trying a lot harder than you could ever know. To assume that she is not, simply because she has not gone out on as many dates as you think she should, is naive and insensitive.

Another cue that blame is being levied is when generalizations, or absolute statements, are made. Statements like "I will never . . ." and "I always . . ." are almost always connected to blaming tactics. If you really believe such things as "I will never fall in love again," "I don't know how to choose well," "I'll never understand," or "I always choose losers," then you might as well pack it in and go home. Blame lurks behind each of these generalizations. Statements indicating that you will never be able to do something or that you have always acted in a particular way not only are pessimistic and inaccurate, but also imply that the reason you fail is because of some flaw in your character.

Blame is even easier to see in the generalizations that damn the opposite sex, such as "All men are dogs," "Men are self-absorbed," "All men want is sex," "All the good ones are taken," "All women want is to get married," "Women today expect too much," "They all want babies, not husbands." If it were that simple, then you wouldn't have to look any further for the cause of your troubles: obviously the opposite sex is the problem! Unquestioned, such generalizations lead to demoralization and a dangerous lack of curiosity about oneself. If the problem lies outside of you, why would you ever bother looking within? Beware of generalizations.

Finally, let a close friend or relative know about your attempts to stop turning to blame to feel better. This will do two things for you.

First, it will make you accountable to someone else. Give your loved one permission to interrupt you whenever you blame yourself or the opposite sex for some demoralizing experience. Joke about it if you can. If your loved one catches you saying something like "All men are dogs," tell her to remind you that you like dogs or that a man on a leash is better than two in a bush, or whatever it takes to get you to laugh at your generalization. Second, it will help your loved one to be watchful of the ways in which she might also be perpetuating the cycle of blame. If you keep the diary we suggested, answer one of the blame questionnaires, read through the other two, talk openly with a loved one about it, and make it a goal not to rely on blame, you can't help but break the cycle.

EXAMINING THE FACTS

When you have broken the cycle of blame, you may still fall back on blaming from time to time, but when you do you'll be aware of it and consequently less likely to persist in it. It is at this point that you will start looking elsewhere for some answers. You will have graduated to the *assessment stage* of being single in a couples' world. You now have an opportunity to examine the facts of your circumstances and the feelings that lie just beneath the surface.

Your circumstances are easy to examine if you take into account the facts we have given you about being single in America today. The statistics we cited earlier reveal much more than the exploding trend toward people spending longer periods single. They speak to the fact that if you have never married, you are not abnormal. If you are single following a divorce, you are also not exceptional. And considering the divorce rate in America, it is safe to say that marriage is a little more scary than it used to be.

Not everyone is getting married, or staying married as the case may be. If marriage is something you want, then it behooves you to understand the reasons why. In our experience we have found that the overwhelming majority of both men and women do have a desire to mate with a partner for a lifetime. But people have other desires as well that can conflict with the wish to be married. That is why examining the facts involves identifying the reasons you have for being single and the feelings produced by your marriage script.

We believe that people do choose to stay single. Circumstances play a role, but so do your expectations and how you act on them. There is choice involved and that is the good news. Because once you understand what it is you are choosing and why, doors open up and your options multiply. You will have taken charge. To identify your reasons for being single, you will have to first challenge the outdated negative attitudes you have about being single because these beliefs keep you from uncovering your true motivations. Sarah held such beliefs but never questioned them until she did so in therapy.

Sarah thought that her priorities were misplaced and that if she were more like June Cleaver, the stay-at-home 1950s television housewife, she would be more likely to marry. She assumed that career and marriage were incompatible. Her negative view about singlehood went something like this: A single woman with a career is unmarried because she is too focused on professional status. The irony is that all but one of the married women Sarah knew personally had careers outside of the home. When we pointed out that most of her friends had successful careers and marriages, Sarah's negative attitude was weakened. Once this blameful belief was deflated, she naturally began to look elsewhere for the reasons she was single.

You can uncover your own marriage script by doing two things: capturing the stray thoughts about intimacy, marriage, and yourself that pass through your mind every day and learning from the experience of other single people in the pages ahead. To help you to begin the process of uncovering your own script take a few moments to complete the following sentences. Put this book down and go get a pen. You will want to be able to look back at what you wrote later on.

DIRECTIONS
Complete the following sentences by filling in the blanks. Don't second guess yourself. *Write down the very first thing that pops into your mind.* Fill in the blank even if what you thought of doesn't seem to make sense. There are no right or wrong answers and your responses will not be scored. Skip those sentences that clearly do not apply to your life. Remember, what you write down doesn't have to make sense.

1. When I am married I will be _____.

2. My mother and father had a _____ relationship.

3. Marriage is _____.

4. When I was a child, the thing I loved most about my relationship with my mother was _____.

5. When I was a child, the thing I loved most about my relationship with my father was _____.

6. As a child, I really hated when my mother _____.

7. As a child, I really hated when my father _____.

8. Marriage can make you _____.

9. My father was very _____ to me.

10. My mother was very _____ to me.

11. I am closest to my _____.

12. The best thing about my parents' marriage was _____.

13. I think my parents probably had a _____ sex life.

14. The worst thing about my parents' marriage was _____.

15. My mother felt _____ married to my father.

16. My father felt _____ married to my mother.

17. The person I imagine marrying will be _____ _____.

18. I will be _____ when I am married.

19. Growing up, I always thought that I would be married by the time I was _____ years old.

20. My mother was _____ being married.

21. My father was _____ being married.

22. Married people are _____.

23. Single people are _____.

Look at what you wrote down. Did anything surprise you? If so, take some time to reflect on what you wrote and where it came from. Did any of your answers trigger a memory? If so, follow them to see where they take you. If you have a friend you can talk to about such things, go over the responses with him or her. Start a dialogue about the topic of what you feel about marriage generally, your fears about intimacy, your experience of your parents' marriage, and most important, your childhood experience of your relationships with your mother and father. The dialogue can be an internal one, but it will be more illuminating if it is with a like-minded friend. Pick someone who is not jumping to conclusions about why you are single and unhappy about it.

As you begin to think of your own script about marriage, turn back to the table of contents and read through some of the more common blameful accusations about singlehood that are expressed in the titles of chapters 5 through 9. Accusations such as "he is stuck on the ideal," "she thinks the grass is always greener somewhere else," "he is too afraid of making the wrong choice to make a move," "she hasn't left home yet," and "he never goes all the way, never makes a real commitment," merely describe outward appearances without really explaining anything. But they offer clues as to what lies beneath the surface. Look for the one that fits best with your experience of being single and read that chapter with special care. In each of these chapters, the marriage script underlying the blameful accusation is revealed in the stories of other single people like yourself. You will learn how each of them came to understand what the real source of their unhappiness was and how this knowledge enabled them to choose which path they wanted to take with confidence. As you read their stories, keep your responses to the sentence completions in mind. Better yet, turn back to the page you wrote your answers on whenever the urge strikes you. You never know where a stray urge or thought might lead unless you follow it. By staying mindful of the thoughts you have about intimacy, marriage, your childhood relationships with your parents, and yourself, you will be able to identify your personal script. Indeed, if you've read this far you have probably already begun to sketch an outline. As you learn from the experience of other singles in the pages ahead, you will find that you can flesh out the outline of your personal marriage script.

TAKING RESPONSIBILITY

When you have uncovered your marriage script and identified the fears that it has spawned, you will have entered the *acceptance stage* of being single in a couple's world. You can now begin to take responsibility for how you react to this script and the feelings it creates. This step involves changing the negative aspects of being single that you have control over: your thoughts and how you respond to the feelings that come from both the cultural script and your personal script.

The cultural script promises, among other things, that marriage will make you an adult, respectable, moral, and socially acceptable. At first glance it may seem counterintuitive that your expectations of how marriage will transform you can worsen your experience of being single, but consider the following analogy and perhaps this idea will seem less odd. Like all the kids in his class Robert, a fourteen-year-old boy who is a rabid basketball fan, wanted a pair of the new sneakers that were endorsed and named after Michael Jordan. Everywhere he went, at school, at the mall, and on television, he kept hearing about how great they were and more important, how cool he would be if he had a pair on his feet. His mother tried three separate times to get him a pair, but the stores were always sold out. In the end, worried about the sorry shape his current sneakers were in, she settled on an equally expensive and well made pair of sneakers. When he came home from school after wearing his new shoes the first time, he looked miserable. His mother asked what was wrong. Pointing down at his sneakers he snapped back, "I felt like a dork. Man, I am such a loser!"

Thanks in part to very effective marketing that capitalizes on the psychology of self-perception, Robert and his peers had very strong feelings about who they would become if they wore the shoes endorsed by Michael Jordan. They would have social status and be considered cool. The other side of that coin was the belief that any other shoes are worn by "dorks" and "losers." This is exactly what advertisers aim for when building positive associations to a product.

As we argued earlier, the cultural script with its mandate to marry is a powerful force that can shape how people act. The technique by which it wields its power is essentially the same as that used by advertisers to sell shoes. Please be assured that we are not equating marriage to a popular brand of sneakers! Nor are we suggesting that you are childish if you care about the symbolism attached to being married. As we have said several times before, we understand that there are many good reasons to get married. What we are discussing here has nothing to do with marriage, it has to do with the ways in which objects can be used as symbols for other things. Even a spouse or a particular type of relationship can be thought of as an object in this context (e.g., if you are close friends with the President of the United States or intimate with a highly admired person in your community).

The culture's script has turned marriage into a powerful symbol with very positive "self-associations." For example, Ellen, the thirty-four-year-old divorced teacher we told you about earlier, felt that when she married again she would be a success. She would have vindicated herself to her family and to her ex-husband. For Ellen, in subtle ways, marriage was equivalent to proving that she was a desirable, capable, and mature woman. It would erase her experience of being a failure, a self-perception that she had lived with since the day she had asked her husband for a divorce. She imagined how good it would feel to bump into her "ex" on the street, looking her best, with a wedding band on her finger and a new husband on her arm.

Positive scripts, either from the culture or your personal history, about who you will become when you marry will also create problems for you after you tie the knot. Expectations about how you will feel about yourself when you marry can result in post-honeymoon blues when you realize that you are the same person you were prior to the wedding day. Less obvious is the fact that positive scripts about marriage can also create problems when you are single. For example, when you are dating, such scripts create subtle pressures that lead to putting yourself and your date under a microscope. See if you can read between the lines of Ellen's account of a blind date to detect the influences of both the cultural marriage script and her own personal script.

"I hate blind dates, but it's the only way I can meet anyone. The worst part is getting ready. I can't stop looking in the mirror to see if my makeup and hair are just right. I change outfits at least three times! It's crazy.

"There was this one date, with this guy Jim; he was great on the phone when we talked and I had heard good things about him. My friend who knew him said he was cute, he had a real job, and he was also divorced. At least we would have that in common. Getting ready for *that* date was a panic. I was so nervous and jittery—I must have changed clothes five times beforehand! The only thing that calmed me down was remembering how many times I had had high expectations before a blind date only to have them crushed the moment he walked through the door. Reminding myself of that works really well. I calm down when I can also focus on the fact that I don't even know this guy and yet I am acting like I am certain I want him to like me. Who knows, chances are better than not that I'll want him to lose my phone number by the time the evening ends!

"Anyway, he shows up, about ten minutes late, and he's actually cute. So I am immediately relieved on that score. But, he's standing there with a bottle of wine in his hand and suggests we have a drink before going out. I was thinking 'that's a little presumptuous' but decided what the hell, one drink in my apartment would be OK. He followed me into the kitchen when I went to get the wine glasses and started asking me about how my day had gone. He was nice, attentive, and seemed genuinely interested in what I do for a living. It all sounds pretty good, right? Well, what I didn't tell you yet was how he was dressed. I didn't see what he had on until he took his overcoat off. Tasteless. The man was absolutely tasteless. His shoes were the worst. He was wearing the most worn out pair of cheap loafers I had ever seen. He must be color blind because nothing matched. His pants weren't pressed and when he sat down and crossed his legs, I saw he had a hole on the bottom of one of his shoes! I don't want to be shallow, I know these things shouldn't matter, but I couldn't help the way I felt. It's like all the air went out of my balloon. I felt so disappointed and even a little repulsed. Nevertheless, I gave it my best shot and tried not to let it get in the way.

"We went to dinner and things started to improve a little, especially after the first drink, but when he ordered I felt my balloon deflate further. He asks the waiter to bring him a bottle of ketchup with his steak! The thing that was so weird was that he was the same person I had talked to on the phone. He was bright, personable, very attentive, and on top of all that he was physically attractive, his face was cute, and he had an athletic build. But I couldn't help thinking that I wouldn't want to run into my ex with this guy. I felt a little embarrassed to be seen with him . . . especially when the bottle of ketchup arrived at the table."

On this first date Ellen could not stop herself from obsessing over whether he was the "one" she would want on her arm. She would ask herself, "Is he someone I would feel proud to be seen with?" The problem with this level of scrutiny is that she got so lost in the details—the way he dressed, his culinary sophistication, and such—that she lost the forest for the trees. She was so focused on the details and on the future that she could not be in the moment, much less enjoy it.

Her personal marriage script, the belief that marriage to the perfect man would vindicate her deep feelings of inadequacy, dovetailed with the cultural script which promised she would become a success as a person when she tied the knot. Both scripts first put her under a microscope while she was preparing for the date, then focused on Jim once the date was underway. In the rare instances when Ellen's dates survived this level of evaluation, if she came away with a good impression about them being "marriage material," she then turned the microscope back on herself. She would review each date in excruciating detail to try to figure out if she had done anything to make herself undesirable.

Such feelings are predictable and to be expected when you've met someone you are attracted to. They motivate you to put your best foot forward. This is a natural stage of courtship. But when the stakes are as high as they were for Ellen, when marriage becomes synonymous with self-vindication and feeling like a success as a person, such feelings hinder rather than help. Worse yet, like a coin, such biases have another side. The flip side of her belief that a marriage to the right man would prove that she was desirable, capable, and mature is that she is currently undesirable, incompetent, and immature because she is single.

Taking responsibility also entails dealing with the feelings and thoughts created by your personal marriage script. This involves testing their relevance to your life today. Ellen needed to learn what the deeper feelings of inadequacy were really about and how to keep from reacting to the anxiety they created. One of her reactions was to not give men like Jim a second look. In the chapters to come, we provide many examples for you to draw from to help you to identify your personal script and learn how to refrain from acting on the negative thoughts spawned by it. Simply making a list of your associations to marriage and singlehood will start you on your way to identifying it. When Patrick, the police officer we told you about earlier, was asked to keep track of the adjectives he used when talking about marriage and singlehood, he uncovered several key biases that he had never known were there. When he realized that he sometimes described his sisters as being "respectable people [because] they're married" he discovered that he was equating marriage with respectability and singlehood with being disreputable. Patrick also said he wanted to "settle down" and that this was synonymous with being married. When he reflected on what it meant to be "settled down" he realized that for him the phrase meant being responsible, having a career and a home. Patrick, single as he was, had already settled down!

Taking responsibility involves identifying your personal script, or expectations about relationships, and learning how to keep it from wielding such power over your sense of self. One of the main assaults you will have to contend with is the emotions that stem from both the cultural script and your personal script: feelings of anxiety, sadness, and anger directed at yourself or the opposite sex. Learning how to respond to these feelings in a manner that keeps you open to solutions, rather than jumping to conclusions, is vital. Only then can you begin to work on the thing you really have control over: the way in which you think and act on your feelings. Once you have identified the marriage scripts that are influencing your life and begun the work of challenging their truthfulness and managing the feelings they give rise to, you can then begin to look elsewhere for a positive sense of self. If you stay focused on the things you don't currently have that you believe would make you whole, then you run the very real risk of letting life pass you by while you wait.

Not Putting Life on Hold

When you have accomplished the main tasks described in the first three steps, you will enter the *assimiliation stage* of being single in a couples' world. You will be ready, willing, and able to stop putting your life on hold. But what exactly does it mean to put one's life on hold? The following lyrics say it best:

> . . . my soul checked out missing as I sat listening
> to the hours and minutes ticking away.
> I was just sittin' around waiting for my life to begin
> while it was all just slippin' away.
> I'm tired of waitin' for tomorrow to come
> for that train to come roarin' round the bend.
> I got a new suit of clothes a pretty red rose
> and a woman I can call my friend.
> These are better days . . .

> BRUCE SPRINGSTEEN
> "Better Days" from the *Lucky Town* album

When we first introduced the last step to being single in the present, we told you about Ellen's reluctance to take a week-long vacation because she preferred to go away only when she could do it with a lover. Such a preference is understandable and healthy. What could be wrong with such a desire? Companionship and love can certainly make life more sweet. Bruce Springsteen's lyrics speak of his joy in finding someone to share his life, a woman whose love helped him to live in the present. But even Bruce would agree with us that the reason he stopped "sitting around waiting for [his] life to begin" was because he took some risks. He stopped putting his life on hold by learning more about what he was afraid of and facing those fears. The result was a new sense of himself ("a new suit of clothes"), an openness to love ("a pretty red rose"), and a marriage to a woman that he felt was truly his friend. During an interview he gave to James Henke of *Rolling Stone* magazine, Springsteen suggests that it was only after he began to face his fears and to examine the facts of his life, that he was able to stop putting his life on hold and open his heart to love. Even if you are unfamiliar with his work, or do not relate to his music, what he had to say in this interview will likely sound familiar and his experience will be one you may relate to.

JH: What was it that woke you up to the fact that you were missing something or had a problem?

BS: Unhappiness. And other things, like my relationships. They always ended poorly; I didn't really know how to have a relationship with a woman. Also, I wondered how can I have this much money and not spend it . . . I couldn't spend it, I couldn't have any fun. So a lot of things started to not feel logical.

JH: Did you ever go to a therapist or seek help like that?

BS: Oh, yeah. I mean I got really down. . . . [During therapy] I realized my life is waiting to be lived. All the love and the hope and the sorrow and the sadness—that's all over there, waiting to be lived. And I could ignore it and push it aside or I could say yes to it. But to say yes to part of it is to say yes to all of it. That's why people [often] say no to all of it . . . I'll skip the happiness as long as I don't have to feel the pain. (*Rolling Stone*, August 6, 1992, p. 42)

Bruce Springsteen had it all. He had millions of dollars, a multitude of faithful and adoring fans, and he loved his work with a consuming passion. But he was miserable. In many ways he had put his life on hold. Rather than blaming womankind, or himself, he took responsibility for his troubles. He began a process of self-examination that ultimately led him to some real answers.

As you can see from his description of this process, the answers were not always simple, but they were valid. As he described it, "The best thing I did was I got into therapy. That was really valuable. I crashed into myself and saw a lot of myself as I really was. And I questioned all of my motivations. Why am I writing what I am writing? Do I mean it? Am I bull-shitting? Am I just trying to be the most popular guy in town? Do I need to be liked that much? I questioned everything . . . it was good. You should do that. And then you realize there is no single motivation to anything. You're doing it for all of those reasons" (p. 44).

Our experience has been exactly like Bruce's. Whether you do it working together with a psychotherapist or on your own, whenever you make the time to regularly examine your beliefs, feelings, and actions, you not only get answers to your questions but solutions to problems. As Bruce began to examine the facts he began to discover things about himself. His needs for approval and connection were as strong as anyone's. We can't tell from the interview what script about marriage Bruce held, but we do know that the interview occurred after his divorce from his first wife. And one thing is clear, whatever his marriage script was, it seems to have led to fear.

Somehow marriage and connection had become synonymous with a fear of loss. This fear was revealed when he said, "Wow, I see. This love is here to be had and to be felt and experienced? [For] everybody on a daily basis? And I knew why [I ran from it], because it's very frightening" (p. 70). He went on to say that it was the fear of loss that had been keeping his heart closed and his life on hold. This fear was also making his concerts notoriously long. He revealed that when he was on stage he felt connected to people, and the relief from his loneliness and "self-loathing" was so great that he didn't want the experience to end. To the delight of his fans, his concerts would often last three to four hours and longer! They would have been surprised to learn that these marathon concerts were born from a deep sense of alienation and loneliness.

We don't know the details of how he accomplished it, but it is clear from this one interview that he examined the facts of his life carefully and took responsibility for his unhappiness by understanding his feelings. And, in exactly the same way we are talking about here, he also succeeded in not succumbing to knee-jerk reactions to these fears. His concerts are rarely as long as they used to be. To paraphrase the song lyric quoted earlier, he stopped responding to his fears, and in doing so, stopped sitting around waiting for his life to begin.

In Ellen's case, she acted on the healthy desire to share her life with someone in an unhealthy manner when she refused to take vacations while single. This is another one of the more obvious examples of how single people can put their lives on hold while waiting for romantic companionship or marriage. Sometimes the self-made barriers to living life fully are more subtle. As you may recall, Ellen's friend had wanted the two of them to vacation together in Mexico. While discussing the various options her friend presented, Ellen remarked, "If we go there without boyfriends every man in the place will think we're looking to get picked up. And you can forget about going to a Club Med. No way. Those places are meat markets . . . they're for desperate women!" Such beliefs not only reinforced her reluctance to take a vacation, but also added to the prejudice that single people who enjoy themselves are somehow emotionally stunted and desperate. Ellen's friend picked up on this when she argued, "I've gone to 'those' places. What are you saying . . . that I am desperate!?"

"No, no, I didn't mean it the way it sounded. I just feel like when I get there everyone will be looking at me and thinking 'how pathetic.' And when I come back I wouldn't want to tell anyone where I'd been."

"So you are saying it's something I should be embarrassed about. It sounds like you did mean it the way I heard it."

"No!" Ellen shot back, "No, no, I mean, I don't know what I mean. I . . . I'm all confused. I don't think you're pathetic or desperate, really I don't. If anything I admire you for putting yourself out there. You really live. But I guess you're right about one thing . . . I do think of singles vacations as being for desperate and pathetic women. Don't get mad! I'm not including you in that. Every other woman, but not you."

They both burst out laughing at this last implicit criticism and feeble attempt at a retraction. Ellen honestly had a very high opinion of her friend. This conversation made her sit up and take notice because she realized that her negative bias about single women who went to places like Club Med didn't really make much sense given the fact that she didn't consider her friend either desperate or pathetic. And she went to "those" places frequently. When Ellen became curious about her reluctance to put herself "out there," as she would describe it, she started to uncover some answers.

Like Bruce, Ellen was afraid, and this is what kept her from going away with her friend. It will come as no surprise that among the things she feared was that she would be perceived as desperate and pathetic. Ellen felt that if she went away alone, or on a single's vacation, she was publicly announcing that she was unattached. She harbored the fear that being unattached meant she was unattractive to men, in the broadest sense of the word. This realization brought her face to face with an even deeper worry she had not been aware of. She wasn't afraid that she was going to get "hit on" by a man while on vacation as much as she was worried that she would not! In other words, she was afraid that her worse fears about herself, that she was inadequate as a woman, would be reinforced further if she received no attention. Once she was able to name the underlying fears, doors opened up to her. The choice of whether to go or not to go was made easier. The stakes were not as high as they were before she understood her fears. Prior to this knowledge, choosing between staying home and going away with her friend was like choosing between being a competent and proud woman and a desperate and pathetic one.

As we described in the previous chapter, there are several other ways single people put their lives on hold. Sometimes it is as subtle as refusing to meet someone new or as obvious as not buying a home when in every other way it makes sense to do so. In the chapters ahead you will read about the various ways other single people have put their lives on hold while waiting for companionship and marriage. Before you read on, make a list of the things you have hesitated doing without a spouse or lover. Next to each item on this list, write down the reasons you wouldn't do the thing you noted. We have found that if you do this, at least nine times out of ten you will come to the conclusion that you have nothing to lose and a lot to gain if you do the thing you are avoiding. The most common reason single people stay on the sidelines is fear. The good news is that whether it is fear of loss, rejection, or some other worry, if you're anything like Bruce and Ellen, your fears can be overcome once you have faced them directly.

Assimilation to a couples' world is complete when you stop putting your life on hold. When Bruce stepped off the stage and Ellen went on vacation, it signified a newfound feeling of belonging and connection to the world in which they lived. Feelings typically perpetuate themselves by influencing our actions. This newfound feeling of connection led Ellen to act in ways that caused her to feel even closer to her loved ones. When she went on vacation she felt closer to her friend and to the community of single people she met while she was away. When she returned home from this experience she found that she did not feel embarrassed. This enabled her to talk about her vacation with co-workers and family, show pictures, and see that no one was responding to her as if she were a pariah. She came back from this vacation feeling less alienated at home.

The following five chapters will help you to identify your underlying marriage script. You may hold elements of one or more of these scripts which are as much about intimate relationships as they are about marriage. Each chapter title expresses a blameful accusation levied against single people that masks one of the following personal scripts: if you marry the perfect partner, you will be OK; marriage is for losers; marriage is just too scary—it's too easy to get burned; marriage will leave you all alone; and marriage involves losing yourself—both your needs and identity will be lost. Some of the chapters will be more meaningful to you than others depending on the script you are following. But in each chapter, you can learn how various single people uncovered their marriage scripts and learned how to live happier and fuller lives while becoming more open to love. In the last three chapters we give you step-by-step instructions on how to avoid friendly fire from friends and family, how to stop competing with your single and married friends, and how to make your needs count in a couples' world.

WHY ARE YOU SINGLE?

5

STUCK ON THE IDEAL

I know he's a great guy, but I just can't get over how insecure he seems and what he does for work. I'd like to not let it bother me this much but I can't help it. My mother says that my problem is that I am waiting for Prince Charming.

        Julia, a thirty-two-year-old administrative assistant

—◦—

Matt needs to grow up. His problem is that he's too picky and never satisfied with who he's involved with. The only women he seems interested in are the unobtainable ones. He better be careful or he's going to end up alone, wandering from one brief relationship to the next, because no one's ever good enough for him.

        Carol's comment about her friend Matt, a thirty-seven-year-old lawyer

E veryone wants the best partner possible. But how do you draw the line between a quest for the best and the pursuit of an impossible dream? If you find that no one who is available to you measures up to your hopes and expectations, then you have probably crossed that line. In our experience, singles who are charged with being "stuck on the ideal" by their loved ones or by an overly self-critical superego rarely understand what this tendency is really all about.

On the surface, two common patterns emerge. One pattern is typified by the single person who appears to be "aiming too high," while the other is embodied by the single who obsesses over someone who appears perfect to them, but is unobtainable for various reasons. Because no one ever seems good enough, these patterns are often mistaken for snobbishness ("No one will ever be good enough for him") or masochism ("She only wants what she can't have").

But in our experience, this pattern is rarely due to being a snob or a masochist. Rather, it stems from a personal marriage script which says, among other things: "If I marry someone perfect it will prove that I'm OK and I can feel better about myself." This script was hinted at when Matt had this to say about Miranda, a woman he was feeling obsessed with: "If I can get her, I'd really be something." And when Julia said: "It's strange to say it, but I feel like if I marry the right guy, I'll become like him. If he's secure in himself and he wants me, then I'll feel more secure about who I am. It's like 'if you're OK, then I must be OK!'"

You're OK So I Must Be OK

O bviously there are many other good reasons to hold out for the "right one," but as you will discover in this chapter—provided you can keep an open mind to the idea—this particular script can keep you from enjoying yourself when single and also hinder you from getting close to someone with whom you could be very happy over the long run. Although most of the scripts you will read about in this book have some common elements—such as their origin in childhood, in the give and take of your relationships with your parents, and in the observations of the quality of your parents' marriage—they differ in other significant ways. One of the more obvious differences is how the scripts are acted out. Julia's and Matt's stories can help you to learn if this script has relevance to your own life.

Julia

"I think my mother worries that I am waiting for Prince Charming," explained Julia, an attractive thirty-two-year-old administrative assistant, currently in a relationship. Julia had agreed to be interviewed to help in our research for this book. One of the hardest things about being single for her was her uncertainty about whether she was holding out for something that didn't exist. She had the same fear, described word for word, as the group of twenty-three-year-old women we wrote about in chapter 1, "My biggest fear is that I am going to end up all alone."

"What is it you think you're waiting for?" I asked.*

"It's hard to say. The external stuff is easier to describe. I want someone who is a man—a real man—secure about himself and successful. Of course he's got to be cute!

"But beyond that, it's more like a feeling. A feeling of comfort and security. Like getting tucked into bed at night, warm and safe in clean sheets. This probably sounds childish," she added a little self-consciously, "it's not that I want a daddy . . . it's that I want to feel protected and safe. What I want is a savior."

"Really? A savior from what?"

"That's a good question. I haven't really thought about it before . . . maybe from worrying. Someone to save me from having to worry. Someone who is secure in himself, who isn't as anxious as I am."

"Does Michael [her boyfriend of two months] make you feel that way?"

"No," she replied, quickly, "I think he worries about stuff as much, sometimes even more than I do. He's a great guy, don't get me wrong, but he definitely doesn't fit my fantasy for who I imagine spending the rest of my life with."

Julia was quick to emphasize that she generally enjoyed being single despite the fact that she was growing worried about ending up alone. Ironically, the trigger for her angst about being terminally single was forged back when she was ten years old. At that time she had written in her diary that she didn't want to get married until she was twenty-seven years old. By that time she figured she would be finished with school, have a career, and have had "worldly adventures and marvelous affairs." When she turned twenty-eight as a single woman living alone, it triggered the growth of a seed of doubt about herself. By the time she first shared her story with us, the doubt had grown considerably and she was feeling many of the things that come with being in the alienation stage of being single in a couples' world.

Typical of people at this stage, she had begun to subscribe to the cycle of blame. When she remarked that "My relationship to the fantasy is much more appealing than anything I could ever have in real life," she revealed a hint of self-recrimination. When she added "Ultimately . . . my fantasy husband will save me from . . . loserdom!" she spilled the beans. She not only felt alienated, but was beginning to subscribe to the theory that she was a failure.

*X.A.

Julia's feelings of alienation as a single person were triggered by missing her marriage milestone and becoming more vulnerable to the stigma and pressures created by the cultural marriage script. But much of the anxiety and discomfort she was feeling about the men she dated ultimately stemmed from her own marriage script which told her "marry a secure man and you will be secure in yourself." But before we continue her story and tell you how she moved through all four stages successfully, we turn to Matt's tale to illustrate how the same script, expressed somewhat differently, was causing him similar headaches.

Matt

Matt, a thirty-seven-year-old, never-married lawyer came to see me* because he worried about his obsession with one woman, Miranda, who seemed only mildly interested in him. They had never dated formally, but they were friends who saw each other once or twice a week and spoke on the telephone almost nightly. Matt felt certain that she was attracted to him as more than a friend. He had confessed his desire for a romantic relationship and she had neither rebuffed him nor conceded similar feelings. Instead, she encouraged him in subtle and ambiguous ways.

Miranda's attraction to Matt, however meager, was all the fuel he needed to launch an intense campaign to win her over. He couldn't stop thinking about her and his emotions were swinging wildly from elation whenever she was responsive to his overtures, to feeling crushed whenever she mentioned she had a date with someone else. I asked him why he thought his feelings for her were so strong.

"If I can get her, I'll have the world! She's so beautiful and sexy. She's the kind of woman who, when she walks into a room, all the guys turn their heads. She's charismatic and successful. What more could I want?"

"And how do you think I might be able to help you?" I asked.

"I was thinking about that on the way over here. Maybe you could help me to get her." He laughed, and continued, "I guess you guys don't do that, huh? I don't know really. I was hoping you would tell me. I do know that I can't go on thinking about her all the time. My

*X.A.

work is starting to suffer because I can't concentrate. When she goes out on a date I feel like I am going crazy. I keep calling her until she answers and then I hang up. That way I know when she came home."

"You hang up when she answers?"

"You would too if you had left ten hang-ups on her answering machine that same night! If I talk to her then she'd know it was me that was calling. It's crazy. I don't think she suspects me, but I feel terrible that I am doing that to her. I have to stop focusing so much energy on her. Something's got to break. Either she goes out with me or I have to find some way of moving on."

Matt had two distinct problems: one was how to get a little control over his lovestruck compulsive behavior and the other was how to get a handle on why he felt what he did so intensely. One way to get a foothold with both problems was to get a picture of how he felt about himself currently and what he thought a relationship with Miranda, or someone like her, would do for his sense of self.

"If she did go out with you, how would you feel about yourself?" I asked.

"I'd feel great. Proud."

"Proud about what?"

"Proud that she was with me. She's a real 'keeper,' someone I would look forward to introducing to my friends."

"Would they think any differently of you if you were with Miranda?"

"I think they would. In fact, when my friend Jimmy met her for the first time, he took me aside within five minutes of laying eyes on her and asked me, 'Are *you* seeing *her*?!' He was seriously impressed. All I could say was 'I'm working on it.'"

"Impressed with whom and what?"

"I think he was impressed by her. Miranda's a real looker, she's successful, charming, she's every guy's dream. Jimmy was also impressed with me. Even when I told him I wasn't dating her! I could tell that the fact that she was a friend of mine and because I thought I had a decent shot at something more—that his opinion of me went up. You can just feel those things. Hell, for that matter *I* feel that way. If I ended up married to Miranda I'd really be something!"

ALIENATION

M att's marriage script was revealing itself. If he could marry his ideal woman, it would change him somehow, it would make him someone special. This expectation begs the question of what the single person who is "stuck on the ideal" currently thinks of himself. Although he wasn't all that aware of it, Matt had a lukewarm opinion of himself as a man. Over the course of our first conversation Matt revealed that he sometimes felt "mediocre and average, just like every other 'suit' on the freeway driving to a nine-to-five." Outwardly, Matt was generally confident despite this underlying current of self-doubt. But he felt that marriage would be a defining milestone in his life. It would be both an achievement and a vindication of sorts. It would prove, mostly to himself, that he was special and that he was a man. And although he did not use this exact word, it would also signify his "citizenship" in the couples' world. He would no longer feel like an outsider, which is how he had been feeling since his thirtieth birthday.

"I never really thought much about when I would get married until I turned thirty," he offered. "But the past few years I've definitely been looking. That's what's so exciting about Miranda. It's really the first time I've had the desire to go that far with a relationship. Don't get me wrong, I don't want to get married tomorrow, it's just that I can see it with her. I can imagine it—whereas before I never could.

"It's almost a relief, because I was starting to worry that I would never feel this way. I felt kind of abnormal. I mean, I should have fallen for someone, really fallen, at least once. I was starting to feel like a freak with my friends. They didn't seem to have the same problem as me."

Like Julia, Matt's single status was beginning to make him feel alienated from his peers. It had begun to signify that he was lagging behind emotionally and that something might be more seriously wrong with him—that he was "abnormal" or "a freak." He was looking for a way out of this feeling when he found Miranda.

It was in the alienation stage that Matt and Julia each began to look for ways to belong. During this period both were drawn to an ideal in an attempt to feel better about themselves. Julia's ideal man held the promise of saving Julia from "loserdom" and Matt's Miranda would save him from being an "average Joe." Both ideals provided them with hope that they could someday belong to, and be respected by, the couples' world. But they still experienced feelings of alienation, especially when they felt that their ideal partners were out of reach.

A Kernel of Truth in Every Script

N ow the tricky thing with both the cultural and personal scripts you follow is that they almost always contain an element of truth. Although both scripts were written in the past, they have aspects that will hold some relevance to your life today. Remember, we never said you had to replace these scripts to start living your life in the present, but you do have to revise them so they're up to date. The fact is that Matt's friends *would* treat him a little differently and he would be seen as more special if he married Miranda. Julia would feel less anxious and be perceived less as a loser by her family and friends if she married someone who fit *her* ideal. So what could be wrong with following the "You're OK so I must be OK" script that they both shared?

One obvious problem is that the ideal mate doesn't exist! Maybe you are wondering: But don't men who are secure in themselves exist for people like Julia to find them? And didn't Matt already find his ideal woman? Maybe they successfully negotiated the assessment stage and discovered what it would take for them to feel better about themselves and to fit in. Perhaps they are not stuck on an ideal so much as holding out for what they deserve? These are valid questions, but so is the experience Julia had while holding out for what she felt she needed. Read on and decide for yourself.

During the course of our conversations, which took place approximately every six weeks over a one-year period, Julia revealed more about her relationship with Michael and learned about the steps we give in this book. During one of our early discussions Julia revealed that she was thinking about breaking up with Michael. At that point they had been dating just shy of four months.

"We have a good time together generally, but I can tell he wants to get serious. I don't think I can do it. I don't know what's wrong with me. He's a nice guy, he's got a decent job and makes a good living at it. I'm thinking about breaking up with him."

"How do you feel about him?"

"Well, I'm not in love," she answered, "but I am very fond of him. He's sweet and sensitive."

"Are you attracted to him?"

"He's very cute."

"OK, but how's your sex life together?"

"Pretty good actually. He's good in bed. In fact, to be perfectly honest . . . the sex is great! The only time it's not is when I am thinking about how insecure he is. It's not so much fun then. And the problem is I am thinking about that a lot more these days."

"You mentioned a couple of things when you told me you were thinking of breaking up—they were the same reservations you told me about the first time we talked about Michael."

"His job and his lack of confidence—right?" Julia interrupted.

"Exactly. Can you tell me more about these reservations?"

"Sure. He works for a real estate company managing commercial properties so he mostly deals with corporate and large business accounts. It's not like he's out trying to sell houses or anything like that. His income is steady and pretty good really. He makes as much as I do. The problem is that I think he's settling because he lacks confidence. He never went to college—well, he did complete one year—and I think that makes him feel insecure. You can tell by the way he talks about his boss.

"He's been working for the same company for five years and the last increase in salary and commission he received was over three years ago. From what he tells me he's done right by them but he can't bring himself to ask for a raise. He sounds scared of his boss. I hate to say it but he sounds like a wimp when he talks about his job."

Julia reveals that she feels self-conscious about thinking that Michael is a wimp. You might be inclined to reassure her and tell her that you agree he's a wimp and that she should "get over it." He's a whiner and whining is never attractive. It's understandable she'd have reservations about him.

We wouldn't argue with you or with Julia for finding Michael's lack of confidence unattractive. It is. But lurking beneath that observation is an undercurrent of less reasonable feelings and her involvement in the cycle of blame. Julia felt repulsed by Michael's insecurities; she felt self-conscious and embarrassed by how intense her feelings about this issue were. Despite all of the things she liked about him, his intelligence, attentiveness, financial success, and sensitivity as a lover, she couldn't stop feeling that he was a loser. She couldn't help thinking that, given the way she felt, perhaps Michael was not the man for her. The problem with that feeling was it kept her from enjoying her time with Michael and from being open to him emotionally. The more immediate problem with this feeling and the thought that sprang from it, "Michael's not right for me," was the fuel it added to the cycle of blame. One part of Julia blamed Michael for her lack of serious interest ("He's a wimp"); another part blamed herself ("Why am I letting this bother me so much?"). The common denominator was a feeling of alienation—from Michael, from herself in the sense that she was confused about what it was she really wanted, and from her friends and family members who felt Michael was great and wondered aloud what Julia's problem was. Julia was left wondering just what she was waiting for.

Julia was teetering on the edge of breaking up with a man whose company she enjoyed, and she was plagued by a good deal of doubt about whether she was doing the right thing. The anxiety this caused made it more and more difficult to see her relationship with Michael clearly and pushed her more toward "jumping ship," as she put it. If she acted, if she jumped ship, then at least she wouldn't be so anxious about what to do.

ASSESSMENT

Both Julia and Matt had begun to question their use of blame and had become curious about what, other than their own shortcomings or the flaws they found in the opposite sex, might be underlying their confusion. In order to *examine the facts* about their situations and to uncover the marriage bias they both subscribed to, Julia and Matt had to learn how to make a critical distinction between feelings and thoughts. It wasn't easy at first because they fell prey to the same fiction that many people do: that feelings should make sense and can be controlled. By muddling the distinction between thought and emotion, they were blind to important clues and facts that could free them from being controlled by the "You're OK so I must be OK" script.

Feelings March to the Beat of a Different Drum

A t this point, a brief digression about the differences between thoughts and feelings is in order. Because people often confuse the two, they inadvertently put themselves in the position of being slaves to their emotions. When the distinction is unclear, you will respond to your feelings when you don't have to and when you'd be better off if you didn't. And importantly, whenever you respond to feelings reflexively by succumbing to impulses like the one Julia had to "jump ship," it becomes harder to uncover what was truly responsible for what you were feeling.

For example, Julia felt turned off whenever Michael complained about his job and how he felt powerless with his boss. When she was completely honest with herself, she had to admit that "disgusted" was the best way to describe how strongly she felt. Julia naturally decided she should do something about what she felt. The first thing she did was talk to her mother about how turned off she was by this aspect of Michael's personality.

Her mother quickly offered, "Maybe he's not the one for you." She agreed that Julia had "every right" to feel turned off by Michael's lack of confidence and encouraged her to follow her heart. She was following the cultural marriage script which says, among other things, "If it doesn't feel right then he's not the one for you." But this conversation didn't help resolve Julia's confusion. Instead, she surprised herself by defending Michael to her mother!

Like most people with conflicting feelings—in this case her attraction and simultaneous repulsion—Julia unconsciously found family and friends who would support both sides of the issue. When her mother took one side, agreeing that Julia should dump Michael, Julia raced to the opposite camp to argue the merits of staying with him. Soon after this conversation, Julia found someone to argue the other side. Her friend Diane remarked, "I hear what you're saying about his lack of confidence at work, but you're also a lot happier than I've seen you in a long time. You seem to like so much about him." Diane's remark did nothing to lessen the confusion and Julia found herself drawn back to her negative feelings about Michael in an unconscious effort to keep the scales balanced.

Julia also acted on her feelings of revulsion at Michael's insecurities by giving him unsolicited pep talks about how he should handle himself with his boss. These pep talks typically ended with tension between the two lovers because Julia's advice was always given with subtle admonishments. In many ways, she was dangerously close to sounding the way her mother used to sound when Julia was a little girl: critical in her attempts to be supportive. But more about this later. The main point here is that by acting on her feelings before she understood fully where they were coming from, Julia missed important information that would have helped her to decide what it was she ultimately wanted to do with Michael. Julia's emotions would continue to rule her actions until she stopped subscribing to five common myths about feelings.

FIVE COMMON MYTHS ABOUT FEELINGS

---

1. *Emotions should make sense.* Wrong. They do sometimes, which makes things very confusing, but more often than not they don't. Feelings do not follow rules of logic. You can feel opposites, like love and hate, at the same time. And two plus two can equal five in the world of emotions. Julia felt both drawn to Michael and repulsed by him. She felt certain that one of those feelings must be right and the other wrong. Only one of them could be a valid description of how she ultimately felt about this man. From this perspective, two plus two equals either four or five; both can't be true. But in fact both feelings were true and equally genuine. However, as you will learn below, one had much more to do with her past than her present circumstances. Until she could understand that both feelings were actually valid, she would not be able to examine all of the facts and to decide which feeling she wanted to act upon.

2. *Always follow your heart.* Wrong again. Think about it and you'll find many instances when you shouldn't follow what your heart tells you to do. Anger is the easiest example to give. Has your heart ever told you to ram your car into that of a driver who just cut you off? Or have you ever lusted for someone else when you were in a relationship that you felt good about and treasured? There are many instances in which you may feel some-

thing strongly, but you would be unwise to follow your emotions. This doesn't mean that you shouldn't follow your heart sometimes. You should, but not always.

3. *It's always better to talk about how you feel.* Not true. Now you're probably thinking, "There is no way Amador and Kiersky are real therapists. Their Ph.D.s are probably in astrophysics. What therapist would tell you to not talk about your feelings?!" Actually, many good therapists will advise you of this from time to time. Until you really understand the source of your feelings and have thought through how they will affect the person you want to reveal your emotions to, it's oftentimes better to wait. You don't have to act on your feelings the moment you experience them. It's just as honest to act on them later, after you've given it some thought.

4. *Feelings need to be defended.* If you've fallen prey to this myth you frequently say "I have every right to feel this way!" But feelings do not need to be defended. You feel what you feel. No one "decides" to feel a certain way. This is another instance where thoughts and feelings get confused with one another. Only your actions, how you've decided to respond to your feelings, ever need justification.

5. *Emotions can be controlled.* You can exert some direct control over what you think, but rarely can you do this with what you feel. Emotions come unbidden—you just feel. It is true that when you change the way you think about certain things you can influence your feelings over time. But it is like the difference between driving a speedboat and steering an ocean liner. Turn the wheel in a speedboat and the boat responds immediately. Turn the wheel on an ocean liner and depending on its speed, it can take literally miles before the course correction takes place. Feelings are often like huge ocean liners: powerful, complex, and very slow to turn in a new direction even when the captain orders an immediate change in course.

Both Julia and Matt had to learn to question these myths before they could uncover their personal marriage scripts. The powerful feelings that stemmed from their scripts didn't make a whole lot of sense on the face of it. But they made a good deal of sense when they were traced back to their origins in childhood.

Julia

Julia needed to take responsibility for what she was feeling. Specifically, she had to understand where the deep anxiety and repulsion she felt about Michael's insecurities came from. Then she had to consider carefully how, if at all, she wanted to act on those feelings. Here is what she discovered.

"I've been doing a lot of thinking since we last met. Especially about why I feel so turned off by Michael's insecurity. I was talking with my friend Diane about it and came to a realization about why it bothers me so much.

"Diane kept asking me, 'why do you think you feel so strongly about the way Michael is with his boss?' At first I thought she was giving me a hard time about it, telling me to get over it and grow up. But actually, she was just trying to help me to figure out why it's such a big deal to me. Well, I think I figured it out.

"I'm the one who feels insecure. In fact, I might even be more insecure than Michael is. I just don't show it, much less tolerate it in others! It's a real raw nerve for me. Diane pointed out that sometimes I get really irritated with her when she's a little insecure. She's right, I do. And it's not just her. I feel that way quite a bit.

"But with Michael it's much worse. Any little chink in his armor and I feel like dumping him. I haven't yet, but sometimes when I am feeling this way it's a real struggle not to."

Julia made an immensely valuable discovery in her conversations with Diane. She found that the main source of her discomfort about Michael had nothing to do with Michael, it had to do with her past and the marriage script that arose from it. This script said that Julia's mate had to be exceptional in several respects, especially with regard to his level of self-confidence. Not that there wasn't a kernel of truth to her observations about Michael. He was a little insecure in this one area. But the intensity of what she felt had to do with *remembered feelings* from her script which greatly amplified the small insecurities Michael had.

In a way, her script gave her a lens to look through that greatly magnified insignificant insecurities and other foibles until they filled her entire field of vision. When she realized this, she understood that the intensity of what she felt had little to do with Michael. Because she was less prone to knee-jerk reactions to her fears, she had to sit with the feelings they created longer. Although it was not always easy to do, as she became more familiar with the anxiety she was feeling, two things happened. Her feelings of nervousness and repulsion about Michael's insecurities became a lot less scary because she had allowed herself to be exposed to them and found that nothing had happened. Second, she began to discover some valuable facts about exactly what it was she was feeling and why.

She found that she had been *projecting* her own sense of incompetence onto Michael. Julia harbored a deep well of insecurity about herself that she attributed to her childhood relationship with her mother. Her mother was doting and in Julia's view "overly protective." Although this resulted in Julia feeling very loved, it also left her feeling both smothered and incompetent. Here was a successful, educated, attractive woman in her early thirties who was disgusted with herself whenever she felt indecisive. It was her one major flaw that she hated and yet could not easily give up completely.

Her mother's admonishments and counsel and Julia's countenance of insecurity and need were the principal ways in which love was expressed between mother and daughter for as long as she could recall. When Julia was in need, her mother was there with advice and support. Unfortunately, the advice was rarely empowering and was often prefaced with admonishments such as "I told you this would happen," or "What's wrong with you? Couldn't you see he would hurt you?" Prior to Michael, Julia had tended to date men who were seamlessly strong. But invariably, these relationships failed when she felt herself slipping into an overly submissive position. In these relationships she found herself acting as she had as a child with her mother: frequently insecure and often very needy. Julia hated this aspect of herself and consequently had a very difficult time tolerating it in others. But when she dated men who were closer to her ideal than Michael was, it was too reminiscent of her role with her mother. Although it felt familiar and comfortable in many ways, she had outgrown the need to be this way in relationships long ago.

This conflict is what gave rise to the appearance that Julia was "stuck on the ideal." She wanted to be with someone who was strong and rarely, if ever, insecure. But she also wanted someone with whom she would not slip into her overly dependent childhood role. That would be a man who let some of his own insecurity show and who did not take a "me Tarzan, you Jane" attitude. Someone who could both respond to Julia's insecurities and relish her strengths.

Because he let his insecurities show, Michael did not trigger Julia's submissive and dependent reactions. Instead, he tapped into a deep well of feelings that had more to do with how she felt about herself than him. In some ways Julia was becoming her mother: critical and intolerant of Michael's anxiety and insecurities. Like most of us, Julia was not happy with the realization that she was reacting to Michael in the negative ways in which she felt her mother had reacted to her. We all fear becoming our parents, at least with respect to those qualities we did not enjoy or approve of. But the truth is that we always adopt some of the bad with the good. We are no more perfect than our parents were and as subject to repeating some of their mistakes as they were to repeating those of their parents. Of course we all put our own unique stamp on these weaknesses, which makes it harder to identify and take responsibility for them.

Julia's ideal, her positive marriage bias, was in many ways a repeat of her relationship with her mother. Remember, her ideal mate would be someone who would be strong, make her feel safe, and "tuck her in at night." What Julia discovered over the course of our conversations was that although she wanted to be "tucked in" at bedtime, she also wanted a partner, an equal, someone who would respect and encourage her autonomy and strength. When she began to see that her marriage script led her to want to be a "Jane" even though she was not someone who could ever tolerate living with a Tarzan, her feelings about Michael's insecurity were put into a new, less anxiety-provoking light.

Matt

Like Julia, Matt also had to take responsibility for the way he was feeling. For him, speaking with a therapist was the first step on the road to reaching that goal, but he didn't know what to take responsibility for until he broke the cycle of blame and examined the facts. The "facts" in Matt's case were nearly identical to those Julia discovered. He too was caught in a conflict that gave rise to the appearance that he was "stuck on the ideal." It was a conflict between the feelings that stemmed from his marriage script and the feelings he had about the reality of his relationship with Miranda.

Several months after starting therapy Matt got his wish. Miranda and he started to date. It was at this point that the conflict rose to the surface.

"She's driving me crazy! There's so much I love about her but I can't depend on her for anything. The other night we went out to a bar together and this guy starts flirting with her. They see what I saw so I am not surprised. But she flirts back! And she does it right in front of me! We had a big blow-up about it."

"What happened?" I asked, wanting more details.

"I went to the bathroom and when I came out this guy was standing next to her talking to her. He was practically leaning all over her! And I could see, from across the bar, that she was not discouraging him. Look, if it was just this one instance I would give her the benefit of the doubt. But this kind of thing has happened before.

"It's strange, but I don't like the fact that she dresses sexy anymore. I used to like it a lot. But now that she's my girlfriend I hate it. I've never been a jealous guy. But she wears these really short skirts with heels and she looks incredibly hot. I know she's always gotten a lot of attention for the way she looks and that's one of the things that attracted me to her. But it's too much. I know I sound like a hypocrite, but I can't help it."

"What would you like her to do differently?"

"I'd like her to consider how it feels to me when she flirts with other guys in front of me. It's bull!" he added, getting angry. "She does a lot of other things that I hate as well. She has this friend Wendy who she goes out with once or twice a week and they always stay out really late. Worse than that, Miranda promises me she'll call by midnight, then doesn't call at all! They're out late, she says she's going to call, but she doesn't. What am I suppose to think? She's driving me crazy!"

As much as he was drawn to Miranda and all that she represented to him, he despised her capriciousness and self-absorption. But the conflict between what he truly needed now (a woman who could understand his needs and be more dependable) and what his marriage script led him to *feel* he needed (someone who turns heads when she walks into a room) was keeping him stuck in an unhappy relationship. It took Matt over six months to extricate himself from his relationship with Miranda, or, more precisely, from the conflict between his marriage script and his present-day needs and desires.

When he examined the facts of his situation Matt made two important discoveries that allowed him to take responsibility for what he could change about his approach to relationships and to himself. The first discovery was that his positive feelings about Miranda were irrational. That is the reason he turned to therapy to begin with. He knew that the feelings didn't make much sense logically because they were so intense. And he was not happy with how obsessed he had become with this one woman.

Later, he was unhappy with the fact that he could not easily bring himself to break up with her, even though her actions and flirtatious nature were making him miserable. His second key discovery took some time to unearth, but it was no less important for being slow to reveal itself. Matt's marriage script was forged, in part, in his relationship with his father. Although Matt's father would probably not believe this to be true about himself, he was a very critical parent. In countless different ways he convinced Matt that he was incompetent and could never fully become a man.

If you think that we are about to go on a parent-bashing rampage, you're mistaken. The point is not that Matt's father had shortcomings as a parent. All parents do. It's that when Matt was a child he built his positive sense of self around certain ideas he had about who he would become when he grew up. As he described it, "I used to say to myself 'wait until I grow up—I'll show him!'" And one of the ideas Matt had harbored, for the most part unconsciously, was that he would marry someone who would impress his father. When he was a boy, his image of such a woman was of someone who was "really, really, pretty." A woman who would turn even his father's head. Marriage would be one of the many ways he hoped to win his father's respect and admiration and to exact a little revenge in the process.

Over time, Matt came to the realization that he no longer needed his father's respect and admiration in the same way he did as a child. He began to accept the fact that he could not change the past. Eventually, he learned to forgive his father for his shortcomings as a parent. By understanding the driving force behind his obsession with Miranda, he felt less compelled to act on it and more drawn to acting on some of the other things he was feeling about her. When he accepted the fact that he would probably always be drawn to women like Miranda, he was able to exert some control over what he did with the feelings that were aroused. He began to demand better treatment from her. Intellectually, he always knew that he didn't need to be with a "head turner" to be respected by other men and to respect himself. But it wasn't until he understood the origins of his marriage script and accepted that he could do little to control the feelings that it created that he was able to make some changes for the better.

ACCEPTANCE

While examining both how they were feeling and the reality of their circumstances, Julia and Matt learned that they didn't need to marry their ideals nearly as much as they *felt* they did. They both felt an intense longing for their "perfect" partners, a craving of sorts, that was insistent and unrelenting. But when they began to understand that this longing and the anxiety that accompanied it were not only illogical, but irrelevant to their present lives and more suited to their childhood needs, they were ready to use our third guideline and move to the *acceptance* stage. They began to shift their focus toward *taking responsibility* for those things about themselves that they could change rather than continuing to pursue impossible dreams and responding to feelings from their past. By mourning what was not possible and learning not to respond automatically to the feelings created by their marriage scripts, they began to focus their efforts on those things they had some control over.

Once Julia and Matt understood the origins of the strong feelings that accompanied the marriage script they learned as children, they were able to change the ways in which they acted on these feelings. Julia still had her vulnerability to feeling disgusted by insecurity, in herself or in a partner. Contrary to what some of our colleagues might think, the feelings did not stop simply because she understood where they came from. But she did learn to react to her repulsion about Michael's insecurities in new ways. By changing the way in which she responded to the feelings, she began to see and to feel things which had been obscured by her previous knee-jerk reactions.

Matt also learned to separate his thoughts from his feelings, so that he didn't allow his emotions to rule his life. He did not completely extinguish the fire he had for Miranda or women like her, but he was able to adjust the flame rather than be burned by it. When dating, sexual attraction was still very important to him, as it is to most people, but it was no longer tangled up with his sense of self-worth. As he put it, "I would rather be single and respect myself than with someone who impresses other guys but treats me like shit."

ASSIMILATION

W hen he took responsibility for the feelings that stemmed from his marriage script, Matt stopped putting his life on hold. He was able to break it off with Miranda and free himself from the conflict he had been in. He began to spend time with friends again, rather than worrying obsessively about whether Miranda would call when she went out with her friends or flirt with other men. Now that Matt was able to give himself what his marriage script had always promised, a positive self-image as a man, the script lost its power to dictate which relationship he would put his efforts into.

Sometimes he is still drawn to women like Miranda, but the pull is less strong and is counterbalanced by an understanding of why the attraction was once so consuming. He now gives himself what his marriage script and fantasy wife used to give: self-acceptance and confidence in his manhood. He now dates women who are more consistent in their desire to be with him. Although he has moments when he longs for the ideal, whenever he stops to examine the facts, the ideal pales in comparison to his real life. He is single, much happier than he was prior to and during his relationship with Miranda, and infinitely more open to getting close to the woman he's currently dating than he could have been before. She is, incidentally, someone he is very attracted to, but not someone he's "trying to get" to make him feel better about himself.

Julia also stopped putting her life on hold when she stopped blindly following her marriage script. By dealing with her insecurities head on, rather than looking outside of herself to feel loved and secure, she learned to rely on her inner resources to provide some of what her fantasy had promised. When she stopped looking for her ideal, she was able to focus more on what she found attractive in Michael. When she focused on the moment and what she had in her life, rather than on the future and what she sometimes felt she needed to feel good about herself, she found herself enjoying Michael more and more. Eventually, she fell in love with him and when he asked her to marry him, she said yes. But more important than the fact of their engagement is the fact that Julia deals with her insecurities very differently than she used to. She realizes she can't change her vulnerability to feeling insecure, but she can take responsibility by changing the way she acts on such feelings. She no longer looks to marriage to make her feel confident and secure as a woman. Consequently she has found herself open to marriage in a way she had never been before.

Both Matt, who was single when this was written, and Julia, who was engaged to be married, had assimilated to the couples' world. They no longer felt that they didn't belong and both felt more open to love. Their personal marriage scripts no longer held them captive and stuck on an ideal, and they were invulnerable to the pressures levied by the cultural script. Neither Julia, who was married when we last spoke, nor Matt, who was happily single, believed they needed to be married to feel good about themselves. They were living their lives in the present, no longer ruled by antiquated scripts from the past and unrealistic hopes for the future.

THE GRASS IS ALWAYS GREENER

He'd better get serious and stop playing around or he'll wake up one day and find himself alone for the rest of his life. He's never happy enough with whomever he's dating. The grass is always greener somewhere else. He drives me nuts the way he gets involved with these poor women and then just discards them for the next one.

Molly complaining about her brother Mark,
a thirty-eight-year-old money manager

◄○►

Her problem is she never gives the guy she's dating a real chance. She falls head over heels at first, then it suddenly fizzles out. I think she enjoys the chase too much to ever give it up. There's always someone better out there for Sarah.

Sarah's friend Jo Anna

A mong the worst things that friends and family say to single loved ones are "You're not trying hard enough" and "You never give anyone a chance." Underlying "helpful" observations such as these is a belief that single people enjoy being single too much to ever want to stop being single. More precisely, they crave attention and love the chase too much to give it up. The implication is that these individuals are frivolous when it comes to love and should buckle down and get serious.

Usually, such descriptions have a kernel of truth to them, in that they describe one aspect of the experience of such singles. Remember what Sarah, the twenty-eight-year-old travel agency owner, had to say about this topic? She said she felt "kind of like a kid who needs to grow up. I think my problem is that I don't always give whomever

I'm dating much of a chance. It's hot and heavy at first, then I sort of get disinterested. I like change and the excitement of the chase." We don't deny that Sarah enjoys being pursued. She clearly does. But both Sarah and her friend Jo Anna, who also accuses her of enjoying the chase too much to stop, are focusing on a very small part of the picture—on the effect rather than the cause. By now, we hope you are asking yourself, "What is the underlying marriage script here?" Because it is the personal marriage script that Sarah is following that is causing her problems, not the fact that she enjoys the chase and that the next relationship always looks more appealing than the one she is currently in. Mark, whom you will hear about shortly, coined the phrase that describes this bias best: "Marriage is for losers."

MARRIAGE IS FOR LOSERS

For a variety of reasons many people are pessimistic about getting married because they have low expectations about the institution. In some instances this does not have to interfere with becoming intimate with someone and making a lifelong commitment to stay together. There are many people who do this without the institution of marriage. But they are still in the minority. Most people who follow the "marriage is for losers" script (a.k.a. "married people are miserable," and "if you're married you've sold out") are not consciously aware of it. As a result, to their own dismay and that of their loved ones, they never seem to give anyone a chance, leaving them frustrated about the prospect of getting close to anyone.

It's not that they decide to not give anyone a chance; that would be a *thought* that they could easily control by saying to themselves "In this instance I'm going to give him a chance and see where it will lead." Instead, what we are talking about here is a *feeling*. They can't help but feel intensely drawn to other people even when they are in a serious relationship. The feeling that the "grass is greener on the other side of the hill" is so intense that it's like a craving for a drug that you're addicted to. And the craving is so insistent that it takes tremendous willpower to stay in a relationship.

What they usually don't know is that their vulnerability to being easily smitten by someone new stems from a fear that if they get too close to anyone they may end up married. The marriage script they follow warns that intimacy will lead to marriage and marriage can only lead to misery and, to co-opt Julia's phrase from the last chapter, "loserdom." Outwardly, such singles appear to be having too much fun dating and jumping from one brief relationship to the next to ever want to stop. Inwardly, people like Sarah and Mark feel torn between a conscious desire to feel close to someone and a reflex to jump ship if a more appealing one passes within sight.

ALIENATION

Mark

Mark is a thirty-eight-year-old money manager who lives in New York City. He is handsome, fit, and he rarely has trouble finding women to date. In fact, his co-workers and friends frequently set him up on blind dates that he gladly accepts. This, coupled with the fact that he never seems to get serious about anyone, drives his sister Molly crazy. Molly is thirty-four and divorced. She would like to date more than she has been able to recently and this adds to her feeling that her brother has an embarrassment of riches that he is squandering recklessly.

Both Mark and Molly agreed to be interviewed for this book. On one occasion, we spoke briefly with the two of them together.

"Molly thinks I'm a real player, like all I want to do is get laid."

"You are!" she interrupted.

"Well, anyway, I don't think I fit the definition. Most of the time it never even gets to the sex part. I lose interest too fast. Don't get me wrong, I love sex . . ."

"See!" she added, laughing. "You're a dog, just like I said!"

"Well of course I like sex! But I pass it up more times than you know. That's my point. It's usually not worth the trouble. It makes it that much harder to get out of the relationship if you've had sex. I know it sounds weird, and I never used to be this way about it until the last five or six years, but I am less likely to do it than I used to be. Although . . . there is one exception to the rule. If it's clear from the start that the relationship is going nowhere, I'll go for it. There's no hurt feelings that way."

When Mark knew immediately that there was no hope for anything but a casual relationship and knew the woman he was dating felt the same way, he was very open to being intimate physically. It may seem that he was splitting hairs when he denied his sister's accusation that all he wanted was to have sex, but in fact his qualification gave us an important clue to his real motives.

"I never heard you say that before," Molly continued.

"We've never talked about it before. Look, if anything I feel like a real loser. I wish I was having half as much fun as you think I am. There's just rarely anyone that I stay interested in long enough to want to deal with the complications that come with being lovers. Remember Carrie?" he asked his sister.

"I liked her. I always wondered why that one didn't work out," she replied.

"That's the longest relationship I've had in a couple of years. We were together for four months. But I blew it. I jumped ship way too soon and I regret it. If I'd known I was going to do that I would never have let things go as far as they did. Too many hurt feelings. We were having a great time. It was good, there was definitely some chemistry there. And I don't think I've laughed as much with anyone I've dated as I did with Carrie. She's hysterical and really smart. But I screwed it up."

What Mark didn't reveal in this conversation with his sister present were the circumstances that led to his breaking up with Carrie. In a later conversation with Mark alone, he revealed that his desire to break off the relationship with Carrie was not nearly as random as he had led us to believe. A specific event triggered the breakup.

"A friend at work asked me if I wanted to be fixed up on a blind date and I couldn't say no. I kept thinking I'm going to miss out on someone better if I don't accept. It was a very intense feeling. It's like when I was a kid and my older brother got to stay up later than me. I'd be lying in bed crawling out of my skin because I was sure that I was missing out on something really cool. It's a very intense feeling and hard to ignore. I gave in to it and took her number from my friend. But I didn't call for a week 'cause I felt so guilty about it.

"The thing about Carrie is that she made it clear that she didn't want to date anyone else and expected the same from me. So I felt guilty about saying yes to being fixed up. I ended up confessing to Carrie before I even went out on the date. What a moron! But I didn't just confess, I told her that I decided that we should break up because I obviously didn't want the same level of commitment she did. I told her she deserved someone better than me. That didn't go over too well. She told me I was full of it and that this had nothing to do with her or what she did or didn't deserve. She was right. The only thing I feel good about is that at least I admitted she was right to her face."

Mark had been embarrassed and understandably reluctant to admit that it was the possibility of meeting someone new that triggered his abrupt breakup with Carrie. He was even more reticent about revealing the thoughts that went through his mind when he contemplated whether or not to accept the blind date.

Carrie was the same age as Mark, thirty-eight, but the woman he was being fixed up with was only twenty-eight. Mark admitted that he had become fixated on the idea that he could date someone much younger than Carrie and had begun to imagine all of the ways in which he would feel more attracted to someone younger. The feelings attached to these thoughts were very intense. Before his friend asked whether he wanted to meet this younger woman, who was described as sexy and very interested in meeting Mark, he had been feeling very attracted to Carrie. There was sexual chemistry and he felt a strong connection to her in other ways. They had similar values and the pace and rhythm of their conversations were what Mark described as "electric." But the idea that he might miss out on someone who was younger, better looking, and more exciting was simply too enticing to pass up. So he broke up with Carrie to go out on this one date.

Carrie would probably tell you that she felt Mark treated her well and he was always honest about what he was feeling. He never led her to believe that he was feeling more than he was and he respected her desire that they be monogamous. He tried to be faithful, but when he felt he couldn't, he told her. She was angry with him for not being able to give her what she wanted and deserved, but felt that he had treated her fairly. If anything, according to Mark, Carrie felt sorry for him. Among her last words to him were "I think you're giving up a really good thing here. I don't get it and I think you're going to regret it. I'm not saying I'm waiting, but if you feel differently you can give me a call."

Only one month later Mark was already wishing he hadn't broken up with Carrie. He missed her company and the connection he had felt with her. More than that, he had never met someone with as strong a sense of herself as Carrie had. But he didn't call her because he still felt that he couldn't guarantee that the same thing wouldn't happen again. His feelings, rather than his intentions, were causing the problem.

More precisely, it was how he was responding to the feelings that was causing the problem. He felt intensely drawn to a fantasy and acted on this attraction by saying yes to the blind date. He then responded to feeling guilty by precipitating a breakup with Carrie. He never gave her, or himself, a chance to sort through what he was feeling because of his knee-jerk reactions to his emotions.

Mark was left feeling like a failure because he thought he had made a big mistake. Being in his late thirties and never married, Mark was vulnerable to the messages given by the cultural marriage script. He felt abnormal and afraid that he would always be alone. He worried that there was something wrong with him, some insurmountable flaw, that would always lead him back to the same place he was in now. Mark jumped at the chance to be interviewed for this book, saying, "It's a drag being single. I'm not having one-tenth the fun everyone thinks I am. My closest friends are all married and we rarely see each other anymore. They think I am out on the prowl, but I feel like a lone wolf who doesn't eat meat!" Mark was feeling alienated from his married friends and ostracized for being a bachelor. His sister was not the only one who had decided the reason he wasn't married was because he was on the prowl. His buddies made similar comments, adding that they were jealous of his single status but that it was time that he settled down. Everywhere he turned, Mark felt out of place.

He was also involved in the cycle of blame. Mark blamed himself, saying, "I think I need to grow up. I'm like a kid in a candy store. Every time I see a hot girl it's like my memory gets erased. Whomever I'm currently involved with just disappears. Whatever I liked about them gets blotted out. I shouldn't be feeling that way at this age. It's so stupid."

During another interview he blamed women and society in general. "You grow up inundated with pictures of women that don't exist. Go to a news stand and all you see are sexy young women on the covers of all the magazines. You don't even have to go to the adult section! It pisses me off. When you meet someone who comes close to the fantasy, she's usually all screwed up because she's spent her life getting attention for her looks and nothing else. It's such a double message. Women try and look sexy and men are told that beauty is what's important in a woman, but you're shallow and a dog if you are too focused on looks!"

Over the course of our interviews, Mark learned about the cycle of blame and began to see how he alternated between blaming himself and women. He was resistant to the idea at first, saying, "It's one or the other, I don't think I blame myself and women." But when transcripts of what he had said were read back to him, he began to see the pattern. Simply acknowledging that a pattern exists will help to identify when you are doing something and help you stop relying so heavily on blame to feel better about yourself. And that is exactly what happened with Mark. He realized that his anger at womankind and society would get him nowhere and did nothing to further his efforts to understand himself better. His self-abuse was similarly ineffective in this regard. As you will see, after he broke the cycle of blame and began to evaluate his feelings and circumstances more honestly, he discovered important facts that freed him from the trap the cultural marriage script and his personal marriage script had put him in.

Sarah

I f you recall what Sarah had to say earlier, in chapter 1, she felt alienated and blamed herself in strikingly similar ways as Mark. Although she generally enjoyed being single, her family and friends' worry over her unmarried status had become infectious. She felt "like a kid who [needed] to grow up." When she wasn't blaming herself she was blaming her parents and society in general. Like Mark, she also complained of getting contradictory messages. "Self-reliance has always been a priority. That's how I was raised and that's what I believe in. But I feel like I got a double message. Not just from my parents, but from everyone. You're supposed to get married. Everyone is supposed to grow up and get married like their parents did."

In therapy, Sarah began to see how her self-blame and her blaming of society and her parents were getting her nowhere. It felt good at first to vent her anger and frustration, but ultimately these accusations left her feeling cynical and demoralized. More important, they kept her from examining all of the facts. She started keeping a diary, as we suggest in chapter 4, and made a list of the self-blaming thoughts that were most common. She, like Mark, found that simple awareness, or mindfulness, of such thoughts was enough to lessen the intensity of her pattern of blame. Once she achieved this, she could move to the assessment stage of being single in a couples' world.

No longer jumping to quick and easy answers provided by blame, she became curious about her experience of alienation. Why did she feel she needed to grow up? Was she so different from her friends who were her age? She also started asking herself what might be behind the cravings she had for new men. Why was it so easy to leave relationships in pursuit of new conquests? She asked these questions without looking through the lens provided by the cultural marriage script which would have made her see these impulses as a sign of immaturity and as flaws in her character. Instead, she saw them for what they were: emotions that she had no control over. Something that could be ignored or understood. She chose to understand them.

ASSESSMENT

When Sarah entered the assessment stage she was free to examine the facts in earnest. The first mystery that revealed itself was why, if she generally enjoyed being in relationships, she so easily became bored with them. Remember what she had to say about this? "It's hot and heavy at first; then I sort of get disinterested." Sarah complained that she had been feeling "bored" with the last boyfriend she broke up with. Whether you are in therapy or not, whenever you give yourself the time and opportunity to examine what you say to yourself about how you feel, certain things become obvious.

Like many people in therapy, Sarah discovered that being bored is not a feeling. To the contrary, boredom is an absence of feeling and usually signifies that there are other feelings lurking beneath the "there's nobody home—go away" experience of boredom. She learned this while talking about her last boyfriend, Rick.

"It was kind of abrupt. We were out having dinner one night and all of a sudden I realized I was double tracking. Do you know what that is?"

"You started thinking about other things?" I asked.*

"Exactly. He was talking and I was following it, but I was also thinking about what I had to do at work the next day. When I caught myself doing it I tried to stop. But I couldn't. As hard as I tried I just couldn't stay focused on what he was saying. It was then that I realized that I was really getting bored with this relationship."

"Do you remember what he was talking about?"

"I don't know, it doesn't really matter, does it? It just became im-

*X.A.

possible to sit and listen to him anymore. I kept thinking about the fact that I had to fire one of our agents. She's really sweet and I felt so terrible about having to do it. My partners elected me because they said I'm better at it than they are but I don't like doing it. It really makes me feel bad . . ."

As Sarah was talking I realized that I had started to double track myself. I was thinking that I only had fifteen minutes between the end of Sarah's appointment and the start of the next one. I had a sudden overwhelming need for a cup of coffee and I was calculating whether or not I had time to run to the corner between meetings. Luckily this dual train of thought didn't go too long before I noticed it. I started searching for the reason my mind was wandering. Was I simply tired? Was it something about what Sarah was talking about? I didn't get far down the list of possible triggers for my boredom when my thoughts were interrupted by silence. Sarah had abruptly stopped talking. I had been looking at her all along, but I thought she may have somehow picked up on the fact that my mind had wandered, so I asked, "Why did you stop just now?"

"I don't know," she answered. "I thought maybe I was boring. I felt like I was whining."

"Did you think I was bored with what you were talking about?" I asked, suddenly very focused and attentive.

"No. It's not you, I just felt like I wasn't talking about anything important."

"Actually, the reason I asked was because I found it hard to stay interested in what you were saying and when you stopped talking, I thought that perhaps you had noticed."

"No, I didn't notice. Was I boring you?"

"I had a hard time paying attention to what you were saying," I replied, trying to skirt the question so that we wouldn't get further derailed from the real topic. "But I don't think it was because you were boring. In fact, it's a compelling topic in its own right. Most people don't have to fire anyone, but I think it may have been an un-conscious diversion. You never really answered my question."

"What *was* your question?" she asked, mulling it over. "Oh, yeah. You asked me what it was Rick was talking about when I started double tracking."

"Exactly," I encouraged.

"I remember now. He was talking about wanting to go away for a weekend together. He was kind of beating around the bush. He never actually got to the point of asking, maybe because I didn't seem interested, but that was definitely where he was headed. He kept talking about this place up in the Adirondack Mountains he liked to go to. He was telling me how romantic it was this time of year. I remember thinking he was testing the water to see if I was interested. Yuck!"

"Why yuck?"

"It just reminded me of camping trips with my parents. My dad loved to go camping in the mountains. I am definitely not interested. Maybe that's why I was thinking about work instead of listening to him?"

"Sounds like a real possibility. But I'm still not clear on the yuck part."

"My mother was always the 'happy housewife' on those trips. She did the grocery shopping, cooked every meal, rolled out the sleeping bags at night, and rolled them up in the morning. My dad would be out fishing or hiking and she would be back tending the home fires."

"Do you think that would happen with Rick?"

"Not at all. I would never let that happen. And Rick wasn't like that. At least I don't think that he was. It doesn't make sense when I think about it. I mean, I wasn't afraid of that happening with Rick."

"Feelings don't have to make sense. I can't tell you what you feel, only you can do that. But I can play back what you've said and you can tell me what the evidence suggests. When you and Rick were talking you got bored. Right?"

"Right."

"But what you uncovered today is that your boredom was actually a kind of mask. It hid what you were feeling. In fact, you were actually feeling something pretty strongly. You felt revulsion, or to paraphrase what you said earlier, the idea of going camping made you think 'yuck!' When I asked you about that feeling, about why you said 'yuck,' your thoughts turned to your parents. In particular, you started recalling the way in which your mother was subservient to your father. You've told me before that she was very unhappy in this role. That she gave up too much to be married. Does all this fit with your experience so far?" I asked, hoping that Sarah was keeping an open mind to the facts.

"It does. I didn't realize it at the time but I did feel revulsion at the idea of going away for a weekend with Rick. But that doesn't mean I was afraid. That still doesn't make sense to me."

"Actually, I think it does make sense in the context of your past. As you said, you don't have any reason to think that you would become subservient with Rick because that's not who you are and he doesn't seem to want that. So in that context, it would *not* make sense that you would feel afraid of assuming that role with him. But then feelings don't always make sense, at least not at first glance. The idea that you were afraid of this makes a lot of sense if the fear is a memory—a remembered feeling that was stirred up by getting closer to Rick."

Sarah's response to these observations was to talk about what it felt like to go camping with her parents when she was a little girl. She actually started to feel some of the old fears in the context of her recollections. As a child she had been afraid of becoming like her mother. She remembered that she used to promise herself that she would never make the same mistake. There was no passion in her parents' relationship and her mother was unhappy with the role she had assumed in her marriage. She regretted getting married so young and wished she had done more with her life. Her mother had been miserable and Sarah was fearful of the same fate.

The fact that Rick had been talking about camping in particular was not some unfortunate twist of fate; he could have been talking about anything. It was the fact that he was "upping the ante," as Sarah referred to it. He was communicating a desire for greater intimacy. They had never gone away together before and spending a weekend together alone would have signified a level of closeness Sarah was not yet prepared for. What Sarah was experiencing wasn't fear of camping, it was fear of closeness. As far as Sarah was concerned, greater intimacy with Rick was one step closer to marriage and marriage was for losers, not for her.

The marriage script she held was insidious in that she had carried it around for most of her life without being aware of it. Growing up, Sarah had been privy to the inner workings of many aspects of her parents' relationship and the resulting script that was written down in her subconscious was not very appealing. Before you jump to blaming her parents as Sarah did at first, consider that when Sarah was being raised, her parents were in the middle of a cultural revolution. Her mother married young, in part, because this was by far the most appealing option open to her as a woman at that time. As women's roles expanded with the feminist movement so did Sarah's mother's expectations and desire for a different life. She was no more to blame for her unhappy marriage than Sarah was for her current discomfort as a single woman. However, Sarah's mother never identified those aspects of her self and her relationship that she could change; hence she was left with several significant regrets. And her daughter was left with a marriage script which argued that "you're a failure as a woman if you're married."

But Sarah was now in a position to take responsibility for her predicament. After that first experience of boredom Sarah had with Rick, her disinterest continued to grow to the point that she finally broke up with him. She moved on to greener pastures. But now, armed with more knowledge about her marriage script and how it led her to equate marriage with regrets and unhappiness, she could begin to do something about the confusion it was causing her. In particular, she learned that her boredom with Rick was a knee-jerk reaction to the fear created by this script. She didn't come to this realization right away; it took time and a greater openness to her feelings. But when she learned that boredom in a relationship was typically a sign that she was feeling afraid, Sarah was finally in a position to do something about it.

Mark

W hen Mark realized that his anger at womankind and society would get him nowhere and that his self-abuse was similarly ineffective, he began to look elsewhere for the cause of his unhappiness. It was at this point that Mark reached the assessment stage and was able to examine the facts more honestly. We wanted to know more about Mark's ideas about marriage, so during one interview the question was posed: "What do you think about marriage?"

"Nothing wrong with it." He smiled as he said this, then added, "I can see it in my future."

"What do you imagine it would look like?" I continued.*

"What do I imagine?" He paused as if in deep thought. "I see a house with a yard in the suburbs, a white picket fence, and kids running around on the lawn."

It immediately struck me that his concept did not also include the kind of woman he would like to marry or the nature of their rela-

*X.A

tionship, so I asked, "What about your wife? What do you imagine her to be like?"

"I don't know. I honestly haven't really thought about it. How could I know what my wife will be like if I haven't met her yet?" he added defensively.

"I'm not asking you to foretell the future. I know you can't do that . . . at least I assume you can't." We both smiled. "But you can imagine it. What do you see when you imagine yourself married? What might your wife be like? What would your relationship with her be like?"

Mark's response to these questions was remarkable in that he couldn't really answer. He kept saying that he'd never thought about it before and that he didn't think he really had an image of the kind of woman he would be with or the quality of the relationship. But he was struck, as I had been, by the fact that his image of what a marriage would be was remarkably devoid of feelings or connection to someone else. His image was as if from the outside looking in and we weren't getting any closer to his marriage bias. So I changed tactics.

"Let's forget about your wife and talk about the house, the picket fence, and the kids in the yard."

"Don't forget the suburbs," he reminded me dryly.

"And the suburbs," I added. "So what do these things make you think of?"

Reluctantly, as if he were a child caught with his hand in the cookie jar, he sheepishly admitted, "My parents. . . . Man, you shrinks think everything is always about our parents!"

"Don't jump the gun!" I countered, defending myself and my profession. "You said it, not me!" We both started laughing.

"Yeah, yeah, yeah . . . OK, I did, but what's the point?"

"I don't know yet if there is a point. I'm just trying to help you keep an open mind to whatever your associations are to the house in the suburbs with the picket fence, yard, and kids."

"Responsibility."

"Can you tell me more?"

"I don't know, that's just the word that popped into my head just then." He paused for a long moment, then continued, "My Dad worked his butt off his whole life. He rarely complained about it, but I know he felt saddled with a lot of responsibility. We had a house in the suburbs growing up, and he's probably still paying for it."

"Do you think he was happy being married?"

"Maybe—maybe not. I know he felt henpecked. Like he was controlled by my mom. She wanted a big house so he got her a big house. She didn't want him hanging out with his friends after work so he stopped doing that. My mom complained a lot about my dad and he just sort of quietly took it. I used to think 'Man, why don't you stand up to her!' But he rarely did."

Over the course of the next several months Mark became increasingly aware of his image of marriage. He had never really thought about it before the question was asked. He uncovered a negative marriage script that had its roots in his parents' marriage. He felt his father never stood up to his mother and that he was generally unhappy in the marriage. We have no way of knowing the accuracy of Mark's perception of his father's experience, but we don't need to. The important point here is understanding what Mark imagined his father was feeling. Because what he imagined, that his father was miserable being married, was the information Mark needed to flesh out his marriage script.

Mark considered his father a loser in some respects. He felt his mother did not appreciate him enough. Once he became open to his bias about marriage, he was better able to recognize it whenever it "reared its ugly head," as he put it. He realized that he thought his married friends were also losers. They rarely went out together anymore and when they did, they often complained about their wives.

Like Sarah, Mark also began to be more open to the feelings this script created in him. The attraction he felt whenever he met someone new was much more intense than the natural allure everyone feels at times for that which they don't have. The pull was as strong as it was because it stemmed from his belief that marriage was for losers. It was an insurance policy against marriage. When Mark saw that a fear of becoming a loser himself was amplifying these attractions, what happened with Carrie began to make more sense to him. It also prepared him for the acceptance stage and for taking responsibility for the feelings and perceptions created by this script and the trouble it was causing him in his life.

ACCEPTANCE

Neither Mark nor Sarah could help what they felt about marriage. Mark feared losing his manhood and Sarah was afraid of becoming passive and subservient. But when they began to accept these feelings rather than trying to distance themselves from them, they began to take responsibility. By becoming more intimately familiar with these previously unconscious fears, they were able to stop themselves from responding to them reflexively. The fact that they had a more accurate idea of where these feelings came from helped tremendously. In Mark's case, he didn't "jump ship" so quickly once he understood that the attractions he felt were like puffs of wind rather than a gale that would capsize his relationship.

Mark told us that he actually called Carrie to ask if she would give him a second chance. With a better understanding of why he felt so drawn to other women, their attraction lost a lot of its power over him. He thought he would not be as vulnerable to acting on such feelings now that he had a better idea of where they came from. Carrie agreed to see him, but with understandable cautiousness told Mark that she wasn't making any promises and warned him that she didn't believe in third chances.

Sarah, on the other hand, had uncovered a different fear but one with a similar effect on her singlehood. She was afraid of ending up like her mother. But like Mark, she would also jump ship whenever this fear intensified. This led to the experience of alienation we described earlier and made what should have been an enjoyable time in her life one filled with doubt and anxiety. When she became more sensitive to picking up on when she was feeling this way, she gained control over how she handled such feelings. She also learned that the attention she got whenever she was being pursued had been the main way in which she had previously sought to allay this fear.

Men are often attracted to Sarah. They typically like what she does for a living and are impressed by her career achievements. She loves to tell the story of how she started her own travel agency with two friends, and how she gets to travel anywhere in the world for next to nothing. The honeymoon period of courtship, that early stage when her suitor was interested in learning all about her, gave Sarah much more than the usual feelings of being desired. It also helped to soothe the fears created by her marriage script. She felt anything but like her mother when she was with a man who wanted to know all about her career accomplishments.

But whenever a relationship began to develop and the attention and compliments of the early stages of courtship faded into memory, the fear of settling for a passionless marriage filled with regrets would intensify once again. Although her anxiety would worsen at such times, it never made it to her conscious awareness. Instead, it triggered a conscious experience of "this relationship has become boring. There's got to be someone better out there."

Because she grew up equating marriage with excessive sacrifice, feelings of regret, and a loss of passion, Sarah's consuming attraction to the honeymoon period of courtship is understandable. When she identified her marriage script, Sarah began to take greater responsibility for her happiness as a single person. Knowing that she held this script helped her to be better at recognizing when she was feeling afraid. She was able to drag the feelings stemming from her script out of the vault and into consciousness where she could deal with them directly in a much more satisfying and less confusing way. She quickly learned how to take responsibility for those things she could change and to accept those she could not. Like Mark, one of the first things she took responsibility for was her impulse to jump ship.

She is currently in a relationship with a man named David. They have been dating for three months. Sarah describes an instance where she came face to face with the task of taking responsibility for the impulses created by her marriage script.

"The passion just went out of it. It was so strange. I realized that the old pattern was starting up again when I came back from London and went to bed without playing back my messages on my answering machine." She had gone to Europe for the weekend as she often did for business. "The last two times I went away I checked my machine from the airport, before I even got home, to see if he had called!"

"Any idea what triggered the old pattern?"

"I thought about it the next morning. The first thing that came to mind was a conversation we had before I left. David said that when I came back he wanted us to go out with his brother and his wife. I didn't realize it at the time, but I think it really freaked me out. I got scared."

"What did you do about it?" I asked a little provocatively.

"Nothing of course!" We both laughed at my question and her answer. One of the lessons she had learned in therapy, repeated over and over again, was that you don't necessarily have to do anything about a feeling. In fact, when you act you often mask what the feeling is really about. Sarah had accepted that she was afraid. She didn't have to do anything about it except feel it—and remember that the fear came from her negative script about marriage. The best thing about fear of this kind is that when you allow yourself to feel it enough, you stop being afraid. Sarah was reaping the benefit of accepting her fears. She checked her machine the next morning. Dave had left a message and she returned the call. Instead of succumbing to her fear, Sarah began to reclaim her place and sense of belonging. She felt more confident about herself in the romantic realm and less defensive and alienated when her mother asked, "So do you think Dave is the one?"

ASSIMILATION

Sarah no longer felt that she didn't know what she was doing and found that she could enjoy time with her parents in a way that she couldn't before. Feeling more sure of who she was and less frightened of the prospect of marriage, she was able to defend herself more effectively from her parent's well-meaning but painful comments. She used many of the techniques we give in chapter 10, "Avoiding Friendly Fire," to educate her parents about how their comments made her feel. Sarah also felt less confused and frightened by her feelings of boredom in relationships.

Her relationship with David had started off hot and heavy like many of her previous ones. And, like before, she abruptly hit a wall of boredom. But instead of responding to it by dumping Dave and moving on, she dug deeper and uncovered a well of feelings that surrounded her marriage script. It was the closeness she was feeling with Dave that was stirring up the now familiar feelings of fear. When she dragged these fears into the light of day she could see clearly that she was not going to settle for an empty, unrewarding, passionless life as her mother had. By accepting these feelings and remembering that they stemmed from memories of her mother's complaints and her own recollections of what it was like to grow up in a passionless household, Sarah had more control over whether or not she would act on them. The impulse to break up with Dave lost its urgency. Instead, she looked for ways to enliven their relationship. We don't know the outcome of Sarah and Dave's relationship, but we do know the outcome of Sarah's story. She came to therapy feeling like a child, incompetent and alienated. She left feeling like a woman, confident and certain that she belonged. She could think much more clearly about what she wanted in a relationship and had every reason to believe she could get it. The fears she had about marriage still lingered, but they no longer ruled her.

The last time we spoke with Mark he was still seeing Carrie and said that things were going well for him. It was clear from our conversation that he was still taking responsibility for his urge to jump ship and the result was that he was feeling less abnormal and alienated. He understood his urge for what it was, a response to his personal marriage script. He no longer interpreted it as a sign of his immaturity and failure as a man. He had accepted his fear.

He was still afraid of ending up like his father and had the urge to jump ship from time to time. But he understood the urge to be a memory and not anything he needed to do anything about right away. By giving himself time and not burning any bridges prematurely, he lost nothing and gained much. If Carrie turns out to be a little too much like Mark's mother, or if some other facet of her personality starts to bother him deeply, Mark can always move on. If that does happen with this relationship, chances are Mark will be moving on for good reasons and not because of some ghost from his past.

AFRAID TO MAKE THE WRONG CHOICE

*All my married friends just seemed to know when it was right. I've been
with Brian for almost six months and I can't help but wonder—is he right
for me? Wouldn't I know by now if he were really the one?*

Katie, a twenty-five-year-old business associate

◄○►

*Sometimes I just don't know what to think about Carl. When we are to-
gether we have such a great time. But I get this feeling that some of my
friends disapprove. They don't come right out and say it but they say things
like 'there's a reason he's still single.' He's been a bachelor his whole life and
that doesn't happen by accident. I feel like I should get one of those stupid
books on how to find Mr. Right.*

Marilyn, a forty-eight-year-old commercial artist

I f you repeatedly ask yourself, "Is he the right one?," the question
may be less about the other person than about a lack of confidence
in your own ability to choose well. Many single people are haunted
by crippling doubts about their ability to choose a partner they can
be happy with. Given the numerous self-help books on how to recognize if you are dating the wrong person and how to find the right
one, it seems that more than a few singles suffer from the fear of
making the wrong choice.

At first glance, the fear of making the wrong choice seems to be
about deciding whether your current love interest is someone "good
enough" for you to give up your independence and the possibility of
meeting someone you'd be happier with. Outwardly, a number of
questions can preoccupy your deliberations. Is he attractive enough?
From a family that's not dysfunctional? Too bitter and cynical about

life? Interested in a similar lifestyle? Successful enough? The focus is on whether your love interest's resume measures up to your requirements for what Katie used to call "a keeper."

On a less conscious level, anxiety about your ability to choose well is usually less about what it would take to make a good fit between you and someone else and more about an underlying marriage script. Marilyn labeled the script aptly when she revealed her belief that "it's way too easy to get burned when you get married."

TOO EASY TO GET BURNED

For a variety of reasons, many single people have come to believe that marriage is treacherous. Undeniably, countless examples of marriages turned sour are portrayed in the popular media. Divorce, infidelity, "getting fleeced," and even murder are some of the bad outcomes encountered by those brave enough, or foolish enough, to get married. But more often than not this script is forged in childhood and then reinforced with every example of a bad marriage that is subsequently encountered.

The "getting burned" script is different from the "marriage is for losers" script in its emphasis on how married life will make you feel and on whether or not you can trust your partner. The "losers" script focuses on how marriage will make you feel about yourself. It tells you that you will feel as if you have given up too much, compromised excessively, and done something that you will not only regret, but will also feel humiliated by. The "too easy to get burned" script, on the other hand, focuses on how you will be hurt when you marry. It will be painful and you will find that you can't really trust your partner or the relationship the two of you have.

Ironically, when people who follow the "too easy to get burned" script are not conscious of it, they oftentimes embrace opposing beliefs such as that married people obviously know how to choose well, and do so without doubts or fears. This is the same type of defensive maneuver, accomplished unconsciously, that William Shakespeare portrayed when he wrote "The lady doth protest too much." Unfortunately, if you believe that married people must have it all figured out, you are likely to amplify aspects of the cultural marriage script which preaches that "if you're single you haven't figured it out yet and you don't know how to choose well." The single person's anxiety and lack of confidence are used as further evidence that she is inherently flawed. This leads to feelings of alienation like that voiced by Katie when she said, "It's starting to feel like everyone has it figured out except me."

ALIENATION

Katie

K atie, a twenty-five-year-old unmarried business associate, came into counseling when she started dating Brian. She felt excited, but also anxious. She had high hopes that he would be "the one," but she also harbored many doubts: she often asked me,* "Can Brian really be it? After all this time of being out there, dragging myself to every singles event in town, could I finally have found the person for me? Somehow I can't really believe it! I know I should be ecstatic, but I just don't feel sure at all. It's making me really nervous."

Brian, a good-looking rising bank executive, had certainly seemed like a good choice at the beginning. He and Katie had a number of friends in common; he had gone to a good school; and he had a terrific job at one of the well-established banks in the community. What was even better was that he seemed very respectful of Katie. He talked to her about work and seemed especially appreciative of her advice on how to handle people, an area that came naturally to her. He was attentive and available, and she felt quite comfortable with him. Katie described him in this way, "He really lets me be myself and appreciates what I have to say. He thinks everything I do is cute . . . even when I'm being a jerk. Can you imagine that?"

In spite of this seeming compatibility, Katie was having a hard time feeling confident about Brian in part, she told herself, because of his family. There were divorces, remarriages, and a mix of religious beliefs in Brian's family. Although Katie's family was also complicated, it was not "like Brian's." Katie's family was Catholic through and through. No one was divorced, and most of her siblings were married with children. It is worth noting, however, that Katie's sister Debbie was a heavy drinker who became nasty when she was drunk, and her older brother, Ian, was considered the black sheep of the family. He

*J.K.

had been out of work more than once and was currently living at home with their parents. But somehow the fact that members of her own family had flaws and problems of their own escaped her whenever she focused on Brian's problems. His family's problems made her worry that maybe he would end up a bad choice as a partner.

"I just don't know if Brian's really right for me. Take religion. His family is barely Catholic, he doesn't even really practice it himself anymore. And his sister is married to a Jewish guy. I think they actually celebrate both Christmas and Hanukkah. I want my kids to grow up Catholic, no question about that.

"And you think that Brian doesn't?" I asked. "I don't really know. But I do know that Brian's parents are divorced. Does that mean that it will be easier for Brian to get divorced? I don't have any idea if I really need to worry about this kind of thing but I guess I must, because I do. It makes me crazy. I feel so stupid about being this worried. Why can't I just figure it out like everyone else does?"

As time went on, instead of gaining clarity for herself, Katie became more and more confused. To handle her increasing anxieties she would repeatedly ask other people for their opinions. "I keep asking my friends what they think of Brian. They seem to love him! What they get irritated about is that I keep asking them about it. They want to know what my problem is. Why can't I just get on with it? They are tired of going over every detail a thousand times. But I can't seem to help it. I go over and over it so much in my mind, it seems to never stop. Some of my friends have gotten disgusted and have told me to stop talking to them about him. Last night Carol told me, 'He's a nice guy, end of story. Either move in or move on.' Everyone else seems to have such an easier time with this. They know when it's right; it's like they can trust their gut. I'm just not like everyone else when it comes to this. I have no idea what my gut is telling me from one minute to the next. I just wish I were like everyone else."

And when Katie would talk to her sisters about her uncertainty, she would slip further and further into the alienation stage. "I am just not like my sisters. Their husbands have turned out to be great, but it took hard work. I would never have married either one of those guys. But, you see, they figured it out for themselves. I'm afraid I just can't do it. I am the one that is sitting here still alone, still feeling like a reject." Katie was blaming herself for her uncertainty and for "causing" the anxious feelings she was having. She made the common mistake we told you about in chapter 5: she assumed that she had direct control over what she felt. This added to her experience of alienation because she was convinced she shouldn't be feeling as anxious as she did. She blamed herself for what she was feeling and for her lack of confidence in whether her relationship with Brian was a good one. But she only did this when she wasn't blaming Brian's family history for making her uncertain. Until she could break the cycle of blame, she would stay stuck in the alienation stage.

Marilyn

Marilyn, a forty-eight-year-old commercial artist, struggled with many of the same doubts and fears that Katie described. Marilyn, however, found her own unique way to manage them. She lived over two hundred miles away from Carl, the man she had recently begun to date. The distance was enough to insure that the time they spent together was mostly limited to weekends. When they did see one another, they enjoyed it immensely, and they could avoid many of the more tedious day-to-day issues that might have caused conflict between them (e.g., time committed to other people and activities, how to manage finances, family issues). In fact, they would usually participate in activities the other person did not enjoy when they were not together. When conflict did occur, they could withdraw from one another, allowing time and distance to diffuse the tensions. This could be a perfectly workable arrangement for two people who wanted a similar level of day-to-day involvement. However, after several months, Marilyn had become aware of some ambivalence on her part regarding this arrangement.

"I've been single a long time now. It's been over fifteen years since my divorce. I know I really love the independence, and the lack of accountability to anyone. But I also feel so lonely at times. With Carl I have begun to wonder what it would be like to get married again. To have him around every day, not just on weekends. To go to bed with him and wake up with him in the morning. Like the rest of the world! I don't think I would be lonely with Carl. We always have so much to talk to each other about. He's so intelligent. I think it could really be nice. He makes me laugh a lot. We really seem to get along."

She and Carl did have wonderful times together. They traveled together well, mostly to out-of-the-way places which stimulated their common intellectual interests. Marilyn was a doer (getting the passports, learning the language), while Carl was the planner (envisioning the bigger picture of what the trip would encompass). When not traveling they enjoyed their local theaters, art openings, neighborhood restaurants, and socializing with a small group of friends, mainly in Carl's community. Over time Marilyn found herself thinking about sharing more of her life with Carl. It seemed like a wonderful idea, something she would dream about, but always off in the future.

As luck would have it, their fairly comfortable situation abruptly ended when Marilyn lost her job. As a commercial artist working in an industry that had been slowly but steadily shrinking in her town, Marilyn believed that she needed to consider her next professional move carefully. It seemed that the future was wide open. Although the new possibilities were exciting, Marilyn also found herself lying awake at night "worried and scared. I really can't believe I was laid off. It isn't that I didn't see what was happening in the company, I did. I knew sales had been steadily decreasing and I knew they were going to have to start laying off staff or close up shop. It's been happening all over. But I never really thought that it would be me. You know, I never made a plan, even though I could see it coming. God, that is so like me." What she was referring to when she said "it's so like me" is her feeling of incompetence.

Her mother added to Marilyn's growing sense of inadequacy and the inevitable experience of alienation that comes with such feelings when she told her ". . . your life is such a mess. No job security, no husband and family. All your life I have worried about you. I always said you'd have problems until you settled down like your sisters. But you never wanted to do that. You've had plenty of chances, but you never wanted to do what everybody else did. You always made such a big deal out of getting married again. You just needed to be different." Her mother's concern hit a nerve. Marilyn did feel alone in the world and wished that she had a partner in life to help her through this frightening time. Although a professional crisis was the trigger for her increasing worry, her status as a single person had become an additional, often more intense, focus of her self-doubt and feelings of alienation.

To handle these feelings, like Katie, she turned to the remedy of blame. She blamed herself for her current job situation, because she had not planned well enough for the layoff, as well as for her unhappy single status, because she always picked losers who were not ultimately who they seemed to be. Other times, Carl would become the target of her fault finding. "I mean when I really look closely at Carl, I wonder why I am with him at all. He's never been married, and probably isn't capable of making a commitment to one person. He's actually quite self-centered. When I think it through, Carl has some pretty serious strikes against him." It wasn't until she learned to break the cycle of blame that she could begin to look elsewhere for answers to why she was feeling so worried and unsure of herself.

To break the cycle she began by looking at what might be underlying her feelings of anxiety other than her blameful belief that she was inherently incompetent to choose well. It was easier for her to begin the process by examining these feelings in her professional life. But as you will soon learn, her insecurities in the work arena had the same roots as her insecurities in the realm of love.

Marilyn had to reconsider the question of whether she had really not planned well for her future at work. Actually, despite what she felt, she had anticipated the layoff and acted in ways that were self-preserving. Marilyn's father had taken ill several months prior to her layoff. During that time he had required additional attention from her, attention which took her away from her professional life. In spite of that, by the time she was actually let go, she had already begun searching in earnest for something new. This was how she knew that her industry was in a general decline in her area, and that it was probably time for a more dramatic professional move.

And what about Carl? He had never married and Marilyn worried that he was "terminally single," a confirmed bachelor. It was true that he had been single his entire life, but this was a superficial, uninformative observation. What did Carl have to say about staying single? As it turned out, among the many reasons he probably had, one stood out. Carl had diabetes and was extremely self-conscious about it. He worried about the possibility of losing his eyesight as his mother, who was also diabetic, had. He often told Marilyn he didn't want to become a burden to anyone else as his mother had become.

Marilyn was able to break the cycle and move into the assessment stage after she recognized that blaming was getting her nowhere. No longer tempted by blame, she had begun to look elsewhere to understand the intense anxiety and self-doubt she was feeling.

ASSESSMENT

B y breaking out of the cycle of blameful accusations, such as "I always make the wrong choices," or "Carl must be terminally single if he's never been married," Marilyn could now begin to examine the facts more fully to find what might be contributing to her current experience of alienation as a single person. She made a valuable discovery when considering her reaction to an offer of help that Carl made.

"I talked to Carl about the job situation, and he has been very supportive. He suggested I might want to look in Minneapolis, which is only twenty minutes from where he lives. He even offered me a small apartment on his property that hasn't been used since his mother died last year. He thought I could try the area out, and have some interviews without having to drive two hundred miles home.

"I hate to admit it, but I kind of freaked out. At first, his offer seemed so giving. Then, I thought, oh no. I know what this is about. He just wants me around for his convenience. It wouldn't turn out to be about helping me; it would be about me taking care of him. I always seem to find men who are users."

"Do you think that's the case with Carl?" I asked.

"It sure felt that way at the time, but then I thought 'just because it feels that way doesn't mean it is that way.' Stepping back I knew fairly quickly that it was another one of my paranoid thoughts."

"Are you going to take him up on his offer?"

"Sure am. Like you always say, I can always change my mind later if my worst fears are realized."

"It kind of leaves us with the question of where the 'paranoid' thought came from. Any ideas about that?"

"Not at the time, but when you were talking just now I couldn't help but think of my parents' marriage."

"What were you thinking about it?"

"How I ended up getting saddled with taking care of my mom. I think of a lot of my fears about what could happen with Carl come from seeing what happened with my parents."

Marilyn's mother had been an alcoholic and her father had turned a blind eye toward his wife's problem. He stayed out of her way, and pursued the things he enjoyed outside the home. It hadn't always been that way. Earlier in his marriage Marilyn's father had been very involved covering up for his wife's drinking. But he made it clear to his children that he felt extremely burdened by the marriage and expected their help. Being the oldest, Marilyn was given the lion's share of the work. In exchange, her father courted her with special attention. But by the time she was a teenager, Marilyn had begun to feel exploited and painfully let down by her father. He burdened her with what she felt should rightfully have been his duties and didn't protect her from being devoured by her mother's needs. Her father had felt "burned" in his marriage, and Marilyn in turn felt burned by having to take care of her mother.

Given her childhood experience, her "paranoid thoughts," as she called them, can be understood as a self-preserving reflex that had been healthy for her at one time. It made sense that getting too close to a love interest would evoke a feeling that things were getting treacherous. At times like these, she felt she did not know who to trust, and feared that she would make a wrong choice as she felt her father had. This fear was amplified by the concern that she would ultimately find herself exploited and let down by anyone she got too close to. Although she hadn't always been aware of the feelings, this is what she felt had happened with her father.

It is probably no accident that she was dating someone who had the complementary fear of becoming a burden on someone else. The fact that Carl worried about how his diabetes could affect a partner did much to reassure Marilyn that she would not have to become the caretaker. It also actually helped her to look at her fears in this area a little more closely. As she put it, "I am afraid of having to be a caretaker, of getting used, and that's exactly the thing that Carl's afraid of for me! My fear is my own; he's given me no solid reasons to feel this way." When she stopped blaming Carl for her anxiety she became curious about what was truly underlying her fear of getting burned. When she uncovered the marriage script she had written in her childhood, Marilyn was able to question its relevance to her current situation. At this point she began to take responsibility for the feelings created by the script. But before we tell you how she did this, we return to Katie to reveal how she too uncovered her marriage script.

Katie

When Katie was able to break the cycle of blame, in which she fluctuated between blaming herself for "having a very serious problem and feeling so anxious all the time," and blaming Brian for coming from a dysfunctional family, she began to examine the facts in earnest and move into the assessment stage. Katie first questioned whether Brian's attitude toward Catholicism was truly a major problem for her. She had to admit that despite his apathy, he was supportive of her desire to be involved with her church. In fact, Brian's point of view was that he had not abandoned his beliefs, only his participation in organized worship. He assumed that when he started a family of his own, he would likely reconnect with the church. What's more, he went to church with Katie whenever she asked and she had to admit that whenever they talked about the substance of their spiritual beliefs, the values they each held, Katie felt they were very much "on the same page."

And what about Brian's attitude toward divorce? Was he more likely than Katie to see divorce as an option for problems later on? To the contrary. As Brian had explained it to Katie, the painful experience of his parents' breakup had made him especially thoughtful about living up to the commitments made in relationships. In fact, he felt it was why he had waited until he was more established and mature before he seriously considered getting married. It seemed that both he and Katie were equally serious about the importance of marriage as a lifelong commitment.

As for Katie's self-blame, could she be exaggerating the difference between what she felt and what her friends and sisters likely felt when they were single? Was she really "dumber" than everyone who has gotten married? When she challenged her self-blame, Katie was able to get some useful answers to her question about why she was so confused about Brian.

In examining her expectations about marriage as an institution, her thoughts turned naturally to the only marriage she had intimate knowledge about. "I don't think either of them were happy. But I always felt more sorry for my mother. Married life had been hell for her because of the way my father treated her. He was kind of abusive, telling her she was stupid. She was chained to that house. He never wanted her to work.

"But she'd always defend him. She'd brag about how successful he was. He was successful, but so what? It never did my mother any good. He never let her spend a dime on herself, or on the house. And of course she wouldn't leave him because she was Catholic. It's just not done in our family.

"My dad's better now; he's not so verbally abusive, but I remember always thinking that I never wanted to end up like my mom. She would never admit it openly, but I know she felt trapped. I don't know how she put up with it for so many years. I would have gone insane if it were me!

"I think on some level I have always believed that Brian, or any man for that matter, would ultimately turn out in some way to be just like my father, and then I'd get trapped and abused like my mother."

With this last revelation, Katie could understand her obsessive focus on Brian, and how it functioned to keep her at enough of a distance from him to feel safe. But unfortunately, it also kept her from confronting her own underlying fear about marriage and ultimately from taking responsibility for it.

ACCEPTANCE

W hen Katie identified her marriage script, she could now see that among other things, being single protected her from the worse fate of a bad marriage. This new knowledge about her motivations for being single helped her to address her worries about Brian in a more positive way. Rather than staying stalled at the crossroads where many single people find themselves today, she could now make a choice reassured by a fuller understanding of the fears she had and a new clarity about the difference between the real versus imagined dangers she might face. She could either put the relationship on hold, and maintain some distance while she learned new ways of dealing with her fears, or she might try to commit herself more fully and work at managing these fears within her relationship with Brian. She chose the latter option.

It's worth noting that for Katie, committing herself more fully meant that she would not give much credence to the sense of urgency her fears created. In other words, she made a concerted effort to not respond to her anxious ruminations over whether she should break up with Brian because he might not be the "right one." She accomplished this by reminding herself that she could "always break up with him tomorrow" whenever she had the urge. She further reasoned that if a pattern emerged in their relationship that she was not happy with, she would detect it and do something about it.

Katie took responsibility for her fears by not acting on them impulsively. She reminded herself that she would never let what happened to her mother happen to her. When Katie realized that she could never acquiesce in the way her mother had, at least not for more than a few hours, she began to trust herself more. Importantly, she also began to trust her relationship with Brian. If he proved to be a bad choice, she believed that she would know and that she would do something about it. She would not get stuck as her mother had. When she saw that her fear of getting burned, which in small doses is a normal and healthy concern, was greatly magnified by the lens supplied by her marriage script, she was much reassured. It felt "really scary" at times, but when she stepped back from the fear and reminded herself of the kind of woman she actually was, the fear had no hold over her. She might make a mistake or two, but she knew how to protect herself. When she took responsibility for her fears about marriage, Katie found that she could afford to venture out and take some chances.

Marilyn also learned to take responsibility for the fears created by her marriage script and childhood experiences as the family caretaker. Knowing, as she now did, that she was vulnerable to feeling panicked about slipping into a caretaker role, Marilyn found that she could handle her worries very differently than she had previously. Before, the fears led only to self-doubt and paranoid thoughts about Carl. But now, with the knowledge of where the fears originated, she felt safer and reassured of her ability to protect herself.

If there is one thing that marks when someone has graduated to the acceptance stage, it is the realization that the only thing you can change reliably is how *you think* and how *you act*. Single people in the acceptance stage know that they cannot change what they feel, nor can they change other people. In the rare instances that it is possible, it takes a long time. Remember the boating analogy offered earlier? Trying to change your feelings, or other people, is like trying to change the course of a huge ocean liner. Turn the wheel but be prepared to wait, it can take miles before your course changes.

On the other hand, changing how you think about things and how you respond to your emotions is more like driving a speedboat. Turn the wheel and be prepared to hold on tight, because the boat will turn on a dime. Marilyn accepted the fact that she could not change Carl into someone who would make no demands on her, never need anything from her. She also realized that she couldn't always stop herself from feeling afraid when becoming intimate with a man. Having accepted what she could not change, she was finally free to take responsibility.

Like Katie, she felt more free to take some risks. She had a very strong impulse to apply for a job, any job, in her town. She was anxious to stay independent and fearful of the strings that might be attached to Carl's offer of the spare apartment. She was drawn to do this despite the fact that work was drying up in her own town and any job she could find there would almost certainly be a step down. Marilyn recognized that her marriage script probably accounted for the intensity of this impulse. If she relied on Carl, if she gave up her independence, she risked getting burned. Although her worries about wanting to stay independent are understandable and generally reasonable, her negative marriage script was still at work. Don't forget, there is always a kernel of truth in every script. But don't be fooled as Marilyn once was. The intensity of her fears and the urgency they created came from the script she held.

Marilyn decided to take Carl up on his offer. She used the apartment he had offered as a base from which to look for work in the Minneapolis/St. Paul area. We should be very clear about her motivations. There were arguably far better opportunities for her professionally there, and her main hesitation about moving was a fear of becoming trapped as her mother and she had been in the past. This fear was magnified by her marriage script and Carl's offer of the apartment. Her father, after all, had also been generous to Marilyn in a manner not unlike Carl's. He provided her with shelter, financial security, and praise. But he exacted a price Marilyn knew she could never again pay to anyone.

"I think now that I've cleared away some of the family cobwebs that were in my way, I can see that I'm not the person I was when I was a child. I can trust myself to not get burned in the way mother was. It's funny, but the more I trust that I can protect myself, the more I can trust men. I didn't have many choices when I was growing up. I am not dependent on anyone like I had to be when I was a child, I am not a little girl anymore. And as far as making the same mistakes my mother made? . . . I am also not her."

ASSIMILATION

M arilyn ultimately found a job in the Twin Cities area. She learned new ways to maintain a safe distance with Carl that did not involve hundreds of miles or avoiding him altogether. Though they were living near each other and saw each other almost every night, they decided to not move in together. Having very similar fears about marriage that they could both appreciate, Marilyn and Carl found that they were growing closer even as they maintained some distance. Indeed, it was probably *because* they maintained the distance they each needed to feel safe, that they grew more intimate.

For Katie, focusing solely on Brian's adequacy as her lifetime partner had kept her from discovering resources which would be truly useful to her. Katie began to attend a workshop on singles and relationships at her church. She was still seeing Brian and feeling pretty good about it. She wasn't certain that it would lead to marriage because she was still unsure about what she wanted out of marriage, but it felt good for now. She was also spending more time with friends, both single and married, but no longer driving herself and them crazy with her ruminations about whether or not she should be with Brian. She felt more at peace with herself and with the choices she was currently making. She described this new feeling in this way: "Why did I think everybody else knew the answers but me? I've learned that everybody struggles, just in different ways, and that eventually everybody figures it out for themselves. I'm scared of making the wrong choice, plain and simple. But I don't have to make any decisions right now. And the fact is, the more time I spend with Brian, the less afraid I feel about the whole thing!"

When we last had contact with them, both Katie and Marilyn felt less alienated for being single, more courageous in the face of the fears they had about intimacy, and clearer about what they wanted out of life. This last bit of knowledge helped them both to feel comfortable with being single. Clarity about what each of them wanted and the knowledge that they were both well equipped to not make the mistakes their marriage scripts warned of opened them to the possibility that they might find some of what they wanted out of life in a marriage. Unencumbered by the past and less worried about what the future might hold, they found it easier to live in the present.

CHAPTER 8

HASN'T LEFT HOME YET

I don't really understand why I feel so upset about breaking up with Char-lie. It wasn't going so well anyway. I feel so depressed and all alone in the world. It's true I talk to my mother every day, but lately it feels like too much. It makes me feel a little pathetic—that we're as close as we are and I'm still single. I never used to feel that way about our relationship.

Lily, a thirty-one-year-old property manager

◄○►

Tom's a little prince. He's a momma's boy if ever there was one. I used to get so angry with him whenever his mother wanted us to come to her house for dinner or for a holiday. What I wanted didn't weigh in. His mom wanted us there, really just him, and so we went. He's way too connected to his family. Not that I didn't love them, I did, but there has to be some limits. I know that's why we never got married . . . he hasn't left home yet.

Stacie, talking about her ex-boyfriend Tom,
a forty-year-old software designer

M ost people are raised in homes that promote autonomy and inti-mate relationships outside the family. But some have childhood experiences that strengthen their familial bonds at the expense of au-tonomy and connection to people outside the family. This can occur in many different ways and for different reasons, but the resulting pattern of emotional dependency on the family is always the same in that it lasts a little too long.

In this chapter we address a marriage script that leaves single people like Lily and Tom feeling extremely ambivalent about mar-riage because of their close connections to family. This script can take on many different faces. The man who people sometimes refer to as a "momma's boy," or a "prince," and the woman accused of being a "princess" or too close to her father to ever get intimate with another man are some of the more obvious examples.

But in fact, these blameful accusations miss the mark in their overemphasis on the single person's supposed lack of maturity. Many single people with this script are mature in a host of other ways, while many who marry are not. Maturity is not really the issue. The real issue is that certain types of relationships with one's parents can inadvertently create barriers to connections with people outside the family. One such barrier is the marriage script we have labeled with the words Dorothy, in *The Wizard of Oz*, chanted to take her back to safety: "There's no place like home."

THERE'S NO PLACE LIKE HOME

Sometimes, this script leaves single people fearful of becoming too intimate with anyone outside the family because they fear losing the home they have counted on for so much and for so long. Other times, it results in an inability to imagine that a marriage could ever be as good as what already exists at home. Lily and Tom are two of the never-married singles who, in our work together, helped uncover some types of connections to one's family that can inadvertently act as a deterrent to happiness in other intimate relationships.

Lily

Lily came to therapy after breaking up with Charlie, the man with whom she had been living for the past three years. At the age of thirty-one, she was alone again. Even though she felt certain that Charlie was not right for her, she was "sick" at the prospect of having to start over again with someone new. During her first session she talked about how it felt to be single again. "I don't understand how I could get to be thirty-one and still not be married! I know I'm fairly attractive, I'm bright, and I've got some great friends so I'm not socially retarded! When I think about it, I get sick to my stomach. All I can think about is what's going to happen down the road? If I end up like my Aunt Sylvia, single forever and all alone, I'll shoot myself!"

Lily believed that the most important thing she wanted to accomplish in life was to be happily married and to have a family of her own. She wanted other things to be sure, but in her eyes marriage and children represented a developmental milestone, a mark of maturity, as it does for most people. After breaking up with Charlie, this goal seemed to be out of her reach forever. She couldn't recall the last time she had been quite so pessimistic and anxious. She felt she had failed and that she was "still a little girl."

She explained why she thought this way: "Just after Charlie left, I started coming home from work and instead of making myself dinner like I used to, or calling a friend, I would turn on the television and have this horrible feeling that this will be my life forever. Work all day, alone in front of the tube all night. I am so tense that I can't eat, all I want to do is roll up in a ball and stay in bed. My friends don't really understand it. They didn't think Charlie was right for me and keep reminding me that I was never all that happy with him. But they're missing the point. I'm not feeling this bad just because of Charlie—it's because of me. It seems that everyone else is happy with someone except me. I am thirty-one. If I haven't found someone yet, why should I think I ever will? Something is definitely wrong with me."

And what did Lily imagine was wrong with her? She felt that perhaps she was too close to her mother: "And to make matters worse, the only person I feel I can relate to is my mother. Since Charlie left over a month ago, she's the only person I talk to every night. We're really close. I know it sounds like a cliché, but my mother really is my best friend. But given how I'm feeling these days, my friendship with my mother is starting to make me feel pathetic, like I need to grow up. I had a boyfriend once, long before Charlie, who said that my problem was that I hadn't left home yet. He accused me of being so close to my mother that there wasn't room for anyone else. I think maybe he was right. I've got to stop relying so much on her, stop talking to her all the time."

Lily has never really experienced the level of closeness, support, and understanding that she has with her mother in any other relationship. She has concluded that she needs to give this relationship up in order to become close to a man. Tom, whom you will learn about next, has come to a similar conclusion about his relationship with his family, and his mother in particular. But the kind of relationship he has with his mother is very different than that enjoyed by Lily and hers.

Tom

Never married and just turned forty, Tom has also become anxious about the prospects of marriage in his future. He is close to his family, in the sense that they really need him and he is willing to oblige. His father died a few years back and his widowed mother is retired and financially strapped. Even if she wanted to work she could not because of multiple health problems. His brother Tim lives two thousand miles away but stays in touch with the family through Tom. Having recently been laid off, Tim is looking for work and worried about his future. Tom spends lots of time taking his mom to the doctor, talking to her every day, and providing her with financial and emotional support. He has a similar, albeit less intensive role, with his brother Tim. They speak every week and Tom has been helping him out financially since Tim's layoff three months ago.

Tom feels both proud and resentful of his role in the family. He says, "Well, I am glad to be there when they need me. In our family we were raised to help each other out. My dad always lent a helping hand to his brothers and my cousins when needed. I like being the one they all lean on. But because I see my mom so much, I often feel like I don't have time for anyone else. I speak to her two or three times a day on the phone. I don't talk to her much about my personal life because there's a lot she obviously doesn't understand. She is my mother after all!

"We usually talk about her, but there's only so many times I can hear the details of her aches and pains without going numb. I'm even starting to talk to her about my aches and pains! Swear to God. It cracked me up the other day when I realized I was doing it. I'm going to start sounding like a seventy-year-old if I keep talking to her so much! But all kidding aside, by the end of the day I just don't feel like talking with anyone else. I feel like my life is passing me by."

Problems with women and inertia in his career are what motivated Tom to go to therapy about a year ago, rather than the feelings about his family he just described. At that time he said, "I want to get on with my life, but I just can't seem to do it. I feel stuck. For years I've wanted to get my master's degree, see if I could move into management, but the inertia feels insurmountable. I have had the application for a part-time program at the university for two years running now. I started filling it out this year, but I didn't finish it. I go to work every day, nine to five, and think about how I'm not doing what I really want to. It's the same thing with dating. I've been seeing this woman Josie for almost a year, but I really don't feel that committed to her. I go through the motions at work, and I go through the motions with Josie. My heart's not in either one."

When asked where he felt his heart was, he answered, "With my family. I love my family. They really count on me, especially after my dad died. But it feels like they're the only people I ever talk to anymore—other than Josie and the guys at work. My mom needs a lot of help. I'm over there three times a week, changing a lightbulb, fixing her dishwasher, and driving her to the doctor. We talk every day, usually a couple of times. She can't drive anymore so I also take her grocery shopping once a week. It's a labor of love. We've got a pretty good relationship, but I'm starting to feel like a deviant. My last girlfriend accused me of being a momma's boy! That really got under my skin. Maybe she's right. I am forty—never been married. But I have to say in my defense, that if my Mom didn't need me for so much, I know I wouldn't be spending so much time with her."

Tom feels stuck, both at work and in love. But unlike Lily, it is not the *intimate quality* of his relationship with his mother that Tom is beginning to feel alienated by, it is the *amount of time and energy* he feels compelled to spend on her. Tom's version of the "there's no place like home" marriage script focuses more on how he defines himself as a man. It's not a feeling that "it never gets better than this" so much as a feeling that "home is where I can be a man." In other words, being a responsible, loyal, and caring son (and brother) was the foundation for his sense of self. It was a large part of the way he defined his self-worth. Unless he could find other ways to feel good about who he was, he would indeed be stuck at home. But not because he was a "momma's boy," as his last girlfriend thought, but because he was "the man of the family."

ALIENATION

Lily

Lily felt alienated because she was unwittingly following the cultural marriage script which said that she must be defective or immature because she was in her thirties (thirty-one to be precise) and still single. She had begun to worry that perhaps her particular defect was a failure to separate from her mother. Maybe she needed to reject her mother in order to "move on" and to feel connected to a man. The fact that Lily was very close to her mother made her feel even more alienated from her married friends who typically complained about their parents. Lily felt that being as close as she was to her mother meant that she was somehow immature. Lonely and demoralized about her prospects for the future, she had come to the premature conclusion that she must be to blame for her current predicament. More specifically, her desire to maintain a close relationship with her mother, to continue to enjoy the support and adult friendship that they shared, must be to blame.

In the past, Lily had turned more readily to blaming men. Although she had dated many different men over the years, she quickly rejected them, because inexplicably they somehow never "felt right." She found it hard to feel very close to the men she dated. In her experience, men were generally "insensitive buffoons." There was at least one exception, a young man she had become very close to when she was in her early twenties. But that relationship ended soon after the two friends had become sexually intimate. And what about Charlie? In this instance, she blamed herself for the breakup.

"I was too hard on him, something I have a tendency to do, I think. Charlie thought so too. He said I expected too much from him and that I was driving him away trying to get it. I wanted him to be someone he wasn't—more sensitive to my feelings and better at communicating. It was unfair to expect him to be either of those things. Charlie's not that kind of guy. He's a sweet man but not tuned in to other people's feelings unless you hit him over the head with them! . . . I pick guys who come up short and then drive them crazy about it."

But despite her newfound compassion and empathy for Charlie since the breakup, she had been much more prone to blaming him for her unhappiness when they were living together. She revealed that there was a long period of time during their three years together when she was certain that Charlie could have given her the sense of connection she wanted, but that he was purposely holding back out of anger. Over time she had given up on blaming Charlie because she had come to believe that he was truly giving her all that he could. And blaming him was not helping her to find answers. But then again, neither would blaming herself.

Lily felt profoundly isolated from her friends, family, and co-workers who were for the most part in couples. She felt that they could only see what was on the surface, a lovely young woman who was free of what they had come to believe was a second-rate boyfriend. The only person who she felt really understood and truly knew what had happened with Charlie was her mother. But when she decided to distance herself from her mother in an attempt, as she described it, "to grow up," she added to her sense of isolation. Lily felt unconnected to her friends and overconnected to her mother, without any idea of how to avail herself of the love and support that these loved ones were offering.

Tom

Tom felt surprisingly similar to Lily. He felt unconnected to Josie and increasingly alienated from his buddies who were all married. Admittedly, his best friend Rick had been married twice, but that was beside the point. Tom had never seriously considered marrying anyone. At least Rick had the courage to take the plunge, not just once, but twice! The fact that Tom had never had the desire worried him and dovetailed with the accusation levied against him by his former girlfriend Stacie. Maybe he was a momma's boy, perhaps he needed to grow up.

He knew that Rick's wife thought so. They were having dinner one night, just the three of them at Rick and Wendi's house, when Wendi said, "I don't get it, Tom, you're such a great guy. When are you going to bite the bullet and settle down?"

"Who says I haven't settled down? I probably have more responsibilities than most people. It's not like I'm out partying until two A.M. every night!"

"You know what I mean. What are you afraid of?"

"Who says I'm afraid of anything?"

"You must be," Wendi countered. "Otherwise you wouldn't be so gun shy."

"Well, since I don't know, why don't you go ahead and tell me, since I'm sure you will anyway," he chided. Rick, meanwhile, abruptly excused himself from the table. Chuckling as he cleared the plates, he said, "I'll do the dishes and stay out of the way while Dear Abby fixes your love life!"

"I'm just trying to help!" Wendi continued a little defensively. "I don't know, Tom, it's just that you seem so unhappy being single and you keep meeting these great women but it never goes anywhere. You're always talking about your mother and brother—honestly, I think you're afraid to leave home! Maybe you just need to get a little braver already. Take some chances. Venture out there and stop spending so much energy on your family. What's wrong with Josie, for example? We think she's great."

Wendi was right about one thing, Tom was afraid, but not about the thing she thought he was. However, before Tom could uncover what it was he was fearful of, he would need to stop his involvement in the cycle of blame. Earlier, we described how Tom had begun to think about what his ex-girlfriend Stacie, and now Wendi, had said. Perhaps he did need to grow up. That was how he blamed himself for feeling unhappy with being single. It also added to his sense of alienation from his friends.

But he also blamed women. He didn't realize it until he was in therapy, but Tom found it hard to not see the women he was dating as burdensome. He had this to say about his current girlfriend: "Josie has been divorced for two years now. She is so needy. Sometimes I think she's afraid to be alone. She calls me whenever anything happens. I mean anything! Today, she called me at work about four separate times: to say hi, that she missed me, that this friend of hers at work was put on probation, and to ask me when I was coming home. I can't drop everything I'm doing just because she's feeling lonely or misses me." But Josie had said some things recently that made it difficult for Tom to hold on to this belief that she was going to be an emotional burden. "She told me that she thought that maybe I didn't ever want to get married. She said that if that was the case, she wanted me to tell her. And do you know why she wanted to know this? It wasn't an ultimatum or anything like that, she just wanted to know because if I didn't want to ever get married, then she didn't want to stay monogamous. She wanted to start dating other guys again. She wasn't saying she would break up with me—in fact she said that she loved me and the time we spent together—but she wanted to get married again and didn't want to put all her eggs in my basket if I wasn't interested in ever getting married!"

Tom found it ironic that he felt more drawn to Josie after she said this to him. But as he discovered later, when he uncovered his marriage script, it made total sense that he would feel more attracted to

Josie following such a statement of her personal autonomy and strength. The take-home point for now is that Tom was able to challenge his irrational feelings and beliefs about Josie and women in general. He was able to see that placing blame with them was overly simplistic and getting him nowhere.

ASSESSMENT

Tom

He was now free to face the real problem. His marriage script fostered two irrational beliefs that he had to learn to challenge if he wanted to move forward. The first was that the only way he will be loved and feel like a man is if he is a care giver. The second was that all love relationships are a burden.

Tom felt stuck at the fork in the road that Sarah described in chapter 2. He wanted to get married, but every time he headed in that direction he felt overwhelmed and burdened by the relationship and retreated to the fork described earlier. In Tom's case, the decision between staying single and getting married was located in a conflict between feeling compelled to take care of others and feeling repulsed at the idea. The lefthand fork was singlehood, which symbolized freedom from emotional burdens and responsibilities; to the right was marriage, which seemed to offer the prospect of even greater responsibilities and burdens than he currently had.

But then why wasn't he chasing the independent women of the world, the ones who would not become an emotional burden? Then perhaps the right fork would feel less onerous and oppressive. The main reason was he was less attracted to them. It's not that he was masochistic, or even that he was simply used to being a care giver and so that was what he was most comfortable with. No. It was because his sense of self-worth, of being a grown man, was intricately tied up with being in the role of care giver and provider.

If he were with a woman who truly needed very little from him in the way of emotional or financial support, he would feel at a loss and among other things, he would feel less like a man. His father was a provider and a care giver. Tom also took care of people in his life. Being with a woman who needed little from him would leave him without a defining role in the marriage. He received so much love, affection, and praise from his family for taking on this role that he couldn't imagine why else a woman would love him. Tom was not simply afraid of leaving home as Wendi had thought. He was afraid of losing his defining role in life.

In this context, it is not that surprising that Tom was generally attracted to women who, in his words, "were needy" in one way or another. Whenever he was in the role of care giver and provider, he felt strong, whole, valued, and loved. But the price was now too high. He had become ambivalent about the role. It no longer worked for him as it had the first time his father had said to him, when he was fifteen years old, "Your Mother and I will be away until Monday. Here's the number where you can reach us. You take care of Timmy. You're the man of the house now, son." Then the role had been appealing. When his father was dying years later, they had several conversations about how Tom was going to have to watch out for his mother and brother. His father was counting on him, even from the grave.

Like many people in therapy, Tom had a brief period where he got in touch with his anger at his parents for expecting and promoting such self-sacrifice on his part. But with forgiveness came a much fuller understanding of his own role in the family play. It felt good to be in the lead role. In fact, it felt great. But the time for playing the part had passed long ago. Tom sorely needed a new script, another way of experiencing himself as a man that did not involve his taking on the role of sole provider and care giver. Without it, he would forever be stuck halfway between the past and the present.

Lily

While in therapy, Lily was asked to challenge many of her blameful beliefs. Was she really expecting too much from Charlie? Was it immature of her to be so close to her mother? Was Charlie truly incapable of being more tuned in to her feelings and better at communicating? Maybe most men are insensitive buffoons. She was able to consider the possibility that, like Charlie, she was also not to blame for her current predicament and how she felt about it. More and more, she was able to refrain from blaming, especially after one particularly cathartic conversation with Charlie.

"We had dinner together a couple of weeks after he moved out. It was so sad. We both wanted it to turn out differently, but we were so unhappy being together. Charlie told me that he always felt so inadequate around me. Like who he was wasn't good enough for me. It made me so sad to hear him say that and I started to blame myself and to think maybe I'm making a big mistake here. It was so unlike him to be that open about how he felt. It was the very thing I used to fight for all the time. But without even knowing it, he helped stop me from jumping all over myself. He said that he believed that we were just not a good fit. As much as he wanted to give me what I wanted, he couldn't do it because it wasn't him.

"I have to give him some credit too. He did try. I remember once I was really anxious about something that had gone down at work. He just kept trying to tell me what to do, how to handle it differently. I was so frustrated and angry that he didn't understand what I needed from him just then. Later, I was telling my mother about the conversation and she tells me about this book, *Men Are from Mars, Women Are from Venus,* that talks about how men and women are different and how important it is to understand and accept those differences. We were laughing at how Charlie and my dad were similar to the men described in that book in that they were prone to try and fix problems whenever they heard of one. Later, I told Charlie about the conversation I had with my mom about this book and asked him to stop being so problem-solving oriented. The only thing I wanted was for him to just listen and to try and understand how I felt. Well, it worked! It was one of the most satisfying conversations I ever had with him. In fact, it worked so well I went out and bought the book. It was a good book, I learned some good stuff, but it wasn't the answer. I read it religiously and followed the advice, but I think that Charlie and I were just too far apart. I think I was from Mercury and he was from Pluto!"

Lily felt that she had given her relationship with Charlie her best efforts. She was no more to blame than he was. They had both given it their all. No longer turning to blame for a remedy to her problem, she began to look elsewhere for answers. She started to look more closely at her relationship with her mother and how it might be hindering her quest for closeness with a man. Since there is a kernel of truth in every script, it is not surprising to learn that indeed Lily's relationship with her mother was creating barriers to connection with a man, but not in the way that she had previously concluded. Unlike her previous theory, what she learned about her relationship with her mother and the marriage script that developed from it did not lead to self-loathing.

Lily was so close to her mother, she believed no other relationship could duplicate its intimacy and rewards. She confided in her mother every day, discussing the ups and downs of the day, what to eat, what to wear. And her mother did the same with her. The more she talked about their relationship, the more unique Lily realized it was. She once said, "You know, it's funny, I never realized how many people don't have such close relationships with their parents. I talk to my mother every day, just little things, but it is a nice part of my day. She can almost read my mind . . . but in a good way!" She added, laughing, "We are always finishing each other's sentences. We have similar values and we really respect and understand each other."

Lily and her mother mirrored each other's feelings. In the dance of their communication, they were highly coordinated and synchronized, like Fred Astaire and Ginger Rogers—with Lily adjusting her moods and comments to match her mom's and vice versa. It looked and felt almost effortless. When two people communicate with mutual understanding, respect, and rhythm, it is very pleasurable. Lily's mother and father had a similar ease of communication and they too generally felt "simpatico" with each other. Lily's personal experience with her mother and her observations of her parents together had understandably created a feeling that truly there was no place like home. This type of connection had become a way to judge that a relationship was on the right track. Or to put it more bluntly, as Lily did, "I can't imagine ever being married to someone I couldn't talk to like that."

When she was with a man with whom she did not feel simpatico, she felt anxious and lonely somehow. She discovered that these feelings stemmed from a script about marriage that she had unconsciously written down from her experiences in the first intimate relationship she had ever had, her relationship with her mother. If she could not experience the same level of familiarity and mirroring with a man that she had enjoyed in her own family, the prospect of spending the rest of her life with him felt bleak and lonely.

But why would she feel that way? It doesn't make sense. Indeed, her feelings about her prospects for the future after her breakup with Charlie also don't make sense. Even if she were in a marriage that was a little less than simpatico, wouldn't she still have her mother and father to rely on for that simpatico feeling? Why the sense of dread and the expectation of loneliness in a marriage?

As it turns out, people who hold a "there's no place like home" marriage script cannot imagine being married and maintaining their connections, for better or worse, to their family of origin. They assume that being married means burning all bridges home. For example, Tom's version of the script told him that when he married, his new wife would need him so much that he would have nothing left to give to his mother and brother. He would lose his place and role in his family. Lily also felt she needed to burn bridges if she was ever going to get married. The culture's marriage script played a role in this case because she feared it was somehow abnormal to be close friends with her mother. She acted on the cultural script by distancing herself from her mother in an attempt, as she described it, to "grow up."

Being as close as she was to her mother, she couldn't help but reveal some of how she was feeling. This resulted in the very thing that Lily feared most: her mother started to feel anxious and defensive. She thought that Lily might have been saying, "Mom, you didn't prepare me for the world; you were negligent." At first, rather than supporting Lily's quest for more emotional independence, her mother impeded it by letting her daughter know how bad she felt about it.

What was particularly sad about this period in the mother-daughter relationship is that her mother wanted the same things for Lily that Lily wanted for herself. But because Lily was trying to deal with her feelings using blame, their relationship had become tense. Lily didn't come right out and accuse her mother of anything, but her mother nevertheless sensed the message conveyed by her daughter's abrupt withdrawal from their relationship. And her feelings of rejection led to Lily feeling guilty and more angry.

Lily had come to see what was underlying her current state of anxiety and her ambivalence about marriage, but she was not yet taking responsibility for the feelings her marriage script created. Instead, she had reverted to blame to feel more in control and better about her situation. She blamed her mother and their relationship for the ambivalence she had about marriage. Although her feelings were generally expressed in subtle ways, she had gone from blaming Charlie, to herself, and now to her mother. But when her mother joined in by blaming herself, Lily realized that she was simply passing along the feelings she had been having about herself. It took practice and a watchful eye, but Lily was finally able to stop relying on blame to handle the feelings created by her marriage script and begin to do the work needed to take responsibility for them.

ACCEPTANCE

L ily's mother was a very caring and devoted person, and the idea that her relationship with her daughter had somehow left Lily feeling ill prepared for life made her feel terribly guilty. When Lily stopped blaming her mother and began to try to take responsibility for the feelings created by her marriage script, she was able to begin to repair the damage that had been done. She told her mother, "You don't have to be everything for me. Just because I'm not confiding in you like I used to doesn't mean we're not still close. I want to start relying on other people more for a while and it doesn't mean that you haven't done a good job. I don't need you to be my mother anymore, but I still want you to be my friend. And right now, what I need from my friends is some breathing room."

"Are you saying that I've been smothering you?" her mother asked, trying to understand.

"Not at all. I maybe thought that at first, but I don't think that way now. I think that I've relied on you for so much that it's hard for me to imagine how I could rely on anyone else. Does this make sense?" Lily had asked hopefully.

"It does. It reminds me of when you were about seven and you got into that huge fight with Jenny from next door. Do you remember the time she didn't invite you to her birthday party? Do you remember how angry and hurt you were and what you said to me?"

"The same thing I always said when I was upset. I told you that I wanted to sit in your lap forever. That I didn't need Jenny or anyone else as long as I had you."

"Remember what I did?" Lily's mother asked mischievously.

"How could I forget!" Lily answered, laughing. "You understood how I felt, I know you did, but then you tickled me until I laughed and straightened your legs so I slid off your lap and landed on the floor. When I tried to climb back on you told me I couldn't come back until I had let Jenny know how sad and mad I was."

"Do you know why I did that?"

"I didn't at the time, I was pretty confused and a little hurt when you wouldn't let me sit on your lap anymore. You'd never done that before! I remember going next door to knock on Jenny's door and feeling like the loneliest kid in the world. Even my mother didn't want me! But I figured it out as soon as Jenny and I made up. And deep down inside I knew that you weren't abandoning me."

Because they had a good relationship and were able to communicate well, Lily's mother immediately understood what it was her daughter wanted. The story she told made it clear that she did not want Lily to be overly dependent on her and that she was capable of encouraging her connections to people outside the family. Although the prevailing pattern between mother and daughter had led to the development of the "there's no place like home" script, all it took was for Lily to step in a new direction and the dance between mother and daughter began to change. Lily's mother was able to understand and respond only after Lily expressed what she needed without blaming anyone for the way she had been feeling.

Her mother understood that she needed to do now what she had done before when Lily was a child: strike a balance between providing a home base for her daughter where she could feel safe and valued and giving her an opportunity to try out her wings. The way she understood the situation, this was now a time for her to step back and let her daughter search elsewhere for connections.

With her mother's understanding and support, Lily was still left with the seemingly daunting task of trying out her wings. Could she trust her own judgment? What could she realistically expect from the men she was dating? Her marriage script had been written down and rehearsed over the course of her entire childhood. The fact that her mother was currently being supportive of Lily's taking responsibility for the feelings created by the script did nothing to lessen its appeal. Indeed, although it was immensely helpful for her to know that her mother understood and did not resent Lily's pulling back a bit, it inadvertently reinforced the feeling that there was indeed "no place like home." In other words, she was still vulnerable to feeling that if her relationship with a man was not as rich and immediately intimate as the one she shared with her mother, then it must mean that he could not possibly be "the one." But that did not mean that she could not do something more constructive with the feelings when they arose.

One of the most constructive things she did was learn to separate her feelings from her thoughts. She realized that this script involved two irrational beliefs: The first is that there is only one type of intimate relationship that is worthwhile—that is, one in which the two people are highly similar and immediately empathic, or understanding, of each other. They share the same tastes and can finish each other's thoughts. With this script it becomes difficult to experience relationships that lack these qualities as fulfilling in their own right. In many relationships friends may have to spell out what they are thinking, rather than assuming the other person will immediately be able to read their thoughts. But this does not mean there is no closeness and that the relationship is inherently less valuable.

The second belief is that if the relationship is not immediately simpatico, then it never will be. Lily may have forgotten that her mother had had Lily's whole lifetime to get to know her. And since she sounds like a caring and concerned person, she may have devoted a lot of her time and energy to learning all about Lily's moods and thoughts. In some sense, the two were experts in each other's characters. But in most relationships this degree of knowledge about another person develops gradually. People need time and opportunity to get to know each other well. And if Lily could accept this fact, she would free herself to enjoy the learning process.

It's important to note that because her mother was so competent at anticipating her daughter's thoughts and feelings, Lily never had to develop certain communication skills that would help her to clearly express her own needs. She was not accustomed to having to work at telling people what was bothering her because her mother was so talented at figuring it out. She wasn't accustomed to the kind of work involved in having to explain yourself to someone who doesn't immediately understand you. It's hard work at times, to be sure, but the kind of work that can leave you feeling closer to another person and more competent and hopeful about your ability to connect.

When she started dating after her breakup with Charlie, she noticed that whenever her date didn't immediately seem to understand what she was saying, she would feel turned off. She told us that she couldn't help but think "if I have to explain myself, then he isn't the right one for me. He'll be like Charlie; he'll never figure it out." To take responsibility, she had to learn to challenge such thoughts and to tolerate the anxiety that was stirred up in such instances.

"I was on a date with this really handsome guy, Will, and we were talking about work. I told him about this fight I had with my boss

and he just didn't get what was bothering me. I could tell he was trying to be polite, acting like he got it, but he didn't. I thought—how
could I ever be with this guy, he doesn't get it . . . he doesn't get me.
What kind of an emotional idiot is he?" It was not surprising to learn
that Will picked up on Lily's frustration with him. But when he asked
her if something was bothering her she had said no. The tension that
had erupted because of Will's slowness in understanding Lily grew
with her reluctance to try to bridge the gap it had created between
them. Lily could not have stopped what she felt even if she wanted to,
but she could have changed how she thought about it and how she
acted on the feelings.

Lily became curious about how she reacted to the feelings she had
in situations like the one she described with Will. She decided she
would try to notice when she got angry, anxious, or turned off during conversations. She found that whenever there were glitches in the
conversation, when the date didn't quite get what she was saying or
had a different point of view, she began to doubt their compatibility.
She would become preoccupied with worry over whether he was
right for her or not and in some instances, such as what happened
with Will, she would become angry.

Upon reflection, she realized that she had a very low tolerance for
being misunderstood and that this stemmed from her marriage script,
as did the resulting anxiety and anger such misunderstandings created. It was a sore spot for Lily. Intellectually she understood that no
man could ever compete with her mother in this realm, at least not
without a number of years of experience being close to Lily under his
belt, but she couldn't help but feel otherwise. However, now that she
understood the real source of these feelings she was better equipped
to do something constructive with them. She no longer felt compelled
to give them the credence she had in the past.

At work, she was quite good at explaining things to her employ-
ees. They often commented that she was a good teacher, so she decided to try using some of these same skills during conversations with
a date. Whenever she felt she was not being understood, instead of
succumbing to frustration and withdrawing, she would try to figure
out what it was he thought she had said. This is how she responded
at work. When she was teaching an employee a new procedure, she
would explain it, then ask him to tell her what she had just explained.
That way Lily knew what she had to do next, if anything, to insure

that the procedure had been learned correctly. Having a good sense of humor made the task even easier for Lily. Here is how she described one of the first times she tried this out.

"It was our third date. Ivan was really growing on me when I slammed into this wall of frustration and worry because he just didn't 'get me.' We had been talking about an argument I had had with my friend Betsy. She has this new boyfriend and ever since he came into her life she's been gone from mine. It's like I don't exist anymore. Obviously, everyone spends less time with their friends when they're dating someone new, but with Betsy it was extreme. I wasn't giving her a hard time about it or anything, I know with a little time things even out a bit, but what was driving me crazy was that I couldn't make any plans with her. It was always 'let me call you back Lil' because she wanted to wait and see if *he* was going to ask her out. So I was telling Ivan about how Betsy kept me hanging all week, then has the nerve to call me Friday at work to see if I still wanted to go out that night. Well, I gave her a piece of my mind and told her I didn't appreciate being treated that way. I also thought it wasn't so great for her to be totally at this guy's beck and call.

"Poor Ivan, he had no idea what he was walking into. He's listening to my story and the first words out of his mouth when I finished were 'She must feel so insecure.' Insightful guy huh? He obviously was interested in what I was talking about and could read between the lines and see that Betsy is very insecure. But at the time, I could have given two shits about Betsy. All I wanted from him was to understand how it felt to be cast aside by one of your best friends and treated callously, and for him to take my side. That's what my mother would have done!" she added, laughing out loud.

"I actually had the thought 'what a moron!' Can you believe it? I started worrying that he not only didn't understand what I needed but never would. When I had that thought, it was like a warning flag went up in my head. I thought this would be a good time to try on my teaching hat. So I did.

"I thought to myself: imagine you're his supervisor, he's new to this, you don't yet know if he's an idiot, be patient and try a new tactic. I must have started smiling at the thought because Ivan asked me what's so funny. I dodged the question and went into my teaching mode. It was such a relief to not sit there and obsess whether he was right for me or not just because his first response to my story wasn't the one I wanted. It's not like he can read my mind. Will I ever stop feeling that way? It's so neurotic!"

Lily was a good instructor and Ivan was a willing student. He came to understand what it was Lily wanted most from him in this particular conversation. He began to empathize with her over her friend's callousness, instead of trying to help her understand it as had been his first impulse. Lily even acknowledged a little of her "neurosis," as she called it, when she explained to him later that it drove her crazy when people didn't immediately understand what it was she was saying. Being skilled at reading between the lines, Ivan asked, "Like when I rushed to explain Betsy to you instead of listening to how bad you felt about it?"

"Was I that obvious?" Lily had asked.

"Not really. At least not until you said 'let me explain this to you real slow because I don't think you're getting my point!'"

She had not spoken these words literally, but Ivan had picked up on her frustration and was confident enough in how things were going to tease her about it. They both had a good laugh at his translation of what she had actually said. More important, they both felt closer to one another for having had the tension between them and resolving it together.

Lily would probably not stop having this "sore spot," as she called it, for a very long time. But she could keep it from ruling her life. She took control when she discovered why she was vulnerable to feeling this way and uncovered where the feelings came from originally, and when she made a plan on how she would act on them in the future. The more times she can tolerate the anxiety caused by her marriage script, the less of a hold it will have on her. It's common sense, really. Whenever you repeatedly face the thing you fear without getting hurt, you become less and less afraid. Knowing that the anxiety came from her script about intimacy and marriage helped her to tolerate the fears. She kept reminding herself that she didn't necessarily need the same level of communication with a mate that she had with her mother. These relationships could be apples and oranges; they did not need to be identical. She also reassured herself by remembering that people can learn if they're willing.

Tom

O nce he understood his attraction to relationships in which he could be the care giver and realized that this role was outdated and no longer worked for him, Tom could begin to take responsibility. His script about marriage terrified him. It said that independence from his family would equal abandonment of them and a loss of his rightful place as the "man of the house." Clearly, these were not rational thoughts. Indeed Tom referred to them wryly when he said, "I was having those psychotic thoughts about my mom and brother again last night. I was talking to Mom about Josie and how things were going. She kept saying that she wanted me to be happy, to find someone, and the whole time I kept thinking 'Oh yeah? Then what's going to happen to you?' I want to believe her and I think I do, but I can't imagine what she and Timmy would do without me.

"Crazy huh? Timmy is fucking thirty-seven years old and my Mom is seventy-two! Who do I think I am? They would get along just fine without me. If you had asked my Mom, Timmy, and me if we could imagine life without our father before he died, all three of us would have said no way, no how. But we survived just fine. It's grandiose to think I'm that important."

Tom went on to notice that he'd had yet another irrational thought. Perhaps you identified it just now. He apparently believed that if he married, his mother and brother would "have to do without him." Why? Tom answered the question this way: "I don't know why exactly. I think I imagine that when I do get married, if I ever do, I won't have time for them anymore." He went on to uncover the reason he felt he wouldn't have time. It would be because to be married must mean that he wouldn't have anything left to give his mother and brother. There was only so much of him to go around and the demands of a marital relationship would be too great. Actually, if Tom continued to court women who were indeed needy, this could very well end up being his fate.

So we return once again to the question of why Tom wasn't drawn to the only kind of woman he could ever tolerate being married to? What was it about women who exuded a sense of confidence and autonomy that was difficult for him? At first, when talking about specific women who fit this description, Tom explained that they were "boring." If you recall what we had to say about boredom early on in this book, then you know this statement was not left unchallenged. Indeed, he eventually found that he was anxious, not bored, when he dated women who were independent and autonomous. It was not anxiety born of feeling threatened by them, but from feeling that such women would have no reason to find him attractive or to love him. Once he became familiar with this anxiety and became more adept at identifying it whenever he felt that way, it lost its hold on him.

Although he came to see Josie as far less needy than he had experienced her at times, Tom still felt they were not a good match. She started dating other men after she asked Tom if he wanted a commitment and he answered her question with "I think I do, but honestly I'm not really sure that I want to get married." Eventually, she found someone who wanted more of the same things that she did and she broke up with Tom. By that time, Tom was already clear about his marriage script and skilled at picking up on the anxiety it created. More important, he was also practiced at not acting on his anxiety by fading away as he had done so many times in the past. Whenever he felt that his "heart wasn't into it," he would stop and consider the possibility that perhaps he was scared and his "heart was shutting down" in a response to the fear. In this way he was able to identify and deal openly with the irrational feelings and beliefs caused by his script about marriage.

Tom described how he took responsibility for such feelings when he told us about an interaction he had with his current love interest, Peggy, a doctor in training, whom he had been dating for several months. "We were lying around in bed on Sunday, reading the paper and drinking coffee, when Peg tells me that she had a big blow-up with the chief resident earlier in the week. He posted the call schedule and he had her on call for the following weekend despite the fact that we had been planning to go away. In fact, she had requested that weekend off almost a month ago. I was about to tell her it was OK with me and that we could do it another time when she told me everything worked out in the end. But apparently it was a real battle for a couple of days. She made him drag out all of the call schedules for the past five months to prove to him that he was being unfair by not honoring her request. She felt a little guilty because one of the other residents she's friends with would have to work that weekend and also had plans, but she felt justified.

"Later, I found myself losing interest in going away with her. It was weird, like the bottom just fell out of it. Then I think 'when did I start feeling this way and what could have triggered it?' Sure enough, it was her story about what had happened with the call schedule. I realized that I felt kind of left out, like she should have called me or something. In my head I thought this is great. Here's someone who is independent and capable of dealing with her own problems. She doesn't have to involve me in every little drama. But in my heart it was almost a panicked feeling. It felt like I was all alone in the world. Like I had been left out of something important. I knew I had hit the nail on the head because I started feeling better about going away with her."

Tom had become skilled at identifying the irrational or "psychotic" thoughts, as he referred to them, that sprang from his marriage script. He could begin to imagine a new role for himself in a marriage, one that did not require him to empty out everything he had in the name of love. He could be a man without always having to be the provider and care giver. Better yet, with this particular script, he didn't have to abandon his family. He could even imagine the possibility of getting some help with the familial burdens he had been carrying. In fact, he met Peggy during one of his mother's visits to the doctor. Peggy had filled in for his mother's cardiologist who was away on vacation. She was already involved in his mother's care!

ASSIMILATION

Lily's lifetime of closeness with both of her parents had many advantages. Her mom was easily able to recognize her feelings and knew lots of the little details of her life, and so she didn't have to take the time to explain many of the circumstances. When she wanted to talk about a problem she could do so without providing a lot of background. Her mother, who had retired, was also much more available than most of the people she was close to. Lily knew she could count on her to be available for companionship and comfort. Although her relationship with her father is not a focus of this chapter, it is worth noting that Lily felt he was fun and always willing to go places with her. When she wanted to learn how to play golf, she asked her father to teach her even though several of her male friends at work were avid golfers. Her father's generosity and attention were very positive for Lily, as they would be for most anyone.

But there are drawbacks to this degree of closeness when it is unchecked and unbalanced with intimacy outside the family. Lily had come to recognize the drawbacks and the fears that came with the "there's no place like home" script about marriage. She was so close to her parents that she had not expanded her range of interests. Mother and daughter liked shopping, talking, seeing movies. But neither had ever taken the time or the risk to learn about the world of sport, for example, or music, or food. When two people's interests are very overlapping, other activities may seem unimportant or even strange. By limiting her intimate social relationships to high levels of contact with her mother, Lily had limited the degree to which she participated in a wide spectrum of other fun, exciting, and potentially people-meeting activities.

Lily took her life off hold when she became more aware of the anxiety caused by the script she held about marriage. Really, as we have said before, such a script is as much about intimacy as it is about marriage. Whenever you long for intimacy and connection, but something inside you makes you fearful of it, you withdraw from the world around you. Lily had come to understand the ways in which she was afraid of losing her family and, more importantly, the many ways in which she didn't give people a chance to build intimate connections with her. With this knowledge she was able to engage more openly with the people in her life outside of her family. She enjoyed the closeness made possible by this newfound courage and optimism, not only with Ivan, whom she continued to date, but also with her friends.

Tom no longer felt the need to grow up and consequently no longer felt alienated from his friends. He felt very much like everyone else. Yes, he was forty and never married, but he had come to learn that this particular circumstance was not nearly as unusual as he once thought it was. He was actively dealing with the feelings created by his marriage script. He was on guard, alert to the irrational feelings and beliefs that he was vulnerable to. He could now see that becoming close to someone else would not necessitate abandoning his family. It did require moving a little farther from them emotionally, but not leaving them altogether.

Tom and Peggy fell in love. It was slow in developing, but the connection between them had grown powerful. His relationship with Peggy developed side by side with his vision of a more mutual role for himself in relationships. He could truly see that it didn't have to be a one-way street for him to feel loved and valued. Peggy did depend on him for some things, but not nearly so much as he used to worry might happen. More importantly, his interest in this independent woman did not collapse under the weight of his marriage script as had happened so many times in the past. Because Tom was watchful of the ways in which he could feel anxious about her independence and personal strength, he was able to keep the fire alive and to take his life off hold.

CHAPTER 9

NEVER GOES ALL THE WAY

All of my close friends are married, and most of them are having their first, if not their second, child. I feel like I'm getting left behind. When Anna and I were together and friends would ask me when she and I were going to tie the knot I'd always say "We're working on it." But that's as far as we ever got. We kept on working at it but never took the next step. She was so needy. I kept hoping she would change, but she didn't. As hard as it was when she broke up with me, I'm glad that she did. We weren't going anywhere but round and round.

Dave, a twenty-nine-year-old restaurant manager

◄o►

I love Alex, but I don't feel ready to get married to him. I've been told by quite a few friends and family that I should know by now, but the fact is I don't. I can't move forward with things the way they are. I've given up so much of my own life to be with him. I quit my job and moved so we could stay together when he got his new job. We spend all of our time with his friends and family and rarely if ever see mine. Do I want to do that for the rest of my life? No. Some things have to change before we take the next step.

Lucie, a thirty-one-year-old high school teacher

Ambivalence is a universal and normal part of being in a relationship. However, single people like Lucie and Dave seem to be more than ambivalent. Becoming close and monogamous with a lover is rarely a problem, it's the fact that the relationship never seems to go anywhere that causes notice. It languishes in limbo, neither moving forward nor dissolving. Friends and family make the observation, more often a reproach, that "you never go all the way." What is not obvious with singles like Lucie and Dave is the unconscious belief that the "cost" of being married is too great to pay.

When Lucie complained that she had already lost too much of her own identity in her relationship with Alex and when Dave worried that Anna was too needy, it suggested that they both held a particularly frightening marriage script. On the face of it, this script differs from the others we have discussed in that intimate relationships are formed but they never evolve into lifelong commitments. You can also spot it by the type of fears that emerge whenever a relationship gets too close for comfort. For women, it is revealed in comments such as Lucie's "I disappear whenever I am in a relationship," while men voice fears like Dave, who once remarked: "Every woman I've been involved with is too needy and self-absorbed. I want a partner, not a child."

I WILL LOSE MYSELF IF I MARRY

It is not that people like Lucie and Dave don't want to get married, it's that they're scared of losing themselves if they do. Although they are in monogamous relationships, they remain unmarried and stuck in their own version of the fork in the road we've described throughout this book. They find it far easier to stay put than to make a choice. Worse yet, because they are vulnerable to the messages proffered by the cultural marriage script, they make themselves miserable while trying to decide.

Although it might appear similar on the face of it, this script differs significantly from the "There's no place like home" script that Tom held (chapter 8). Tom's script did not make him afraid of losing himself in marriage. Instead, it made him fearful of losing his place in his family. That script focuses on the connections to one's family of origin and how those relationships can throw up barriers to connecting to someone outside the family. The script that is the subject of this chapter centers on the premise that you will lose your individuality, your needs will be ignored, because of the manner in which you get close to people. Lucie and Dave are good examples of what happens when you abide by this script. After several "close calls" (i.e., relationships that became intimate and nearly resulted in marriage), they both began to recognize some fears they had about intimacy that were clearly irrational, at least on the face of it.

ALIENATION

Lucie

Attractive, energetic, bright, and an exceptionally talented high school teacher, Lucie should have had no trouble finding someone with whom she could spend the rest of her life. Or so her friends and co-workers say. She is friendly, easy to talk to, and doesn't seem to have an enemy in the world. In fact, most people were surprised to learn that she was still unmarried. Her supervisor often remarked that he just couldn't understand why Lucie wasn't married yet. She had been in a relationship with Alex for three years. They lived together for well over two years, and Lucie said she wanted to be married but that the relationship was not where it needed to be for her to be willing to take the next step.

At work, Lucie was well liked. Her supervisor, whom she is friendly with, observed that "Lucie could have the pick of the crop. There are a lot of men who would be thrilled to call Lucie their own. Something has got to be wrong with Alex. She should move on." Like her supervisor, Lucie sometimes blamed Alex for her reluctance to marry, which was drawing some unwanted attention from her friends and family.

The fact that she recently passed her marriage milestone caused Lucie to feel painfully out of step and disaffected with those around her. She sensed a subtle indictment of her character and maturity. "Every time someone asks me why Alex and I aren't married yet, I can hear what's being said between the lines, 'What's wrong with you? If he's not right for you move on. Either shit or get off the pot.' But I'm scared to get off the pot. I've invested so much in the relationship and I do love him. And I am terrified of never finding anyone, of ending up all alone."

Her best friend had doubts about Lucie's desire to be married. "I know everyone wonders why Lucie and Alex haven't tied the knot. But, you know, I don't think it's so complicated. Lucie could be married if she wanted to be. I think it's pretty clear that she just doesn't want to be. She doesn't know how to compromise and she doesn't want to. She's happier being single." Lucie felt misunderstood and increasingly alienated from her friends and co-workers, who joined the chorus in her head that chanted "What's wrong with you? . . . why aren't you married yet? What's wrong with you? . . . why aren't you married yet?" But she took some refuge in the belief that the problem has been with the men she has been involved with and a masochistic tendency on her part to choose men, like Alex, who demand too much and give back too little. Her alternation between blaming herself and blaming the opposite sex was so rapid that the boundaries between the two poles had become blurred. In other words, Lucie believed that the men she got involved with were inherently bad for her and that she had a tendency to choose bad men.

Alex, whom she has been involved with since she was twenty-eight, was an easy target for her blame. Lucie felt he was emotionally "cut off" and frequently self-absorbed. In fact, Alex was not someone who could easily reveal what he was feeling and did have a tendency to take Lucie for granted. One incident stood out in her mind as paradigmatic: "I remember planning a birthday party for him, a really big bash with all his friends, and he came really late. I mean over an hour late! I thought, what the hell is going on here? I felt like he was so disconnected and inconsiderate. It felt like I didn't exist." Other incidents—like the time he planned a vacation without her—left Lucie feeling, "It's always about *his* plans, rarely about *our* plans." In an effort to understand how she ended up in this relationship Lucie said, "The only conclusion I can come to is that I am drawn to self-absorbed and selfish men." But this conclusion did little to further her cause and only added to her sense of alienation.

When asked whether she could have foreseen how the relationship would evolve when they were first dating, Lucie had to admit that probably no one could have. Things started out well for the couple and Lucie felt that Alex was not nearly as insensitive as she now felt he was. In fact, he used to be quite focused on her needs and capable of being selfless.

But was his capacity to be giving simply a result of the honeymoon phase of courtship or did something happen along the way to make him more self-centered? Both explanations are likely true. Lucie's natural inclination in relationships was to empty herself emotionally. She said, "I've given up so much for this relationship. I moved to the apartment that Alex wanted to live in; I basically supported us when he was between jobs; and I worked hard socializing with his friends and family. When he got his new job in Boston, there was never any question, at least not in my mind, that I would follow him. It got to the point where I felt he just expected it. I don't know exactly when it happened, but right before we moved to Boston it seemed like he stopped putting me before the other priorities in his life.

"I need Alex to be more there for me. I know he loves me, I know he tries to give me what I want, but he doesn't seem to know how. Maybe I played a part in that. I am not very good at making my voice heard. When he came late to the birthday party I threw for him, I didn't say anything to him about it for a couple of days and when I did, I softened it up. He never really heard how hurt and angry I was about that."

Clearly the problem was not simply that Lucie picked self-absorbed men. Alex had shown that he was capable of being selfless and giving. But somehow their relationship had evolved into a one-way street. The more Lucie focused on Alex, the more he expected it. Curiosity about why she focused so much on Alex's needs, and why she was reluctant to voice her own, helped her further to relinquish her dependency on blame for answers. It also opened the door to some valuable territory that she had not yet explored.

Dave

Like Lucie, Dave is often described as someone who "never goes the whole nine yards." He gets involved, "but never closes the deal." He had been feeling pressure from family and friends who told him Anna was good for him, and as his good friend Greg put it, "You should just go for it." But if it was as easy as simply deciding to "go for it," Dave would have done so long ago. His reluctance to marry was not a decision, it was a feeling, and Greg didn't understand the depth of the fear Dave was up against.

Dave had been involved with Anna for two years. Prior to that, he had been unattached for nearly three. He wanted to be married and wanted it to work out with Anna, but found that he couldn't bring himself to propose marriage. Making matters worse was his fear of ending the relationship. He worried that if he couldn't make it with Anna, then who could he make it with? Perhaps he'd never find anyone. The pressure to decide had been mounting as he approached his thirtieth birthday, a common marriage milestone for many. When he looked around at his married friends and colleagues, he wondered if maybe there was something really wrong with him. Even his little brother was married.

Dave was also involved in the cycle of blame: "When feeling at my worst, I think that the common denominator is clearly me. That's the bottom line. I just can't make a relationship work. I've broken up with every woman I've been with who wanted to make a commitment to me. I have never felt so inept at anything in my entire life. It's depressing." Other times, Dave was heard to say, "So many of the women I've dated seem so totally into themselves. They may be sweet, friendly, and giving at first, but in the end, I get used. Like Jen, who used me to make her ex-boyfriend jealous. I doubt that he was ever truly her ex. He made a major play for her once we were dating and she eventually went back to him." Previously, he generally blamed himself for being blind to the obvious. But in more recent years, he turned more and more to blaming women, accusing them of being self-absorbed and manipulative.

It is worth noting that when he was asked to describe his relationships one by one, he realized that in fact, only a few of the women he dated fit this unflattering description. Others he had not gotten to know well enough to judge, and still others were not self-absorbed after all. "You know, there were probably one or two of the women I've gotten close to that could have worked out. They really weren't all 'vanity cases.' Do you know the TV commercial? This woman is talking about herself incessantly and she pauses and says to the guy she's talking at, 'Enough about me, let's talk about you. How do you think I look tonight?' No, only Suzie was that pathetically self-absorbed!" This exercise, which was meant to challenge his negative generalization about women, got him thinking that maybe no one was to blame for his being unmarried. It was a fact to be understood in the context of his desire to be married. It was not something that anyone needed to be blamed for.

When he had been focused on fault finding, he wasn't paying any attention to how it felt to be in these relationships. He quickly discovered that he often felt a little panicky whenever the relationship became more serious. He felt as if he had to be on his toes watching every little move his lover made to insure that she was not going to get angry with him or disappointed. This realization led naturally to an important question: "I never really thought about it, but I'm always on edge when I'm in a relationship. Why is that? Like with Anna, I am so focused on her moods. If she's in a bad mood it ruins my day. I can't leave it alone, let her be bitchy or blue, I'm always in there trying to fix whatever it is I thought I did wrong. Sometimes she yells at me, tells me to just leave her alone, that everything doesn't have to do with me. I am always so sure that I must have done something to put her in a bad mood. I wish I was more like Greg. When his wife's in a bad mood he doesn't take it so personally. I don't know why I do that." With some newfound curiosity about why he was feeling the way he did in relationships, Dave was one step closer to uncovering the source of his ambivalence about intimacy and marriage.

Assessment

Dave

Whenever Dave felt more confident that he wanted to be with Anna, she would get distant and pessimistic about their relationship. When she was feeling in love and sure about their future together, Dave was typically angry and withdrawn. They went back and forth like that for two years. When Dave first talked about the pattern, he blamed Anna for it. She only felt close to him when he was angry and distant. But over time, he came to see that it truly "takes two to tango." The two of them had found a degree of emotional distance in their relationship that they both could tolerate. Dave's insight into the fact that he often felt "on edge" in relationships, blaming himself for his lover's bad moods, helped him to see that he too needed a certain degree of distance when he was with Anna. But all this begged the question: Why? It is beyond the scope of this book to explain in detail *how* he answered the question while in therapy, but we can tell you *what* he discovered.

Dave couldn't help but feel that relationships carried a high cost to his personal identity. His marriage script was written and practiced in his childhood relationship with his mother. Dave's father left his mother for another woman when Dave, the eldest of three sons, was five years old. His mother turned to him for solace and sometimes inappropriate emotional support. She related to Dave more as a spouse than as a son. Making matters worse, she suffered from an undiagnosed clinical depression for most of Dave's childhood. When someone becomes depressed, it affects everyone around them. This is particularly true of the depressed person's family. Dave did what any-one, particularly any child, would do when a loved one is depressed. He willingly rushed in to fill the void.

But Dave was in over his head. There was nothing he could do to lift his mother's mood for more than an hour or two. Nor could he make an appreciable impact on her pessimistic outlook on life. Dave often felt afraid that his mother might fall apart. One particular childhood memory poignantly describes the origins of the edgy feeling Dave felt as an adult in romantic relationships. "There was a father-son dinner at school when I was thirteen and Joe DiMaggio from the Yankees was going to be the guest of honor. I think it was a fund raiser for the baseball Little League or something. Anyway, I was real depressed because I wanted to go but I couldn't because at that time we only saw my dad for one month every summer and on some of the holidays. He lived too far away. I felt lousy when I came home. I remember crawling under the covers when I got home and crying. I also felt embarrassed for not having a dad who would take me and probably humiliated for crying about it all. When my mom came home I heard her slamming doors and I remember wiping my tears and jumping out of bed. I didn't want her to see me crying."

One of the things that Dave discovered about himself in therapy was that he almost always put women's feelings ahead of his own. He learned that this pattern had been set early on in his life. Oftentimes, when he felt sad, his mother would become anxious. But not for Dave so much as for herself. She could be very sensitive and loving, but before she finally got diagnosed and treated for depression, she was frequently overwhelmed by her own feelings of sadness and anx-iety. Like many clinically depressed people, she could only see her own experience of sadness and hopelessness. She had blinders on to the needs of her son. If Dave cried she would say, "Oh no, Davey, don't be sad, I need you to be strong. Not you, you're my reason to go on living." At that time in his life, Dave could not count on his mother to help him with what he was feeling.

"So I wiped away the tears and was just getting out of bed when she knocked on my door real loud and swung it open, yelling, 'I don't deserve this! Why are the garbage cans still on the curb, your jacket is on the floor, and where are your brothers? You're supposed to be watching them!' I said I was sorry, picked up my jacket, and went out to get the garbage cans and look for my brothers. Later, I went into the kitchen and she was talking to her friend on the phone. She was sobbing, I mean really intensely, her shoulders shaking, and she was saying that she felt so alone that she had nothing to live for anymore. I went over to her and threw my arms around her and held her. I was so scared. I thought that somehow I had caused this reaction. I know now that it was the depression and not me, but I didn't then. So I tried to console her, but she barely noticed me—she was crying so hard. I remember thinking, I've got to take care of her or everything is going to fall apart. The last thing on my mind was what happened at school.

"She finally calmed down and got off the phone. She gave me this crushing hug that felt like it would last forever. She kept saying 'Thank God I have you, thank God, you're my reason for living, thank God.' It's sad to say, but I never realized that she wasn't even thanking me—God was getting all the glory. I didn't exist beyond what I could give her at that moment."

This single event was not responsible for the marriage script that Dave held and the walking-on-eggshells feeling he had in relationships with women. It was only one of countless interactions with his mother that left him with the feeling that whenever you get close, you risk losing yourself. In his relationship with his mother he was no longer a twelve-year-old who missed his father, a child who felt embarrassed that his father could not take him to meet Joe DiMaggio. Instead he had become his mother's comforter, her confidant, and her "reason to go on living." Although this particular memory did not by itself account for the fears Dave had in relationships, it became his touchstone. He used it to help him take responsibility for the anxiety and dread his marriage script created.

As a child, Dave had succumbed to the myth that he needed to be selfless, to have no needs of his own, to sustain his mother's love and to keep her functioning. The way in which Dave lost himself in his relationship with his mother is such a common response to a loved one's depression that one of us has co-authored a book on the subject. Over the course of his childhood, Dave learned to put aside his feelings and needs in the mistaken belief that this was what his mother needed to survive. In fact, his caretaking often left her feeling very guilty. Ironically, her feelings of guilt at how much she leaned on her son worsened her self-esteem and ultimately the depression. When Dave learned, later in life, that his mother had suffered from a depression for most of his childhood, the pieces began to fall into place. It gave him a clearer understanding of the role he had taken with her, and the role the depression had put him in. This knowledge helped keep him from focusing all his energy on blaming his mother for what had happened, and thus freed him to identify the origins of his script about marriage.

He came to see that his fear about taking a similar role with a wife, that of a selfless and exploited partner, was based more on memory than reality. He really had very little to worry about because as an adult he could set limits in a marriage. Dave was no longer the boy he once was. He was a man with very different needs than those that led him to adopt the script that he did when he was a child. With clarity about both the fears and the fact that he did not have to accept today what he had little choice but to accept while he was growing up, Dave was now able to take responsibility for the fears rather than reflexively acting on them.

Lucie

As Lucie described several different relationships, a clear and consistent pattern emerged that was hard for her to miss. Although a strong and assertive woman when on her own, she had a way of becoming passive and forfeiting many of her own priorities when involved with a man. For example, she described her relationship with Ben, with whom she had lived for a year while in her mid-twenties: "Ben and I worked together, but no one at school knew about it. That was so weird and difficult. I basically had to pretend I was single when I wasn't! Ben was administration and I was faculty. He was concerned that it wouldn't look good if the other teachers knew.

"I gave up a lot to be with him. He pretty much defined our life together. When we moved in together we lived in his apartment. Mine was every bit as comfortable and convenient as his, but somehow we ended up at his place. We had so much furniture that I left most of my stuff in storage. I should have known then that this was headed in the wrong direction. It only got worse. He would go to work before me so there wasn't any worry about "appearances," as he would say. The whole situation was absurd. He was so worried about appearances and his job. But what about me and how I felt? I went along with it though. In the end, he broke up with me, not the other way around. In a way I was a little relieved."

As she talked about different relationships she had been in, Lucie naturally became curious as to why she was prone to "disappearing," as she referred to it. At first she jumped to the conclusion that she was masochistic, but that explained nothing and was actually off the mark. Among the common threads running through her account of previous relationships were an excessive focus on the needs of whatever man she was involved with and censored expressions of her own wants and desires.

In Lucie's case, we can track the development of this pattern to her childhood relationship with her father. A loving but rigid man, Lucie's father was emotionally withdrawn. Although there were many interactions between father and daughter that could shed light on Lucie's current script about marriage, one that occurred when she was eight years old stood out in her mind. "My father never came to me, I always had to go to him. When he came home from work my mother would find me and say 'go give your father a hug.' When he walked through the front door I would be waiting for him to give him his hug. It's funny, I never thought about it before, but it really was his hug, not mine, it always felt like a duty, not something freely given.

"One morning, we were sitting at the kitchen table and he was going over my homework. Every morning he went over it with me. Education was very important to him; I have to give him credit for that. I think it's a big part of why I became a teacher. But he was often very critical. I remember this one morning when I had gotten nearly everything wrong on my math homework. He kept shaking his head and calling me 'dumb Dora.' After he finished going through it he told me I was stupid and I wasn't trying hard enough. He threw my worksheet on the floor disgusted and said I should be ashamed of myself and that he didn't know why he should waste his time going over my assignments with him if this was the crap I was going to produce. I had such a hard time with math and he knew it! I had worked so hard on that assignment and I felt he was being really mean and unfair. When he left the kitchen I was in tears. He saw it and so did my mom. She consoled me after he left for work, saying he didn't mean it and I really should work harder because I knew how much he wanted me to succeed, but I was inconsolable. I was crying more out of frustration and anger than anything else.

"Later that day, when he came home and my mom did her 'your father's home' ritual I didn't come out of my room. I acted like I hadn't heard her. I was mad at her too, for not taking my side. But then she never stood up to him for herself. I don't know why I would think she would do it for me.

"When I came down later on he was sitting in his chair reading the paper. He ignored me when I came and sat down on the sofa. I don't know how we got into it but somehow I got him talking—or arguing, to be more precise. I told him that he wasn't fair and that I hated him. My mother overheard me, rushed into the room like the Tasmanian devil and yanked me up by the arm. She pushed me toward my room and told me to stay there until I could be more considerate. I remember she said 'You don't talk to your father that way!' The whole time this was happening, my father didn't even respond. He ignored me as if I hadn't said anything. I was just a little kid, for God's sake! Children should have the room to feel that way every now and then.

"When I was allowed out of my room I saw that my father had ended up in the den in front of the TV. When dinner was ready he told my Mom that he wasn't hungry. He was sulking like a big baby. Eventually, she brought him his dinner and they ate together on the couch. She was so mad at me. She made me eat alone in the kitchen. She said my father didn't deserve what I said to him. He sulked for a week! Literally a week! I felt so alone. My mom was really mad at me the whole time and kept telling me I should make up with him. But I didn't want to. I kept thinking, 'What about what I deserve!' Didn't that matter to anyone?

"But no one sulks like my father, and eventually he wore me down. I had no choice but to take a lesson from my mother. Don't rock the boat and keep your mouth shut and everything will be fine. When I apologized to him it was like I had been allowed back in the family. He stopped ignoring me, my mother was warm with me again, and everything was back to normal. I didn't have any other option back then. He even apologized. Not for calling me stupid, but for being so cold. He said he hated it when things were bad between us. At times like this he would even warm up a little, give me a hug and tell me I would always be his little girl."

In her relationship with her father, Lucie learned that she must diminish, even relinquish, her own needs and feelings or risk losing the love and acceptance everyone wants. That relationship, and her observations of her parents' marriage, formed the script about marriage that she now held.

Worsening the ambivalence she felt about commitment in adulthood was the fact that for much of her childhood she harbored high hopes that she could change her father. It is clear from Lucie's recollections that her father was not entirely at ease with his coldness and gave some indication that he would have liked to have been warmer, but the fact is he was not. Some armchair psychoanalysis to explain his tendency to be emotionally bankrupt was helpful to Lucie as she struggled to understand her father's apparent lack of interest in her. Developing a richer understanding of his limitations helped her to not take his shortcomings so personally. But this was also a dangerous trap. With each insight into her father's character, or Alex's personality for that matter, she was drawn further into the silence she had kept most of her childhood. She became like her mother who would try to explain Lucie's father to her in an effort to silence her and to repair the rift between father and daughter. But when Lucie used such insights to forgive, rather than to silence herself, she began to move forward and to take some risks emotionally.

ACCEPTANCE

Lucie

The fact that Alex could be "cut off," as she described him, had actually been helpful to their relationship at the very beginning. It kept him at enough of a distance to protect Lucie from the fear she had about closeness: that closeness equals death to your own needs. This anxiety would have kept her from dating him at all had he been more readily emotionally present. However, this emotional distance, necessary at the beginning, ultimately added to her deep ambivalence about whether or not to move forward with the relationship.

But with a fuller understanding of why she had been drawn to Alex, she no longer saw herself as masochistic and Alex as emotionally bankrupt. Options she had never seriously considered opened up to her. Previously, she felt she had to choose between submission and forfeiture of her own needs and persisting in the hope that she could change him. Now, with her sights set more confidently on her own needs in the relationship, she found she had other choices. She could learn to accept that Alex was not someone who would readily communicate his feelings or an interest in what Lucie felt and stop trying to change him. And she could accept the responsibility and risk of voicing her needs despite his limitations. Or she could move on, confident that she would not be left all alone in the world and with a clearer understanding of what it was she really needed to feel fulfilled in a relationship. In either case, she could take responsibility for the fears created by her marriage script and begin to move forward.

Dave

D ave could see that with Anna "never being in emotional sync" kept her at enough of a distance to allow him to stay in the relationship. When Anna was ready to commit, he was not. When it looked as if she might leave, it felt safe for Dave to commit. But as he began to discover what he was afraid of, he found it easier to be close to Anna, and simultaneously less threatening to walk away from the relationship should he feel the need.

The script he learned in his relationship with his mother demanded that he walk on eggshells in his relationships. Anna did not want him to do this; in fact it made her feel guilty a good deal of the time. Now, however, whenever Dave felt the inclination to be overly solicitous with Anna he turned to the touchstone we described earlier. He recalled the terror he felt as he hugged his mother and reassured her she would be all right. With his feelings properly labeled for what they are, memories, he reassured himself further by thinking "Anna is not my mother and I am not her son."

Anna detected the shift in Dave's openness to her and to himself. She acknowledged that something had changed for the better. In fact, Dave had become more vulnerable in that he was increasingly honest about how he felt in the relationship. From his perspective, he was feeling more inclined to make a commitment and told Anna so. Although he felt she was less sensitive to his needs than he would ideally like, he was willing to compromise, and the shift in his approach to her had helped her to become more giving to a small degree. No longer feeling as if Dave was always frustrated with her and feeling victimized, she felt less guilty and criticized. Their relationship seemed to be moving toward marriage.

ASSIMILATION

O nce she understood the history behind her fear of voicing her own needs in relationships, Lucie was able to put such feelings into a useful perspective. They were memories, they were not the reality of her current situation. She was not running the same risk she had when she tried to tell her father what she felt and needed from him. As an adult, the biggest risk she now had to take was tolerating the anxiety that came with letting Alex know how she was feeling.

Nevertheless, it was not always easy to accomplish this feat. Her fears often led her to believe that she would end up feeling as alone and unloved with Alex as she had with her father. Worse yet was the belief that the isolation was permanent—that she would always be stuck in her room or eating in the kitchen alone. But fortunately, Alex was cut from different cloth than her father, and more important, Lucie had come to believe that she would not accept in adulthood what she had no choice but to accept as a child. The more she took the risk of voicing her needs, the more opportunities she created for Alex to be responsive.

Her relationship with Alex changed slowly but surely. Lucie felt that he would never become the "touchy feely" kind of man she sometimes thought she would like to be with but somehow was never drawn to. But she saw that obscuring her own needs in the relationship had led to a self-fulfilling prophecy. The more she focused on Alex, the more he expected her to think only of his agenda. When she stepped in a new direction, Alex could either follow her lead or stumble. As it turns out, he matched her step by step and the impasse was breached. Approximately a year after Lucie stopped catering only to Alex's needs, he asked her to marry him and she accepted.

But do not be misled by the outcome. Lucie stopped putting her life on hold when she understood the fears that stemmed from her marriage script and began to take responsibility for them. She very seriously considered the possibility that her relationship with Alex would not progress to marriage, but was no longer overcome with dread and fear at the prospect. Indeed, it was because she no longer focused so much on him that she felt free to either move forward or move on.

Dave, on the other hand, missed his chance to propose marriage to Anna. No longer feeling stalled in the relationship, he was seriously considering proposing. He had talked about it in therapy and with several friends in a way he never had before. But abruptly, from Dave's perspective, Anna broke off the relationship. At first he was bitter and slid backwards to the alienation stage of being single, but his cynicism about women and even his inclination to blame himself for not reading the writing on the wall were shortlived. Having previously mastered all four stages of being single in a couples' world, he was less likely to repeat the same mistakes.

As he did with his mother, Dave was able to forgive Anna for not being able to give him what he would have liked. He truly loved her and felt that to be true to that love he needed to accept her essential nature—as is. She too was frightened of closeness in strikingly similar ways to Dave. It was the reason they were able to come together in the first place. He described it perfectly when he said, "It's like we were both blind. We both had the exact same limitations. If one of us had been deaf and the other blind, we might have been able to make it work." Anna was not right for Dave nor was he right for her. He now knew this with certainty. He knew with equal certainty that he still wanted a partner for life and a family of his own. By not succumbing to blame and cynicism, he kept his heart open. He also refrained from putting his life back on hold as he had during the majority of the time he and Anna had been together.

Freeing Yourself from the Past

You have, we hope, learned some vital lessons from the experiences of Lucie, Dave, Tom, Lily, Katie, Marilyn, Sarah, Mark, and the other single men and women we have told you about. Being single in the present is a goal worth striving for. If you are living your life in the present, you have achieved some peace and self-acceptance. You have freed yourself from being ruled by your past because you have embraced it. You have a much clearer idea about the script you wrote in your childhood and how it directs you to perceive and experience intimate relationships. Perhaps your script leads you to fear losing yourself in marriage or, on the other end of the spectrum, it promises the reward of finally realizing your value and self-worth when you marry the perfect partner. Regardless of which script, or combination of scripts, you found relevant to your own circumstance, you have seen the tremendous value of cultivating a curiosity about your feelings and their origins and a reluctance to blame. If you have not yet identified your script, do not lose heart. Because if you are committed to the task, if you can stay curious about your emotions and where they may come from, it will reveal itself in time.

In the three chapters to come, you can learn even more from the experience of single people like yourself who have dealt with the pressures and stigma that stem from the cultural marriage script. You will also learn from the experience of their loved ones. These three chapters shift our focus almost exclusively back to the cultural script and what single people and their loved ones can do to avoid its damaging influences. These chapters are written both for you and for those loved ones who unwittingly make being single in the present a much harder task than it ought to be.

HOLDING YOUR OWN
IN A COUPLES' WORLD

10

AVOIDING FRIENDLY FIRE

You broke up with him! Sweetie, I hate to be the one to tell you this because it makes me sound so old, but you're not getting any younger. What was wrong with this one? He was a gem as far as I am concerned—successful, handsome, and he had great manners. I don't understand what you were thinking. I think you need to learn to compromise more. You're simply too picky.

Grace's advice to her daughter Sarah, a twenty-eight-year-old travel agent

—◦—

You know, you don't have your whole life if you want to have kids. Do you want to be my age with a couple of toddlers running around the house? Don't you think it's time to buckle down and get serious?

William, father of Matt, a thirty-seven-year-old lawyer

—◦—

You know work isn't everything. If you keep focusing on your career you're never going to find anyone. I think men are intimidated by you. If you tried harder I am sure you could find someone.

Mother of Debbie, a thirty-four-year-old account associate

M ore often than you would like, you have probably been hit by friendly fire from the people closest to you. What we mean by this term in this context is probably self-evident. In the event that it's not obvious, let us define friendly fire as an assault accidentally launched against single people by loved ones who are trying to be helpful. It can take the form of words or deeds, or both. Whenever you feel criticized or undermined by a loved one *because you are single,* it can draw you back into the alienation stage.

No book on being single in a couples' world would be complete without some words of advice on how to cope with the negative impact the cultural marriage script has on your connections to the people in your life. Friendly fire is one of the more pervasive and damaging products of the cultural script. Because it so often alienates single people from their loved ones, the following chapters deal with special instances of friendly fire that come from both family and friends. Here, we pay special attention to the assaults commonly launched by family members.

If you are single and reading this chapter, you will find that there is much you can do to protect yourself from these assaults. Not unlike a soldier in a battlefield, your main task will be to make sure your side sees who you are, not who they think you are. Remember, your loved ones are probably following a cultural script which tells them that you are someone to be pitied and you must be desperate to be married. When your real experience is acknowledged and understood, you will find that your loved ones can stop blindly following the script and become more effective at seeing who you really are. Their natural inclination to be supportive will then be directed to *you*, rather than to what the culture's script led them to believe you are. But you can't do this on your own. After you finish this book, consider asking your family members who are stuck using the culture's script to read this chapter. Much of it is written for them.

If you are a family member of a single person, please remember that *we are all on the same side!* We are not out to blame you. But we think that we can help you to become more effective in giving the support you'd like to give.

In our culture, being single has always been a family affair. Virtually no group of people is more emotionally invested in the single person's marital status than is her family. Undoubtedly this is a mixed blessing. Sometimes, it is a family member who is the most savvy and supportive during tough times as a single person. However, we have talked to hundreds of single men and women, and it is clear to us that many feel they cannot turn to family members for support. Yet these same singles will acknowledge that their families' intentions are often well-meaning. How, then, can family members learn to act on their intentions so that their efforts are experienced as supportive rather than as callous and critical? The first step is to learn how to identify friendly fire.

KNOWING WHEN IT'S FRIENDLY FIRE

If you are the single reader, the best way to know if it's friendly fire is to simply ask yourself, "Did it hurt?" For example, Matt, the thirty-seven-year-old, never-married lawyer we told you about in chapter 5, had a telling experience with his parents that he recounted one day in therapy.

"I decided to not ask Susan [his current girlfriend] to come to Thanksgiving. She was hinting around that she would go and I considered asking her, but I just don't think we're there yet. At least I am not."

"What do you mean?" I asked,* thinking I might already know the answer, but wanting to know for certain.

"You know how they'll be—they'll put her under a microscope. I don't feel like Susan and I are tight enough with each other to weather it just yet."

"How was it staying with your parents?"

"It was good. They were really OK. My sister was there with her husband and the kids. It was good to see them too. But I got really down in the dumps on Friday. I didn't get out of bed until almost noon. I think I just needed to be alone."

"Did anything happen the night before?"

"We had the Thanksgiving dinner thing. It was fun. Although, come to think of it . . . I probably started to feel a little depressed during dinner."

"At what point? Do you remember what the conversation was about?" I encouraged.

"I am not sure. But I know we were talking a lot about my sister's kids. They're really great. Sammy is four and Ben is two; they are both so affectionate and fun to be with—not like when they were babies. I hadn't seen them in almost six months. They were so much bigger.

"My mother and father were talking about how quickly they grow. My mother was saying things like 'It seems like it was only yesterday that your sister and you were their age.' And my father was saying things like 'You better get on with it, Matt, you don't want to be my age with two toddlers running around the house!'"

*X.A.

"Can you remember what else was said?" I thought we might have found a trigger for Matt's blue mood.

"I think so . . . I think they started asking me about whether I was dating anyone now. Yep, that was it because I remember my father repeating the 'you don't have your whole life to settle down' speech. And my mother kept saying 'I just want you to be happy.' I said I was happy, then I told them I was dating someone to get them off my back. And of course they started asking all sorts of questions about Susan. My mother's first question was 'Is she pretty?' I must have made a sour face or something because I remember my sister caught my eye and gave me this look that said 'Do you need my help?' And I did!"

When asked whether anything happened the night before that might account for his mood on Friday morning, Matt's thoughts turned to the Thanksgiving dinner conversation. He went on to identify that his blue mood did indeed start at the dinner table and that the various comments and questions his parents had about his singlehood triggered it. Matt was hurt by what was said. He felt pressured by his father, who accused him of not trying hard enough to find someone to marry. His father's critique of Matt's motivation is ironic, since Matt had come to therapy and invested a good deal of money and time in an effort to understand his patterns in relationships. He was anything but lazy!

His mother also didn't help his mood. When she said "I just want you to be happy" when Matt had already been feeling happy, it made him feel invisible and in a subtle way abnormal. He caught himself thinking, "Maybe its a bad sign that I'm happy with not being married." And her first question about Susan, "Is she pretty?," reinforced a negative pattern that he was trying to break out of. In chapter 5 we describe this pattern in detail, but suffice it to say that if Matt's mother understood her son better, that question would not have been the first one asked if it were asked at all. His sister, on the other hand, was tuned in to Matt's feelings. That's why she did not participate in the friendly fire and why she had offered to help.

It is beyond the scope of this chapter to go into detail about why these comments and questions were particularly hurtful to Matt, and the reasons are largely irrelevant for our purposes. The main point is that his parents' concern left Matt feeling defective, pressured, and a little demoralized about being single. If they had known that their questions and comments had this effect, they may have realized that they were involved in some friendly fire.

If you are a family member of someone who is single you have a couple of sources of information you can draw on to determine if your well-intentioned efforts are hurtful. The first is obvious: your single loved one. If you are curious about how your actions and words affect him, you will very naturally minimize your involvement in friendly fire. Matt and his parents were out of tune with one another. His parents were not curious about how their actions in this realm affected their son and Matt was not telling them. Don't make the same mistake. Be curious about how your single loved one feels when you talk with her about her singlehood or love life and you will be a step ahead of the game.

You can also learn from what other single people have told us. Look over the following list of some of the worst things family and friends say to single loved ones. Do you make comments or ask questions like these?

FRIENDLY FIRE CHECKLIST
Put a check mark next to the remarks you have made when talking with a single family member.

_____ "You're so pretty, I don't understand why no one has snapped you up!"

_____ "If you really tried you'd meet someone."

_____ (When you get together after being apart) "So . . . are you seeing anyone?"

_____ "I think your problem is you're too picky."

_____ "You're too focused on your career, that's why you're alone."

_____ "Guys are intimidated by you."

_____ "What are you complaining about, he's really nice and he has a great job."

_____ "Just once, I wish you could find a decent guy."

_____ "By your age, all the good ones have already been taken."

_____ "So when are you going to settle down already?"

_____   "Your problem is that you don't ever want to get married."

_____   "Be careful, if you wait too long you'll be sorry."

_____   "Your problem is that you don't know how to compromise."

_____   "At least you don't have to worry about a biological clock."

_____   "You'll find someone when you're not looking."

_____   "What are you complaining about, she's really cute and we love her!"

If you answered yes to one or more of these questions, you may be involved in some friendly fire. If the reasons why some of these items are on our list aren't clear to you, read on to see the advice we gave to single readers on how they can respond to such comments and questions. The responses we offer are meant both to reveal the implicit hurtful message that is given between the lines and to inject a little tension-relieving humor into the interaction. But don't forget to ask your single loved one. Even if she can't illuminate the reason why we have included a particular item on the list, it will at least begin a dialogue between the two of you about the issue of friendly fire.

So what causes friendly fire? As you will soon learn, it is essentially the same thing that causes friendly fire on real battlefields. The single person is not seen for who she is, but for the kind of person the cultural script would have her loved ones believe most single people are. In the next section we offer some answers to this question and following that, some advice for both singles and their family members on how they can deal with the problem of friendly fire.

What Causes Friendly Fire?

In some instances friendly fire is obvious and you can use your common sense to identify it. Saying "You're just too picky," when your sister's last date turned out to have bad breath, body odor, and made her pick up the check; or asking "Why is this such a big deal? You broke up with him over a year ago!" after learning that your daughter is depressed because her ex-boyfriend just got married last week, are clearly instances of friendly fire. But just what is it that underlies such assaults?

Whether it is obvious or subtle, it always stems from blind adherence to the cultural script and a failure in empathy. For family members, becoming aware of and exercising greater empathy is key to avoiding inadvertently adding to your single loved one's experience of alienation. If you are single, making sure that your feelings are expressed and that your loved ones know what you really need, rather than what they think you need, is one of the best ways to protect yourself.

But what exactly is empathy? You can empathize when you understand your loved one's situation, feelings, and motives. It is the ability to stand in someone else's shoes and truly feel what it is like to be them. When you do, feeling compassion is almost always unavoidable. And when you feel compassion, it is difficult to be hurtful, intentionally or otherwise.

Empathy is how we bridge our differences in order to form supportive bonds. Unfortunately, in families, bridging differences is often forfeited in favor of concern for, and self-absorption in, our own feelings about something. And most families have many thoughts, opinions, and feelings about the fact that a loved one is single. Like Sarah's mother, who you will read about below, your family members may feel anxious about the fact that you are single, or envious, or even embarrassed. But whatever the feelings may be, they always make it more difficult to be empathic.

HOW TO AVOID FRIENDLY FIRE

Sarah and Grace

It is common for mothers to be anxious about adult children who are single. This alone certainly does not constitute friendly fire. However, when a mother repeatedly tells a son or daughter "Be careful, if you wait too long you'll be sorry," it's likely that her own anxiety is keeping her from understanding her child's feelings about singlehood. This lack of understanding, the loss of empathy, is what sets the stage for the occurrence of friendly fire. Take Sarah's mother, Grace, who often inquires about Sarah's "dating situation" and warns her that time may be running out.

Grace, a woman who married "late," at the age of thirty-five, has always wished that she had married earlier. She felt like a consolation prize for a husband who reminded her of this throughout their marriage. Grace wants to spare her daughter the humiliation she felt, but she also feels a bit embarrassed that at age sixty-five she does not yet have a son-in-law, much less grandchildren.

Sarah, on the other hand, sees herself as "only twenty-eight" and with plenty of time to get married. She loves her job, and doesn't worry much about finding a husband, except when her mother "starts in" on her. At these times, Grace and Sarah can hardly have a civil conversation. Each one feels angry, hurt, and misunderstood. How, then, can Grace and Sarah maintain greater empathy for one another, and avoid getting caught in friendly fire? A good start is to do an empathy check.

This involves finding out what each other is really thinking and feeling rather than making assumptions about it. If you are a family member, it's time for an empathy check when you have just spoken to a loved one regarding some aspect of being single, and you walk away thinking, "What is going on here? I was trying to be helpful but it seems that whatever I say or do makes it worse! I just can't win." If you are single, it's time for an empathy check when you walk away from an interaction with a family member feeling worse about yourself for being single and angry with your loved one.

Although friendly fire is initiated by the single person's loved one, the single individual can either maximize or minimize how hurtful it is by what he does next. That is why the empathy check is most effective when it is used by both family members and the single person. It consists of three questions that may seem easy to answer, but that are frequently difficult to answer honestly. Experience has taught us that this strategy is well worth the time and energy because of the payoff in terms of healthier and happier relationships between singles and their family members.

EMPATHY CHECK

1. *What am I feeling and where do the feelings come from?* If you are the family member, ask yourself how you felt when you were single. How do you feel about your loved one being single? Does it make you nervous, embarrassed, impatient, or sad? If you are the single loved one, ask yourself how the interaction made you feel about yourself. Did it make you feel demoralized, abnormal,

devalued, or angry? Are you vulnerable to feeling these things in general or is what you are feeling specific to your interactions with this family member?

2. *What assumptions have I made about the other person that I have not checked out with him or her?* If you are the family member: Do you think that your loved one is unhappy about being single, feeling lonely, or desperate to get married? The only way to know for certain is to ask. If you are the single person: Why do you think your family member is saying or doing what they are? Are you considering all of the possibilities or have you assumed ahead of time that you already know the answer?

3. *What can I do to repair the damage and reconnect?* Ask yourself, what can I do to find out what the other person really feels, needs, and wants? Then ask yourself if you can fulfill any of these needs.

An interaction between Debbie and her mother, whom we quoted above, illustrates a how a single person, hit by some friendly fire from her well-intentioned mother, employed the empathy check to minimize the hurt, to repair the damage to the relationship, and to redirect her loved one's efforts in a more positive direction.

Debbie and Margaret

D ebbie, a thirty-four-year-old account associate at a large marketing firm, has never been married. She has had one serious relationship which she had hoped would result in marriage, but it was not to be. It took Debbie a great deal of time and soul searching to come to terms with what happened in that relationship, but after a year, she was now at peace with what happened and where she was today. Recently she found herself thinking about dating with an optimism she had not felt in a long while. She could see that she was someone who could both enjoy life now and be open to being with someone if the right opportunity came along.

Currently, she was very focused on her job which was offering her an intellectual challenge and the possibility of a big promotion. She loved her work and she was considered a rising star at her firm. Her success in her career was having a very positive impact on her self-esteem and gave her life a sense of purpose and meaning. All in all, Debbie felt things were going pretty well.

Debbie's mother, Margaret, has been a housewife for almost thirty-five years. She often worries about Debbie, who she thinks has had bad luck when it comes to men. Margaret holds out the hope that Debbie will be the "successful one." For Margaret, that means getting married and having a family, which she believes will make Debbie happy and secure for the rest of her life. Margaret's other daughter, Sarah, has been a much greater source of pain and anxiety for her than has Debbie. Sarah, who is five years Debbie's junior, has already been divorced from a man Margaret always considered "beneath her." Sarah has never quite gotten herself on her feet, and she is financially supported by her parents, who are well off enough to do so. It is hard for Margaret to feel hopeful about Sarah.

Sarah and Debbie are Margaret's only children, and in her eyes she has not been much of a success as a mother. She worries that it is her fault that neither daughter is married, that somehow she didn't do a good enough job raising them. She worries that somehow she has put their futures at risk. Margaret is convinced that Debbie's focus on career and independence is going to hurt her in the end because Margaret is following the cultural script which tells her that no unmarried woman can ever be truly happy. This was generally true when she was growing up. In fact, her own sister Jody was divorced and had to work all her life. She felt that she had never really established herself as a respected member of the community and consequently went with "low-class" men who took advantage of her. She was frequently on the brink of poverty and had to turn to Margaret and her husband numerous times for "bailouts." Margaret's sister Jody was the main role model she had for what singlehood was like for a woman. It was not an appealing lifestyle in Margaret's view.

Ever since Debbie and her boyfriend had broken up last year, Margaret had been feeling especially anxious about her daughter's future. She had been thinking more and more about her own sister, Jody, and was feeling increasingly desperate to help the daughter she holds out the most hope for.

It was under these circumstances, in the context of Debbie feeling good about herself as a single woman and her mother feeling anxious and guilty about her daughter's marital status, that Debbie and her mother found themselves in the midst of *friendly fire*. They spoke on the phone regularly, and during one of their conversations, Debbie mentioned that she was feeling more positive about things since her breakup a year ago. She made a point of saying this because she was hoping that it would make her mother feel less worried about Debbie's future. But Margaret misread the message and instead saw it as a request for help to find someone new.

"So I am telling my Mom how good I am feeling about work and about being single, and you know what she says? She says she has this great idea about how I can meet someone. It's a dating service where you meet guys for a cup of coffee. She didn't even ask me, she sent them a check and I have six dates coming to me. Can you believe it?"

"I take it you're not interested?" I asked,* smiling.

"Of course not! First of all, I am feeling good about myself right now and I am incredibly busy with work. And besides, there's someone at work I am a little interested in. If I wanted her help with finding a date I would have asked her. It's probably overkill, but I was furious with her for doing this!"

"What do you think made you so mad?"

"First of all, she made it sound like I was desperate or something. She said that with this service I'd never have to worry about a date working out. I'd always have the next person to fall back on. It will be security for me. She says 'that way you can go out and not worry about it being a life and death thing, because there is always the next guy on the list. Then she tells me she doesn't want me to end up like my Aunt Jody, who never knew where her next date would come from!"

Unexpectedly, Debbie was furious. She could not believe that her mother saw her as such a loser and so desperate. She continued "Does she really believe I can't do this by myself? And since when did this become a life and death issue? I was so shocked I didn't even really respond. I got off the phone as quickly as I could—and what the hell does any of this have to do with Aunt Jody? It's ironic because I was just starting to feel good about being single. I thought if I could convey some of that to her she would calm down. It only made me feel worse and probably her, too, because I was anything but grateful for what she had done."

Clearly good intentions on the part of both Debbie and her mother

*J.K.

turned into some confusion and hurt for both of them. Margaret's lapse in empathy evoked a similar response in her daughter. Margaret was, after all, truly just trying to be helpful. Worst of all, it left them feeling helpless and disconnected from one another.

While talking about this interaction in therapy, Debbie learned about our empathy check. She decided it was worth trying. It was pointed out to her that when emotions are hot, as they were in this instance, it can help to have the three questions in front of you when you speak about the incident. She felt it was a bit "hokey" but the idea generally made sense to her, so she tried it. What's more, she asked her mother to do it with her the next time they saw each other. Debbie read each question out loud and mother and daughter agreed to listen to each other's responses without interrupting or trying to respond. Here are some excerpts from what Debbie had to say about how they answered each question.

What am I feeling and where do the feelings come from? Debbie reported that her mother answered this question by saying, "I know I keep comparing your life with that of my sister, but I can't help it. Jody's life was so tough after her marriage ended, I can't bear to think of you ending up that way. . . . Your not being married by now makes me feel like a failure as a mother. I have already failed with Sarah. . . . Last but not least, I think that you can never really be a success as a woman if you aren't married and have a family. Everything else is secondary."

Debbie responded to the same question by saying, "I called you to let you know that I was really doing well, and I felt like you completely missed it. It's been a long time getting myself to this place, and I just wanted you to see how well I was doing. I wanted to tell you about what was happening at work, but I never got the chance. I know you worry about me, and my hope was that when you heard how great I've been feeling you would feel less worried. . . . Your 'gift' made me feel like such a failure in your eyes. And you were obviously still worried."

What assumptions have I made about the other person that I have not checked out with her? Her mother had this to say: "When you said you were feeling better, I thought maybe you were hinting that you wished you had someone new to go out with. That you were ready to date again. You haven't dated in almost a year. I thought you were not coming right out and saying it because you didn't want me to feel worried. So I assumed that you would see my offer as a gift. . . . Maybe I was also trying to give myself a gift to help me feel more secure. I worry that you're going to end up all alone."

Like her mother's response to the question, Debbie's answer also began to shed some light on what had happened: "When you told me you signed me up for this thing, I thought 'you think I am desperate and that I can't meet someone on my own.' I guess I wonder if you think that I am a loser. . . . I think you're much more worried about the fact that I am single than I am."

What can you do to repair the damage and reconnect? "I can start by apologizing for not listening to what you were trying to tell me and for assuming so much," Margaret had said. "Even though I get nervous for you, I never wanted to hurt you. I am very proud of you, do you know that? I tell my friends all the time what you do at work. . . . In the future I will try not to be so quick to 'start in,' as you would say, about your romantic life. I have to try to keep in mind that my feelings might be getting in the way of your feelings. Maybe you can remind me when I don't. That shouldn't be too hard for you!"

Debbie answered the question by saying, "I know you really worry about my not being able to support myself if I don't hurry up and get married and that you're scared I'll end up like Aunt Jody. But you know, I am not Aunt Jody. She barely squeaked out a living. I am set financially; I have security. You should really try not to worry so much about that aspect of my being single. And as far as my happiness goes, I am a lot happier single than Aunt Jody ever was when she was married! . . . In the future, I think I can try and not take it so personally when you do things like this. I have to remember that sometimes you worry about things that have nothing to do with me."

Debbie and her mother had both responded in a way that is common when one's own feelings get in the way of staying in touch with those of another. But they were each able to get back on track by taking the time to find out what the other had been feeling. It wasn't the first time they had had difficult moments when talking about facets of Debbie's singlehood, and it surely wouldn't be the last. But Debbie and her mother both felt they had a fuller understanding of each other's motives and feelings and, more importantly, a new appreciation for the importance of staying curious about each other's feelings.

Ultimately, one of the worst aspects of friendly fire is its power to draw the single person back into the alienation stage. Alienation from your family can be one of the harder things to have to deal with when you are single. To help you to be better prepared to deal with the problem on an ongoing basis, we give some do's and don'ts for avoiding friendly fire.

AVOIDING FRIENDLY FIRE

DO   Look out for friendly fire
       Find out what your loved one really feels
       Use the empathy check to reconnect

DON'T Blame each other for a negative interaction
       Assume you know the other person's motivations
            and feelings
       Try to raise the dead

All but the last item are self-explanatory and follow from what we have said above. But "don't try to raise the dead" refers to the special problem of a relative who is not as responsive as Debbie's mother Margaret was. Matt had such a relative: his father. Matt's dad simply could not rise above his own experience. What little we know of him is that he too was raised by a man who was very critical. Unfortunately, despite countless attempts, Matt could never get his father to see the ways in which he was critical and hurtful to his son. Matt had to focus on steering the conversation away from topics that would likely trigger criticism from his father. More importantly, he learned to not take his father's comments so personally. The more he knew about himself and his father, the more he understood that the critical statements had nothing to do with Matt.

USE HUMOR TO BE SEEN AND HEARD

In most instances, avoiding friendly fire can be as easy as letting your loved one know how you feel. In other words, don't ever take it lying down! Make a point of talking about hurtful interactions. Of course, sometimes you may only have a moment in which to respond—not enough time to sit down and talk it through. In those instances, try using humor as much as possible. Humor is a high-risk/high-gain strategy, so be careful about how you use it. If you remind yourself that your loved one was raised to follow the same cultural script that you were following prior to reading this book, then you'll be on safer ground. It will be easier to not take it personally when stinging comments are made. The humor you use will be aimed at getting your loved ones to laugh *with* you about the outdated attitudes they hold rather than make them feel that you are laughing *at* them.

Consider the following two lists of the worst things family and friends say to single women and men. We've provided some responses that you can use to educate your loved ones about what it is they are communicating between the lines and to help you both to see the humor in what is being said. Remember, in most cases your loved one is merely abiding by an antiquated cultural script and does not intend to be hurtful. Although they are intended to reduce friendly fire, the responses given below can either help or hurt in your attempts to better your relationship with a loved one. It all depends on how you use them and whether healthy humor is a part of your relationship.

Ten Worst Things Said to Single Women and How to Respond

1. "You're so pretty, I don't understand why no one has snapped you up!" *Response:* "Maybe it's my intelligence and personality they don't like?"

2. "If you really tried you'd meet someone." *Response:* "You think? I always thought if I sat on my couch every night eating chocolate that Prince Charming would eventually find me."

3. When the first words out of their mouth when you get together are: "So . . . are you seeing anyone?" *Response:* "I've been well, thanks for asking."

4. "I think your problem is you're too picky." *Response:* "You're right. Better to be with someone I am miserable with than to be single."

5. "You're too focused on your career—that's why you're alone." *Response:* "Maybe if I went on unemployment and moved back home with my parents men *would* find me more attractive."

6. "Guys are intimidated by you." *Response:* "Maybe I *would* be happier with a man who prefers his women unintelligent, unemployed, and insecure."

7. "You'll find someone when you least expect it." *Response:* "Really? Then today's my lucky day because I haven't been expecting it for years now!"

8. "What are you complaining about? He's really nice and he has a great job." *Response:* "You're right, I shouldn't let the fact that I am not in the least bit attracted to him get in the way."

9. "Just once, I wish you could find a *decent* guy." *Response:* "But you know how much I love losers."

10. "It's difficult for you because by your age, all the good ones have already been taken." *Response:* "Thanks for letting me know that I'm not one of the good ones."

TEN WORST THINGS SAID TO SINGLE MEN AND HOW TO RESPOND

1. "So when are you going to settle down already?" *Response:* "I've got a job, loans to pay off, monthly bills, and a home of my own. Now that you mention it, I really should stop playing around and get more serious about my life!"

2. "Your problem is that you don't ever want to get married." *Response:* "So that explains why I got depressed at the last two weddings I went to without a date!"

3. "Be careful, if you wait too long you'll be sorry." *Response:* "Thanks, I really wasn't feeling enough pressure as it is."

4. "Your problem is that you don't know how to compromise." *Response:* "Sure I do. I'd like to tell you what I really think about your opinion. But instead, I'll just listen politely and nod my head."

5. "At least you don't have to worry about a biological clock." *Response:* "Good point. So what if I have kids in my forties. I'm sure by the time I'm in my seventies I'll have the energy and the inclination to raise a couple of teenagers."

6. When the first words out of their mouth when you get together are: "So . . . are you seeing anyone?" *Response:* "I can see you. Do you see me?"

7. "You'll find someone when you're not looking." *Response:* "I guess I could walk around with a blindfold on."

8. "What are you complaining about? She's really cute and your parents love her!" *Response:* "You're right, I shouldn't let the fact that *I* am not attracted to her get in the way."

9. "I think your problem is you're too picky." *Response:* "I agree, I'm better off being with someone I am miserable with than being single."

10. "If you really tried you'd meet someone." *Response:* "Thanks for the insight! It never occurred to me that I should try."

Make sure that you are seen for who you truly are by not taking friendly fire personally, and by voicing how it makes you feel. With a little care, friendly fire can be eliminated from your interactions with loved ones. The next chapter focuses on friendly fire between single friends and family. Here as well, the key is to be curious about how each other is feeling and to take some steps to improve your communication. But when friendly fire occurs between friends or relatives who are also single, there are a few unique problems you need to be aware of.

COMPETITION AMONG FRIENDS

I'm not competitive! Lisa's the one that's competitive. We were at this party together once and I lost track of her. I found her talking to this guy so I walked over to say hi. Is it my fault he started paying more attention to me than to her? I didn't go over there to steal him away. Lisa accused me of being competitive. I think she blew what happened way out of proportion.

Molly, a thirty-four-year-old divorced television producer

◄○►

Sometimes I think Jo Anna gets jealous of me when I'm dating someone and she's not. She makes these little comments like "That's so great that you're seeing him. I didn't think you were his type." And my all-time favorite, when I first met Tom and I was really high on him, was "I give it one month, tops." But if you asked her, she would tell you she doesn't have a competitive bone in her body.

Sarah, a twenty-eight-year-old travel agent

◄○►

Billy and I are very up front about the fact that we compete for women. It wasn't always that way. I used to deny that it was as big a problem as it was. Now we have a system when we're out together so we don't butt heads.

Patrick, a twenty-seven-year-old police officer

C ompetition is either a dirty word in your vocabulary, or an inescapable fact of life. When single friends compete with one another, it can result in the worst kind of friendly fire, especially when the competitive feelings of envy and jealousy are not openly acknowledged. As you know, one of the toughest things about being single can be the sense of alienation, of not fitting in, that the cultural marriage script promotes. At its core, this experience is one of not feeling connected to anyone.

Loved ones who are single can be an invaluable source of connection. In fact, any single person can be if you can identify with their experience. That is one of the reasons we have shared the stories of so many single people in this book. It is also why we have alerted you to the ways in which the cultural marriage script may alienate you from the population of single people out there by leading you to believe that they are abnormal and flawed in some way. The cultural script is also apt to make it more difficult for you to connect with single loved ones in another, less obvious manner. Oftentimes, it will pit you against one another.

The cultural script demands marriage and abhors singlehood. It can create tremendous pressure to couple whenever you are single. The script warns "Don't get left behind," "You only have status when you're in a couple," and "You're a loser if you're single." When single people succumb to such messages, they feel envy, jealousy, and sometimes even competitiveness with other singles they are close to. Add to this the fact that courtship is, in many respects, a kind of competition and you have a recipe for significant tensions between single loved ones. Learning how to deal with these tensions and maintain the connections you have to the single people in your life is what this chapter is all about.

Men and women frequently differ in how they handle competitive feelings, and nowhere is this more evident than in the realm of dating. Much research has been done on sex differences and the findings are consistent: boys and men are typically more open about their competitive urges than are girls and women. Indeed, males are encouraged to cultivate such feelings while females are more likely to be discouraged. But that does not mean that men don't encounter problems with competition in their friendships with single friends and relatives. They do; the problems are just a little different.

We will show you how to identify when you are being competitive, how to get a loved one to acknowledge his or her own competitiveness, and what you can do to keep it from undermining the trust in your relationship. If you are single and close to a friend, a sister, or a brother who is also single, envy, jealousy, or competition is very likely to become an issue if it is not already. Our goal is to help you to see that such feelings are a natural part of your relationships that can be especially intense when two people are striving for the same thing. When it is not handled in a healthy manner, competition can catapult both of the single people involved into the alienation stage as the connection they once felt with each other is weakened by the hard feelings that arise.

Whether or not you think competition is a problem in your relationship with a single friend or relative, we encourage you to read on and learn to recognize the warning signs. If it already is a problem, try to put aside any beliefs you have about who is to blame. If you can, you will learn that competitive feelings are almost always inevitable in this context and like most difficult feelings, they can be turned to strengthen, rather than weaken, the trust and love you have for one another.

HURTFUL COMPETITION

Depending on how they are expressed, envy, jealousy, and competition can be healthy for your relationship or hurtful to it. Here, we examine when these feelings are hurtful. There are two main situations in which competitive feelings usually get played out. One common scenario is when you are talking to another single loved one about a current love interest. Stinging comments such as "I never thought he'd go for you—that's so cool," "Maybe you're aiming too high," or "She was flirting with me, not you," are made that suggest an additional motive not discussed in the last chapter on friendly fire. The observation made by Sarah above, that Jo Anna only made jealous comments when Sarah was dating someone and she was not, is one clue you can use to identify hurtful competition. But regardless of whether one or both of you is dating anyone, friendly fire from another single person should always suggest the possibility that he or she is feeling competitive. The second, more obvious situation where these feelings get expressed is when you and your loved one are interacting with a member of the opposite sex.

Molly and Lisa

You may remember Molly from chapter 6. She's Mark's sister, the one who complained that there are too many women for the number of men available. During the course of our conversation with her, it became apparent that her friend Lisa felt that Molly was very competitive and envious of Lisa at times. We asked to interview Lisa to get both sides of the story, but we start with Molly's perspective first.

"It's happens a lot. We're out together and Lisa gets real sullen and quiet. When I ask her what's wrong she says 'nothing.' But it's obvious to me that I've done something to make her angry. It's so annoying that she won't tell me because it ruins the evening. Sometimes it takes days just to get her to tell me what it is I did wrong.

"She keeps getting mad at me. She says I compete with her. She's dating this guy Peter now and I think she's purposely keeping us apart because she's afraid I'll flirt with him or steal him or something."

"Have you ever dated anyone she's dated?" I asked.*

"No! But I dated this guy Don for a few weeks that she was interested in. He worked with Lisa. I knew that they had lunch with each other a number of times, but they weren't dating. I didn't know she had any interest in him until after he asked me out.

"I met him at this party they had where they work. I got cornered in a boring conversation and I kept looking around for Lisa. I found her talking to this guy in the corner of the room so I excused myself, saying I needed to talk to her about something. I get over there and it turns out to be Don she's talking to. She had told me about him and I knew she thought he was cute, but she never said how handsome he was. When he took my hand in his to shake it and looked into my eyes, I thought, 'I'm going to melt!' And sometimes you just know the feeling is mutual. I could see he was feeling something too. We had this intense chemistry right off the bat.

"The three of us started talking but before long Lisa wandered away. Don eventually asked me for my number and I gave it to him. I didn't think twice about it and I certainly didn't think Lisa would care. When she had talked about him before, she never gave me any clue that she was interested.

"She was real low key the rest of the night. I remember trying to talk with her about the fact that Don asked for my number because I was real happy about it. But all she could say was 'whatever.' So I didn't bring it up again for the rest of the night. The next few days whenever we talked on the phone I could tell something was wrong

*X.A.

but she kept denying it. It was like pulling teeth to get her to tell me. In fact, it wasn't until Don and I went on our first date that she told me what was going on. So she finally tells me that she was annoyed with me at the party. She said that I was flirting with Don and competing with her! I don't get it. Don was flirting with me, not the other way around. And even if I was, so what? They weren't dating, and how was I supposed to know she had any interest in him? I'm still not clear what her interest is in Don and I definitely don't understand what it is I did wrong."

Depending on your experience with this kind of interaction you have probably already sided either with Lisa's view of what happened or with Molly's. The reason Molly doesn't understand what she did wrong is because there really is no right or wrong in situations like this, there is only being sensitive or insensitive to your friend's feelings. Clearly Molly was insensitive to what Lisa felt for Don. But before you rush to lay blame on whose fault it is that Molly didn't know what her friend felt, consider Lisa's side of what happened.

"I know she'll probably never admit it, but Molly has always been competitive with me. I think she gets envious when guys pay attention to me and has to get the attention for herself. Don is one of the better examples. I know she thinks I never let on that I liked him, but I think sometimes she sees what she wants to see. Honestly, I've always felt that Don was probably not interested in me. I know men are attracted to me but I don't think that I am Don's type. But even so, anyone watching us talking together that night could see that I liked the guy. He's really handsome, charismatic, and we were having a great time until Molly slithered her way in between us. Don't get me wrong, I love Molly and we've been friends a long time, but I don't think she's honest with herself about the effect she has on guys.

"Not that I don't hold my own. I do. But when Molly flirts, most guys can't help but respond to it and that's what happened with Don. She comes over, I introduce her, and she just keeps looking directly into his eyes the entire time we're talking. Even if I had the courage to scowl at her to get her to stop I couldn't have because she looked in my direction maybe twice in ten minutes! So I left. I thought, I am not going to compete with my best friend over this guy. It's not worth it—the friendship is too important.

"The next day at work Don asked me what had happened and I made some lame excuse. He seemed really concerned that he had done something wrong but I told him he hadn't. But I couldn't shake the feeling that maybe Molly had done something wrong. I think she just had to have the attention I was getting from Don. He's a charmer and I just bet that's what put her in gear. She couldn't deal with the fact that I was getting attention from him and she wasn't, so she got what she wanted. Did she mention that she actually dated him for a few weeks?"

"Yes she did. It sounds like that was kind of hurtful?" I replied.*

"Not really, I didn't think he was interested in me anyway. Besides, she's my best friend, there are other guys out there, but only one Molly. I just try and stay clear of situations where she'll compete with me."

I thought that perhaps Lisa was minimizing how hurtful this interaction with Molly and Don had been so I asked her about her current boyfriend. "Do you mean like you're doing now with Peter? Molly mentioned that she believed you weren't letting her meet Peter because you're afraid she'll flirt with him."

"She said that? I didn't think it was that obvious. We've been dating for a couple of months, nothing very serious yet, but yeah, I am a little afraid to have him meet her. It's kind of pathetic that it's come to this, isn't it?"

"Have you tried to talk with her about it?" I asked.

"Not about Peter, but about Don I did."

"Why not about Peter?"

"She'll just tell me I'm being paranoid and it won't go anywhere but downhill from there. And anyway, how do you tell one of your oldest friends something like that? When I did talk to her about Don, all she could say was that I should have told her, that she didn't know. Well, I don't think I should have had to say anything. She should have figured it out. You'd have to be blind not to see I was interested in him!"

Molly obviously had been blind. The axiom "love is blind," or more accurately in this case "lust is blind," made it close to impossible for Molly to see what Lisa was feeling. That fact, coupled with the fact that Lisa had never explicitly told Molly that she was interested in Don and wanted her to steer clear of him, made matters worse for the two friends. So then Lisa must be to blame for what happened, right?

*J.K.

Wrong. Communication in a relationship is the responsibility of both parties, never only one. As Molly said, "This has happened many times before." If she had heeded the familiar warning signals, much pain could have been avoided. So it is Molly's fault after all? That would be the logical conclusion.

But when you consider that later that evening and in the days following the party Molly repeatedly asked Lisa if anything was the matter, it's difficult to lay blame solely with her as well. She even asked her about the specific warning signals, Lisa's quietness and sullen mood at the party after giving Don her number. According to Molly, if Lisa had admitted what she was feeling at that time, she would not have pursued her interest in Don. If and when he called, she would have told him she'd met someone else. So whose fault is it? If you're getting confused trying to sort this out, you can imagine how Molly and Lisa felt.

To get a better handle on this painful set of interactions, we can turn to our guidelines for being single in the present. These guidelines are not only helpful for uncovering your personal marriage script. They can also help you and your loved one excise the influence of the cultural script from your relationship. Lisa and Molly were feeling alienated from each other and stuck in the cycle of blame, and this was keeping them both from seeing the ways in which the cultural script was pitting them against each other.

But what were the facts to be examined in this instance? Molly was indeed feeling competitive with her friend and Lisa was much more hurt and angry about it than she let on, perhaps even to herself. These feelings did not stem from an underlying personal marriage script as much as from the cultural script and the natural dynamics of courtship. The cultural script creates pressure for single people in a variety of ways. It demands marriage and abhors singlehood. If you and your loved one are interested in the same person (a.k.a. a "potential mate" by the culture's script), the script warns, "Don't get left behind" and "All's fair in love and war." And because courtship is, in many respects, a kind of competition, you have a recipe for significant tensions between single loved ones.

But does courtship necessarily involve competition? If you are a woman you will be more inclined to scoff at this idea than if you are a man. In fact, you are probably not competing in the same manner as a man would. For women, the competitive aspects of courtship are often more subtle and less conscious. But whether you want to or not, you compare yourself to other members of your sex and you compare your love interest to other members of his or her sex. And while comparing you inevitably compete. Some people, like Molly, feel this aspect of courting more acutely than others. But until Lisa and Molly could break the cycle of blame and examine the facts of how they really felt more honestly, they would never be able to take responsibility for how they acted on these feelings.

They each had different tasks to complete if they were going to take responsibility. Molly would need to learn how to act on her competitive urges in a more constructive manner and Lisa would need to learn how to talk about her anger more directly. If they had joined forces rather than working at odds against each other, they could have dealt with the competition in a more satisfying manner for both of them.

There are few emotions as powerful as those that exist in the realm of sex and love. In previous chapters we have encouraged you to make a distinction between what you *think* and what you *feel*. That lesson is rarely as important as it is in situations like the one encountered by Molly and Lisa. Remember, feelings don't always have to make sense and oftentimes they are much stronger than the circumstances suggest they have any right to be. Molly and Lisa had been friends since childhood. They were extremely close and there was a history between them of mutual support, admiration, and loyalty. We could never adequately describe the love these two friends had for each other because it was forged over the course of many years and experiences together. But it was precisely because of this love that Lisa and Molly could not fathom the idea that they would intentionally do anything to hurt each other. Nevertheless, both Lisa and Molly were acting in ways that are hurtful. Let's consider Molly's feelings and how she was acting on them first.

Molly was very used to getting attention for her good looks and flirtatious manner. To some extent, she relied on such attention to feel good about herself. Because the focus of this chapter is not on why some people are more competitive than others, we won't delve into Molly's past to uncover the reasons she has learned to rely on such attention for much of her self-esteem. What's important here is to understand that this is a pattern born out of a kind of necessity. It is the reason why whenever another woman was getting attention from a man, Molly began to doubt herself and feel insecure. At times like this she became anxious about her self-worth. But because she had

not yet taken responsibility for these feelings, she acted on them reflexively. To feel less anxious and preserve her self-esteem, Molly
tried to redirect the man's focus so that it was on herself. She wanted
what the other person had, in this case the attention Don was giving
to Lisa, and that is the essence of competition. Although Molly didn't
walk over to Lisa and Don to compete with her friend, when Don
stopped paying attention to Lisa and started noticing Molly, the race
was on. And Don's attention was the prize. The fact that she wasn't
aware of this aspect of what she was doing did not change the fact
that competition was a part of the picture.

Meanwhile, Lisa was not being fully honest with herself about
how much Molly's actions in such instances bothered her. But the
fact that she didn't want Molly to meet her current boyfriend because
she feared Molly would flirt with him reveals the depth of her hurt
and distrust. We wondered, as you may be now, why Lisa didn't
make it clear ahead of time that Don was going to be at the party and
that Molly should consider him "off limits." Or why she didn't in-
terject herself into Molly and Don's conversation, rather than become silent and slip away. Finally, why didn't she admit to Molly the
way that she was feeling? We could focus on many aspects of Lisa's
experience to arrive at some answers, but the most important facet in
our experience was that she didn't know how to begin to talk about
her feelings.

People can be mirrors for one another. They can help you to see
things about yourself that you would never see otherwise. It was
striking how easily Molly and Lisa could reveal things to us that they
could not tell to one another. If they could have been more honest
about how each of them was feeling, the other would have had an
opportunity to see an aspect of herself she could not see otherwise.

Lisa never told Molly the extent to which she felt distrustful of her.
Molly sensed it, but she didn't know for sure. Because Lisa was reluctant to reveal her hurt, Molly had less of an opportunity to see her
actions in terms of how they made Lisa feel. If she had, she might
have seen more clearly the ways in which she was being competitive.

Meanwhile, Molly was reluctant to reveal how hurt she was feeling about Lisa's apparent distrust. Lisa was surprised to hear from us
that Molly knew of her reluctance to introduce her to Peter and that
she felt saddened by that. If Lisa had known how hurtful the way in
which she was dealing with her anger and distrust was to Molly, she
might have reconsidered the manner in which she was dealing with

those feelings. Also, if she had been able to talk about these difficult feelings with Molly while they were happening, she would have given her friend a chance to see herself from Lisa's perspective.

Neither Lisa nor Molly were clients of ours, so there were few avenues for us to help them with their problem. However, we did talk to them about the distinction between thoughts and feelings that we have written about in this book. We encouraged them both to consider the possibility that *they could be very close friends and feel competitive with one another.* These two things were not mutually exclusive. Feelings have a life of their own and if they could begin to accept that feelings of envy or jealousy could exist between them but that this did not have to signify that something was wrong with their friendship, then they would have taken the first step toward doing something about how the competition was affecting their relationship.

Both friends reported that simply talking with us and thinking about the issue got them talking to each other about it. Molly and Lisa agreed that it didn't matter who was right or wrong. What mattered to both of them was that they had respect for each other's feelings. Lisa got Molly to agree to a plan that would keep the competition to a minimum: If they met a man whom they were both interested in, whomever he showed the most interest in would get the go ahead. If it wasn't obvious, they would excuse themselves and go to the bathroom together (provided one was available) to discuss it. Molly thought it was "overkill," mostly because she still wasn't convinced she was all that competitive, but if it would make Lisa feel better about their friendship she was willing to try it.

However, the last word we heard from them was that they had fallen into one of the common pitfalls that exist when you first try to deal openly with the problem. As you can imagine, their proposed "solution" is likely to create more problems than it solves. Below, we tell you about two brothers who made the same mistake and a few others not encountered by Lisa and Molly, but found their way out by using the guidelines we have already told you about and some strategies we have developed for healthy competition.

DEALING WITH THE PROBLEM TOGETHER

You may have wondered whatever happened to Patrick, the twenty-seven-year-old police officer we told you about in chapters

3 and 4. We pick up his story here because it has much relevance to the present topic. When we first met Patrick he hadn't been on a date in over six months, but over the course of therapy he learned to stop blaming himself and women for the intense feelings of alienation he was having and learned about his underlying marriage script. In Patrick's case, it was the "There's no place like home" script we told you about in chapter 8. As he moved through the stages of alienation, assessment, acceptance, and finally assimilation, he learned to take responsibility for the feelings created by this script and ultimately stopped putting his life on hold. One way he did that was by dating again. He also stopped isolating himself from his family. As you may recall, he had been avoiding family gatherings, especially with his sisters, because of his sense of alienation—they were married and respectable, he was not.

Patrick and Bill

It was during this period that Patrick and his older brother Bill began to spend more time together. Bill was recently single and the two brothers, only one year apart in age, would go out "cruising" a couple of nights a week. It was in this venue that they began, in Patrick's words, "to butt heads."

"Billy is such an jerk sometimes. We were out at Coogan's [a sports bar in their neighborhood] again last night. I was talking to the bartender I told you about and he muscled in on me again." A couple of weeks earlier Patrick had mentioned that he had been flirting with Fancha, the bartender at Coogan's. He was very interested in her and felt that he was making progress. He hadn't asked her out on a date yet because he wanted to be more sure of her interest before doing that. He continued, "Billy had been talking to this girl that was sitting next to him, but when her boyfriend arrived he spun around on his stool and started talking to me. I had been talking to Fancha, but she left right when Billy turned around 'cause she had to take this guy's drink order. No big deal—he wasn't butting in like he did before 'cause she wasn't even talking to me—she was busy. At least at first. But sure enough whenever she came by to talk with me he wouldn't let me get a word in edgewise. He knows I like her. What's his problem?"

"Have you talked to him about it yet?" I asked,* knowing he had been reluctant to bring the topic up before.

"I did. I probably should have waited until I was less pissed off. He told me I was dreaming, that she wasn't interested in me, she was flirting to get a bigger tip. And then he says that she flirts with him too and that I don't own every woman who's out there!"

"It sounds like that wasn't very satisfying?"

"It wasn't. I tried to explain that I had been talking to her a lot lately and that it was different. But he just laughed at me and told me to grow up. He really got under my skin. He just doesn't get it."

"What is it he doesn't get?"

"That she's more interested in me—talk about denial!"

Bill did not deny that he was competing with his brother for Fancha's attention. He was competing, and what's more, he was not about to apologize for it. But was he in denial about Fancha's fondness for Patrick as he suggests? Was she more interested in Patrick? We'll never know for certain, and neither will Patrick or Billy without asking Fancha herself. But at this point in their debate over how to handle their competition the question is completely irrelevant. The "she's more interested in me" argument is one of the more compelling pitfalls that loved ones competing over a common love interest fall into. It puts the control over how they handle that competition in the hands of someone they've just met, rather than keeping it with the two of them where it belongs.

What gave Patrick the "right" to claim Fancha for his own and to make her off limits? His claim was based on the argument that she had flirted with him. Billy quickly countered with the observation that she flirted with him as well and that her motivation for flirting with either of them may have been purely professional. As you can imagine, or perhaps recall from your own similar experience, this tactic leads only to further frustration and hurt feelings. The implicit message is: "I've already won, so you might as well go home and lick your wounds." Patrick wasn't being mean spirited or manipulative. He truly believed, and for all we know he may have been correct, that Fancha was interested in him and not Billy. But to ask Billy to rely on Patrick's assessment of Fancha's feelings is asking too much. Patrick didn't need to take that tack if he had exercised the rights he actually

*X.A.

has. He had a right to expect that his brother, whom he also counted as a friend, would care about how he felt and try to be responsive.

The brothers were already one step ahead of Molly and Lisa in their acknowledgment of the competition. But they were stalled in resolving what to do about it because "competition" was a dirty word in Patrick's vocabulary. Although he acknowledged the competition, he felt it should have been over before it ever started. Billy should have backed off, as Patrick believed he would have, had the shoe been on the other foot. Like Lisa, he was taking the moral high ground and suggesting that he would have been more responsive to the cues than his brother was being. In this instance, Billy was being unfair, Patrick thought, and had no right to compete with him. In a roundabout way, Patrick was saying that the moment you notice yourself competing you should stop. Patrick's strategy for dealing with situations like the one he found himself in with his brother betrayed an underlying belief that competition is a bad thing and should always be avoided.

KEEPING THE COMPETITION HEALTHY

But this belief was keeping Patrick from taking responsibility for his feelings and doing something more constructive and satisfying with them. Until he can accept his own competitive feelings for what they are, an inevitable and healthy part of courtship, he will continue to "butt heads" with his brother. Even worse, he will never learn that how he feels is the only right he needs to invoke to convince Billy, or any single friend, to be responsive to his wishes.

Ask yourself whether you think that competition is necessarily a bad thing in situations such as these. If you think that it is, you are probably prone to reacting to competitive feelings in a hurtful rather than a healthy manner. Patrick answered the question by saying that "It always leads to trouble. I don't see how competition can be a good thing in this instance."

"When is competition a good thing?" I asked, noting his use of the qualifier 'in this instance.'

"Football, sports, things like that."

"What's different about competition in that setting versus the situations you and Billy get into?"

"There are rules, it's organized . . ." He paused, then added, "It's not personal."

"What's personal about how you and Billy compete?"

"I think he does it because he's jealous of me. He's always been jealous of me."

"And what's personal for you?"

"For me? I guess . . . I don't know if it's personal for me. He's been mad at me before when we've gone after the same girl, but I've backed off when he's told me to."

"Any instance stand out in your mind?"

"Sure. One time, we were at Jones Beach and we were talking to these two girls we met at the snack stand, but we were both interested in the same one, I think her name was Nancy. I felt a little bad for the other one . . ."

"You felt bad for the other one?" I interrupted.

"Sure. It was hard not to be more attracted to Nancy and her friend seemed a little put off about how much attention Billy and me were giving her. I remember she rolled her eyes at one point when Nancy said something funny. The three of us were laughing but she wasn't. She looked peeved. It was a little tense. I thought that this must really suck for her and so I guess I made a point of trying to include her. Anyway, where was I? Oh, yeah—they were definitely into hanging out with us but I think they needed to talk about it because the one I was worried about says she's got to go to the bathroom and Nancy says, 'I'll go with you.' After they left, Billy tells me that he's really into Nancy and asked me if I was cool with it. I said sure and stayed out of his way when they came back."

"Why did you say you were 'cool' with it?"

"Because I was. Billy was talking to her more than I was."

"Why do you think that is? Was she more interested in him?"

"At that point I'd have to say she was interested in both of us. I think she was into the fact that I'm a cop. Some women are impressed with that. But I kept including her friend—I felt bad leaving her out of the conversation. She was having a bad time with the scene and like I said, Billy and me were much more interested in the other one. I guess I was a little worried about her feelings getting hurt."

Because of his discomfort with competition, Patrick appeared to have ended the race before it started. He felt uncomfortable competing with his brother and watching the two friends compete with each other. You might be thinking that he's a "nice guy" and he was being sensitive to the friend that was getting less attention. He *is* a decent man. He's gentle and concerned about other people's feelings. Remember what he said on his first day in therapy? He was proud that he was a New York City police officer who had never had a civilian complaint filed against him. Patrick felt that everyone deserved to be treated with respect and kindness until they gave you good reason not to. He was being sympathetic and kind to the shy friend who was losing the competition for attention that she was in with Nancy. But did Patrick's sensitivity have to preclude him from pursuing his interest in Nancy? And was he truly "cool" with the understanding his brother and he arrived at?

As it turns out, he wasn't as comfortable with his decision as he let on. In fact, he had continued the competition but in a less conscious and obvious way after they parted from Nancy and her friend. Patrick revealed that on the drive back from the beach Billy and he got into an argument over what had transpired at the snack bar. Patrick accused his brother of being insensitive for ignoring Nancy's friend. He even got Billy to admit that he was being rude. By the end of that conversation Patrick felt he had taken the moral high road while his brother had been selfish and unkind. He was still competing over Nancy. If he couldn't have her, then he would spoil it for Billy. Because he was unaware that the competition had not ended at the snack stand as he had convinced himself, he acted on it in a manner that was hurtful rather than healthy.

"I felt good about the way I handled it. There's other women out there."

"It sounds like you feel you handled yourself better than your brother did?"

"Absolutely. Unlike Billy, my main concern was about how bad she was feeling, not on how to get to Nancy."

"This may sound like a provocative question, but bear with me for a moment: If your main concern was with how bad she felt in that situation, why didn't you say something to Billy when they went to the bathroom?"

"I did!" he replied, apparently frustrated that I didn't remember.

"I'm sorry, I guess I wasn't listening closely enough. What did you say?"

"I told you already, I said I'd back off—he could have her," he answered defensively.

"I'm not sure I understand. How was your backing off helping to cue Billy in on how bad Nancy's friend was feeling? Because it sounds like you decided to handle the situation on your own."

"I see your point. I guess I was deciding to deal with it myself."

"I don't know that I was trying to make a point so much as trying to understand what your motives were for giving up your interest in pursuing Nancy."

"The whole situation just felt too uncomfortable. It was making me nervous and Billy was talking a mile a minute. Sometimes it's hard to get a word in edgewise when he's jacked up. I don't know. I guess I really just didn't want to butt heads with him on this one."

What Patrick went on to discover was that his anxiety was about his own competitive feelings as much as anything else. He didn't want to give up his interest in Nancy as readily as he thought he did. That is why when he stepped aside so Billy could pursue Nancy unhindered, he did it in a morally superior way. His withdrawal from the competition was anything but supportive. He wanted Billy to feel guilty for pursuing Nancy and paying less attention to her friend. If he hadn't, he would have taken the opportunity to alert Billy about how Nancy's friend seemed to feel left out and annoyed. The competition for Nancy's attention was every bit as personal for Patrick as it was for his brother.

At first he felt a little ashamed when he realized that he wanted his brother to feel guilty. According to Patrick, "Billy's a good guy. He wouldn't do anything intentional to hurt anyone. I know he felt bad about Nancy's friend after I hit him over the head with it. He was hot for Nancy, he wasn't as sensitive as he usually is—it's not like it's a crime." Over time, Patrick traced the roots of his negative attitude about competition with his brother and came to see that it felt more personal, for both of them, than it should have.

Growing up, the two boys were taught that they should always stick together. "Friends come and go, but family is forever" was their father's creed. Competition between the boys was discouraged. Consequently, they had few opportunities to learn how to compete with one another and still feel like teammates. Just as two pitchers on the same baseball team strive to beat the opposition while trying to beat each other's personal best in order to make the starting lineup, Patrick and Billy could stick together and still compete with one another.

When he stopped blaming his brother and himself for being competitive, Patrick began to examine the facts honestly and opened the door to experiencing the competition in a different light. He found that he felt more competitive than he had previously known. In the instance with Nancy, he had never really "backed off," as he had thought. More aware of his feelings in this realm, he was now able to take responsibility for them. When he eventually accepted his competitive feelings as a sign of emotional health rather than disease, Patrick was ready to talk about the problem with his brother. He used the main principles of the five guidelines given below to talk with Billy about dealing with their competition.

Guidelines for Talking About Competition

1. *Exercise your rights.* What you feel is all the right you need to bring the topic of competition to the table. You don't need anyone else's opinion to buttress your own, "objective" evidence, or anything else to ask that your loved one discuss your feelings with you. You feel what you feel and that is the only fact needed. The focus should be on voicing what you are both feeling without rushing to place judgments on who has the right, or not, to feel what they do.

2. *Don't take it personally.* Don't take your loved one's competition personally. That doesn't mean you can't respond to it, ask her to stop, or have feelings about it. But if you can see competition as a natural, healthy part of courtship, it will hurt less and you will be able to do more together to handle it constructively.

3. *Weigh the evidence.* Working together, try to determine who feels more strongly. Listen carefully to each other. Try to not be defensive. Put yourself as best you can in your loved one's shoes. You will need to disengage from the heat of the moment and put your feelings in perspective. For example, you may feel very attracted to a new acquaintance, but perhaps you are already dating someone you feel good about while the loved one you are deliberating with has been depressed because she has not had a date in over a month. Our point is not that something like this should necessarily outweigh your desires in such an instance. Rather, it is that

you will both feel better about whatever agreement you reach if the full picture is acknowledged and considered in your deliberations.

4. *Make a decision.* Decide whose feelings are more important in this instance. If you can't reach an agreement, consider flipping a coin. At an impasse, if one of you is willing to flip a coin but the other is not, then the reluctant gambler clearly has stronger feelings and should be given the go ahead. Never leave the decision up to your common love interest, as this is a recipe for further conflict and more hurt feelings.

5. *Devise a plan.* Talk about how you will deal with the situation at hand. Anticipate how you will deal with snags such as when one who has stepped aside gets flirted with. Also, make an overall plan on how to talk about such situations when they arise in the future. For example, Lisa and Molly agreed ahead of time that if one of them felt the need to talk about escalating competition, all she had to do was announce that she was going to the ladies room and the other would follow. Patrick and Billy had a similar rule, with the added proviso that neither of them would assume it was OK to pursue a new interest they had both just met until they had checked in with each other, conducted a "men's room check," as they called it.

After talking it through, Patrick and Billy agreed that some sort of plan for the future would be helpful. Their first plan was the one Molly and Lisa had come up with. If they met a woman they were both interested in, whomever she showed the most interest in would get the go ahead. The first time they tried this they took so long in the bathroom arguing about it that when they came back out to the bar she had left. They had forgotten to weigh the evidence. Or, more precisely, they tried to weigh the wrong evidence which was much less reliable than what they were supposed to be considering. By focusing on what each of them perceived this woman to be feeling, rather than on what they were feeling, they got stalled (no pun intended). It was a valiant first attempt at working together as teammates, but it needed some fine tuning. Below are some ground rules for healthy competition that Patrick and other single people we have worked with have found very helpful.

GROUND RULES FOR HEALTHY COMPETITION

DO   Talk about it
           Use humor
           Remember you're teammates

DON'T   Ignore it when it happens
           Take it personally
           Let the love interest decide

By following these ground rules and the guidelines given above, you can turn hurtful competitive interactions like those experienced by Patrick, Bill, Molly, and Lisa into something very positive for your relationship. Remember what Patrick said about what sets football and baseball apart from the kind of competition he had with his brother? The main difference was that competitive sports had rules and it wasn't personal. If you develop some rules you can both agree on and remember to not take it personally, you may find that you actually enjoy competing with your loved one! It may sound strange, but the experience can be one of feeling like teammates rather than adversaries. Sometimes your loved one is in the starting lineup and you're cheering on the sidelines. Other times you get to play and your loved one provides the moral support.

Single people too often become alienated from one another for a number of reasons, not the least of which is competition. By learning to recognize when it is happening, you will be in a much better position to take responsibility for your participation in it and to not let the cultural script alienate you from one another. When you do that you take charge of how the competitiveness affects your relationships and even your experience of the opposite sex. Both Lisa and Patrick had said that their love interests were "not worth it." They devalued Don and Nancy in their attempts to withdraw from the competition. If you make such comments, consider the possibility that they stem from resentment over the control you've handed over to the Dons and Nancys in your life by letting them decide how you will deal with competitive feelings in your relationship. Instead, take charge of such feelings and turn them into a healthy part of your relationship with your single loved one and into an enjoyable aspect of being single.

FEELING INVISIBLE

We used to talk every day and see each other a few times a week. But ever since Sallie started seeing Tom it's like I turned into the invisible woman. At best we talk once a week and I rarely see her anymore. And when we do get together it's always around their schedule or at their apartment, never at mine. Even if she doesn't insist on bringing Tom, he's there in spirit. His schedule dictates when Sallie can see me and he even affects what we do when we finally do get together. Sallie and I used to go to the movies together a lot, but now every time I ask her to go she says "I can't, I promised Tom I'd see that with him." I know things change whenever a friend gets involved with someone and I like Tom a lot, but I can't help feeling abandoned. She's was my best friend! It's like my whole life has been reconfigured and I'm not supposed to have any feelings about it? The message I get is that I am only supposed to be happy for her, I can't also be angry.

Liz, a twenty-six-year-old loan officer at a bank

◄○►

I know Terri feels like a third wheel. She told me I don't consider her needs and that she feels hurt. I know her needs count! But what about mine? I have a husband and a daughter to think about. They have to come first. Frankly, I am exhausted at the end of the day. I have a lot more going on than she does. I wish I had Terri's life! She's responsible to no one but herself. The bottom line is . . . if she doesn't come over to my place then we usually don't see each other. I wish she didn't take it so personally!

Jenny talking about her friend Terri, a thirty-three-year-old social worker

◄○►

Ever since my divorce, I've been feeling like the odd man out with Jack and Cathy. When I was married the four of us used to get together and I enjoyed it. I still see them, but now it's different. I feel like everything we do is on

their terms, not mine. My needs don't count nearly as much as theirs. I'm
starting to feel more like their stepchild than their friend.

Adam, a forty-one-year-old manager of a sporting goods store

A common experience that goes hand in hand with being single in a world of couples is feeling invisible. Many single people have told us of feeling like Liz. Although they understand that a newly coupled friend will have less time to spend with them than before, the shift in focus feels extreme and the single friend feels abandoned.

The invisibility experience of other single people like Terri and Adam takes a different form. In this case, the experience is one of feeling your needs do not count as much as those of your coupled loved ones. In its extreme, the experience is like that expressed by many New Yorkers when a fellow pedestrian ignores the fact that he just bumped into you and continues single-mindedly racing down the sidewalk: "Yo! What am I, invisible?" Other times the feeling is more subtle: your needs may be acknowledged, but they are not given as much weight as those of coupled people. This feeling of invisibility eats away at the fabric of the single person's relationships with friends and family and at his self-esteem.

But what about Jenny and other coupled people like her? Don't they have a valid point of view? Or have they all been corrupted by the mandate to marry? Once coupled, do they breathe a sigh of relief and say to themselves "Thank God I'm not single anymore," and then strive to distance themselves from their past? For some people who were miserable when they were single this is undoubtedly true. If they succumbed to the stigma created by the mandate to marry when they were single, then they will be doomed to promote it when-ever they are coupled. But the fact is, any intimate relationship takes time, energy, and emotion away from other relationships. Add chil-dren to the equation and you're talking about someone with very limited emotional and logistical resources for friendships outside of the family unit. Perhaps single people should just "get over it" and stop being so self-centered!

This chapter was written for both single people and their friends and family. If you are single, you will learn how to communicate your needs more effectively, how to not take it so personally when a coupled friend is self-absorbed, and how to feel more visible in your relationships with coupled friends and family.

If you are coupled and have been given this chapter to read by a single friend or relative, be assured that we are not out on a witch hunt and that we have your needs in mind as well. We have been both single and coupled and are personally familiar with both sides of the problem. In our work as therapists, we have found that the problem is not that you and other coupled people like you don't care about your single loved ones. The problem is blind adherence to the mandate to marry and poor communication of each other's needs. The goal of this chapter is to help you to improve the quality of your relationship with your single loved one. Whether you are single or coupled, the goal is easily reached with a little education and effort.

Whether you are single or coupled, we encourage you to read this section and the entire chapter. The advice we give will be useful for both single and coupled loved ones. We will start with some guidelines for the single reader. We will then discuss two typical experiences that single people have—abandonment and feeling as if their needs don't count—and show how our guidelines can be used. Then we'll turn to what couples can do to improve the quality of their relationship with a single loved one while insuring that their needs are also met. In this section, we also provide some "Do's and Don'ts" for coupled loved ones.

ADVICE FOR THE SINGLE PERSON

You know the problem. Whether your best friend has recently coupled and you feel forgotten, or the time you spend with coupled friends and family leaves you feeling like an outsider, you can't help but feel invisible. Try as you might, despite having read the preceding chapters and making progress, whenever you interact with certain coupled loved ones you feel sucked back into the alienation stage of being single in a couple's world.

The problem is not only universal but almost always inevitable. The mandate to marry and the mechanics of intimacy create a schism between single people and their coupled friends and family. But that doesn't mean that the situation is hopeless. You do not have to forgo the closeness you once enjoyed. The guidelines we give below can be used to improve your relationships with coupled loved ones regardless of the situation you find yourself in. Whether a previously single friend has joined the ranks of the coupled and you are left feeling abandoned or the time you spend with coupled friends and family leaves you feeling alienated, the advice we give here can help.

When You Feel Invisible

We refer to the guidelines that follow as the "four E's" to getting seen. They focus on helping you to: identify those needs and desires you can realistically hope to get met in your relationships with coupled loved ones; become more sensitive to each other's experience of the problem; talk about your needs in a constructive manner; and learn when and how to compromise. After introducing you to the four E's we will illustrate how each of them has been used successfully in the lives of other single people who were feeling invisible.

The Four E's to Getting Seen

EXAMINE YOUR NEEDS. This task may seem obvious, but it's not as straightforward as you might think. What's involved here is identifying the needs you have in your relationship that you can realistically hope to get met. If your loved one recently married, or has a newborn baby, and you feel you want as much time with this person as you used to have, you are going to be disappointed. The trick is to start with what's possible, not the impossible.

EMPATHY CHECK. The empathy check we told you about in chapter 10 on friendly fire is key here as well. Before you talk about what you want from your coupled friend or relative and how you've been feeling, make sure that you know what your loved one is feeling. Does he feel guilty about letting you down, angry because he feels pressure from you, defensive because he feels criticized by you, or overwhelmed with the emotional demands that come with being in an intimate relationship? If you want your loved one to understand and listen to your experience, make sure that you understand and listen to his.

EXPRESS YOUR NEEDS. Pick a time when neither of you is stressed and choose only one thing to focus on. Start off with communicating your desire for a better relationship. Follow this by talking about what you learned from your empathy check. Make sure your loved one knows that you understand the demands she has on her life. After doing these two things, tell her how you feel and what you want her to do differently.

EXPECT TO COMPROMISE. As the two of you begin to talk you will quickly discover that in order to improve the relationship you will both have to compromise on what you expect from each other. Like the first guideline above, this may seem blatantly obvious, but it is not as easy to do as it is to say. To compromise, you both have to articulate a clear vision of the kind of relationship you want to have and work from that point forward. Then follow the advice given in the lyric from the song by the Rolling Stones, "You can't always get what you want, but if you try sometime, you just might find, you get what you need." Stay open to what is being offered, even if it means that you have to compromise on what you wanted originally.

Feeling Abandoned

The experience described by Liz at the start of this chapter is all too common. It is inevitable whenever a close friend who was single gets seriously involved with someone new. Liz had come to therapy for other reasons, but her feelings about what was happening in her friendship with Sallie were the topic of more than one session. Liz was hurt by how much Sallie's relationship with Tom interfered with their friendship. She even felt a little used.

"When Sallie was single, we were really tight, we spoke on the phone every day. In fact, after her last breakup we spoke nearly two to three times a day! I was in a relationship then but *I* didn't just disappear. I don't get how she can be this way. I know what it's like when you start a new relationship, it takes time and energy, but I never cut her off like this. At best I talk to her once a week! And when we do talk, I feel like she's not really interested in what I have to say. Honestly, I am getting less and less interested in what *she* has to say. It's Tom this and Tom that, Tom and I went . . . blah, blah, blah. I like the guy, but I'm starting to wish they never met!

"Now that she's got Tom she's dropped me like a hot potato. She was my closest friend and I thought that I was hers. But I am starting to wonder if maybe she was just using me because she was lonely and we were never truly friends."

"Have you spoken to her about how you're feeling?" I asked.*

"Yep . . . Boy, was that a fiasco! She got really angry and told me to grow up."

"How did you bring it up?"

"Not in the best way possible way I'm sure. I have to give you a little background—I called her last Monday when I got home from work. She had just walked in the door so she asked if she could call me right back and I said sure. An hour later and she still hadn't called. I was feeling really angry because I really needed to talk with her, I was having such a lousy day. Remember what happened on Monday?"

"Of course," I reassured her, remembering how terrible she had felt that day. Bob, her current love interest, had called her at work to cancel their date for Saturday—no explanation, just a message on her voice mail. I saw her the next morning. She was feeling very lonely and confused about why Bob had "blown her off," as she described it.

Liz continued, "Well, when she didn't call I said, 'screw it,' and went out to rent a movie. When I got back from the video store, still no call. I could barely watch the film I was so hurt and angry. It's not the first time she's forgotten to return a call since she started dating Tom. I wanted to call her again, but I felt too mad and a little pathetic, like I would be begging for attention. So I didn't. I tried to watch the movie instead.

"Wanna know what I rented?" *Friday the 13th*. I hadn't seen it since it came out years ago. But I had such an urge to rent it when I walked in the store."

Remembering that many young couples were murdered in this movie, I couldn't help but pursue the tangent, "Why do you think you had the urge?"

"I knew you would ask me that! I knew why I rented it the moment the couple having sex in the bunk bed got killed. I cracked up laughing! I can always dream—huh?"

"Sure can," I answered smiling. "But it sounds like besides the

*X.A.

anger, you also felt pretty hurt by Sallie's insensitivity to what you needed from her."

"Yeah, I did. Too hurt. I should have waited to talk to her. After I saw you last week she called me at work. I think it was on Wednesday. She acted as if nothing had happened so I asked her what happened Monday night. Why hadn't she called me back? Know what she said? She said that Tom called and asked her to have dinner with him. It was a spur of the moment thing and she forgot that I called. That was bad enough, but what really pushed me over the edge was when she said 'I'm sorry that I took so long to call you back, but I don't remember saying I'd call you back the same night.' I lost it. I told her that I thought she was really selfish and that she didn't care about anyone but herself."

"What did she say?"

"Nothing at first, I had too much to say. I told her that I felt like our friendship didn't mean anything to her and that I felt used by her."

"How did you end it?"

"She told me to grow up and accused me of being jealous. She said that I should be happy for her and that if I couldn't be, I was no friend of hers. Then I had to get off the phone—my boss had just walked into my office. Sallie called me at home that night and left me a message. No apology, just a 'call me.' But I haven't returned her phone call yet. It's really sad—maybe I'm testing her, but I just can't pick up the phone to call her. It's too humiliating."

Liz and Sallie's friendship was in trouble. Liz was feeling that perhaps they were never truly friends. She was beginning to think that Sallie never really cared for her at all and found it humiliating to reach out to her. She wondered how it ever got to this point and what she could do, if anything, to repair the friendship.

The first question she needed to answer was what did she want from the friendship? She needed to step back from her feelings and *examine her needs*. When the question was posed to her, she said, "I'd like things to be the way they were before."

"In what way—specifically?" I asked.

"I want us to talk like we used to. She was the only person I used to talk to every day, I really miss that. I'd also like to spend some time with her alone. A couple of weeks ago we had dinner together and she asked if Tom could join us for dessert. I said fine with me. But he showed up before the entrées were even on the table. I never got the chance to talk about what I wanted to talk about. And when he's not with us, he influences what we do together. The last three movies I suggested we see together got vetoed because she promised Tom she would see them with him. Should I go on?"

"Please."

"I'm tired of hearing about how great he is. I wish, just once, when we do talk that she would either talk about something else or at least talk to me the way she used to."

"Which way is that?"

"She used to talk about how she felt in relationships. The last guy she was seeing, before Tom, made her feel really insecure. She was really open about how it felt to be with him. I was a shoulder to cry on, someone she could trust; now I feel like maybe she doesn't trust me enough to tell me those things. We have always talked honestly, about things that mattered, not the superficial garbage she tells me about now."

Although Liz acknowledged the fact that her friendship could not be exactly what it used to be now that Tom was in the picture, she was probably asking for more than Sallie could deliver. What was it she wanted from her friend? She wanted more time alone with Sallie. She wanted Sallie to go to the movies that Liz wanted to see, even if they were ones Tom had asked Sallie to reserve for him. She also wanted Sallie to show more of an interest in what was going on in Liz's life. And she wanted her to be more open about how she was feeling in her relationship with Tom. In many ways, Liz wanted the same level of intimacy she'd had with her friend before she got involved with Tom.

So, what was reasonable to ask for and what was not? At first, Liz felt that everything she wanted was reasonable to expect from someone who was a true friend. But as she began to look at her "wish list" more closely, Liz found that she was working in a vacuum. She didn't really have a clear idea about what was going on in Sallie's head. She needed to do an *empathy check* before she could know what Sallie could, and could not, deliver. Here is what Liz learned from her empathy check.

"I called Sallie like we discussed. I started by saying that I was sorry about being so mean on the phone. I told her I was calling because I valued our friendship and because I felt it had been really tense lately. I told her I wasn't sure how she was feeling about me and our friendship—and I wanted to know." Liz paused, waiting for a response from me.

"What happened?"

"It worked. She didn't get defensive. She started by saying she was really sorry and then asked me how I was doing but I stopped her. You would have been proud of me. I said that I had called because I wanted to understand how she was feeling about our friendship. I think she was worried I was going to jump down her throat again, but I convinced her I just wanted to understand how things had gotten so tense between us and wanted to know what she was feeling about it.

"She said she felt guilty about me a lot of the time. She knew that she wasn't spending as much time with me and calling me as much as she used to and it made her feel bad. But she also felt like I was pressuring her and trying to make her feel guilty, and that made her mad. I hadn't realized how 'under it' she was feeling. She talks to Tom every night, even when they've been together. On top of that, they see each other four times a week. She said by the time she hangs up with him, or comes home after spending the evening together, the last thing she wants to do is talk with someone else for an hour. I understand that and more or less anticipated it, but hearing her say it made me feel a little better somehow."

"It felt less personal?"

"Exactly. Then she told me that she sometimes feels like calling me just to say hi and because she misses me, but she doesn't do it because things are so tense between us. She worries that either I'll feel hurt because she only wants to talk for a few minutes or she's too angry with me and doesn't want to open up a can of worms."

"A couple of times now you've mentioned that she's angry with you. Do you know what she's angry about?"

"She thinks I'm jealous because she's in a good relationship. She thinks I should be happy for her and doing things to help her make a go of it with Tom. It's really ironic, but she feels like I'm not being supportive. She feels the same way about me that I've been feeling about her! But I am supportive, at least I am trying to be. I think Tom is really good for her and I've said as much. But she thinks I am jealous and that if I really loved her I wouldn't feel that way—I should just be happy for her."

"Do you think you might be jealous?"

"Of the fact that she's in a good relationship? No. I don't think so." She answered thoughtfully, looking as if she were considering the question carefully, "I feel happy for her. Sallie deserves someone who treats her well and who really loves her. Tom's a good guy. But— I can't believe I'm going to say this—I think I am jealous . . . but of Tom! I feel like he took my best friend away from me. Sallie doesn't confide in me anymore. I couldn't put my finger on what felt different talking to her these past few months, but that's it. She still talks about Tom and what they're doing but I am not getting the details anymore. She also isn't leaning on me the way she used to. We used to talk a lot about the guys she was dating, about problems at work, or how her sister drives her crazy—but not anymore. I can't help but think that she's relying on Tom for those things now. I feel silly caring about it, but I do. She's getting closer to him than she is to me and I am jealous!"

"Did you tell her that?"

"No, not exactly. But I told her that I wanted to understand how she felt and that I was glad she told me everything she did. Even if some of it was hard to hear. She asked me how I was feeling about all this and I told her I wanted to wait to talk about it because I wanted some time to think about it. But I did say that I thought we would work it out and that I would call her in the next day or two."

Liz was now in a much better position to *express her needs*. She had a much clearer understanding of what Sallie was feeling and what her motivations were for withdrawing from their friendship. The empathy check had also left Sallie feeling less angry and curious about what Liz was feeling. Liz revisited her "wish list" of things she wanted from Sallie and revised it with the information she gleaned from this last conversation.

There were four main items on her list: more time together alone, seeing movies that Liz wanted to see, Sallie showing more of an interest in what was going on in Liz's life, and being more open about how she was feeling in her relationship with Tom. Given what Sallie had said in their last conversation, Liz doubted that Sallie could free up more time than what she had already. But she did think it was reasonable to ask that when they did get together that they have some time alone. She also thought it was reasonable that every now and then they see a movie she wanted to see, even if Tom would be disappointed. Liz felt she probably wouldn't even have to ask for the third thing on her list because she believed Sallie would naturally show more of an interest in her life if they could resolve the tension between them. But the last item was probably not reasonable to expect.

It made Liz sad to admit it, but Sallie was moving away from her and toward someone else. Tom had become Sallie's new confidant. Liz had to admit that not only did Sallie have less time to talk with her than she used to, but she probably didn't need to talk about the same things. She didn't need her in the way she used to. Tom was already providing Sallie with the support she needed. Also, because her friend's relationship was going so well, Sallie had less to feel insecure about and, hence, no need to talk about her insecurities. It was not likely that she could expect the same type of intimacy they enjoyed before.

But this didn't mean that Sallie and Liz were no longer close. In fact, when Liz told Sallie how she was feeling and what it was she wanted from her, she ended the conversation feeling closer to her friend than she ever had before. Liz didn't have this conversation until a week after her empathy check because she wanted to speak with Sallie face to face.

"Well, I finally had my talk with Sallie," Liz began during our next session together. "We had brunch last Sunday. I started by saying that I had given the problems we were having a lot of thought and that I valued our friendship. I asked her to try not to get defensive, then I told her what I had been feeling. I told her that I felt like she just dropped me after she met Tom and that I felt abandoned. She got really defensive when I said that and said that she didn't drop me. She told me she thought I was being oversensitive."

Liz had made the mistake many people do when talking about hard feelings with one another. She focused on what Sallie had done and *labeled* it rather than focusing on how she felt. The trick is to use "I" statements that focus on how you feel, rather than focusing on what the other person did and what you think her intentions were. Rather than talking about Liz's feelings, their conversation quickly deteriorated into an argument over what Sallie's motivations were for withdrawing from the friendship. Sallie was responding to Liz's implicit accusation that she had "dropped" her friend because she had no further use for her. Luckily, Liz realized her mistake and recovered the lost ground quickly.

"My heart sank. I thought, Oh God, here we go again—back to square one. I realized what I had done. I had accused her of not being a good friend, of dumping me and using me for her own needs. I asked her to stop and let me explain. I apologized for what I said. I told her that I didn't really think she didn't care for me—if I did, I wouldn't be there talking to her. I thought she did care and what I had meant to do was talk about how I felt. I told her that I had been feeling abandoned, but that I didn't think she actually had done that to me. That was just how it felt. I told her that I thought we had been out of tune with each other and that I had a better sense of what she had been feeling and wanted her to know my side of it, how I was feeling."

"How did she respond to all that?" I asked.

"She listened. She calmed down. So I told her what I felt—I started by saying that I missed her and wanted to spend more time with her. And when we do get together I wanted us to do it alone more often than we had been. Not that I don't want to see Tom from time to time. I do and I told her so. But I made it clear I needed some time with just her alone.

"Then I brought up the movie issue. You know what she did? She almost started to cry! She said that she hadn't realized she had been doing that and understood how hurtful it felt. We used to go to so many movies together, especially foreign films, and she knew how much I loved doing that with her. Sometimes we would spend liter-ally hours talking about a film that we really loved or arguing over whether it was well directed or not. She understood immediately—it was such a relief. She apologized, saying that she saw how badly that must have felt. When she said that, I realized I had left the most im-portant thing off of my list. I just wanted to know that she saw me, that she understood how it felt to be in my shoes. I felt that she did.

"As we were leaving the restaurant she asked me if I would go see *Il Postino* with her. Now it was my turn to try and hold back the tears! I had asked her to see it about a month before, but she said no because Tom wanted to see it with her. It was such a lovely gesture."

Liz had been feeling discarded before she spoke with her friend. She felt used and as if Sallie didn't see, much less care about, how she was feeling. But she was able to get herself seen in her friendship by following the first three guidelines we gave above. She very naturally implemented the fourth guideline—expect to compromise—on her own. Several months after this initial conversation about the changes in their friendship, Liz had a painful interaction with Sallie. She had asked her to go to a concert with her and although Sallie readily agreed and the tickets had been purchased for some time, she nevertheless canceled just three days before. The reason, as you may have anticipated, was related to Tom. His boss had asked him if he and Sallie would have dinner with him, his wife, and one of their clients and her husband. Tom immediately called Sallie to ask her if she was free, as this was an important opportunity for him in several respects. When she reminded him that she already had plans with Liz he told her to keep the date and that there would be other opportunities like this one. But Sallie knew that in the year they had been together, this was the first time Tom's boss had included him in something like this, so she asked him again what he really wanted to do. This dinner was very important to him, he admitted, but so were Liz's feelings and Sallie's friendship with her. Being familiar with the tension they had previously, he didn't want to do something hurtful. He wanted to be supportive to their friendship. They went back and forth about it for a while, weighing the opportunity against how they thought Liz would feel. Ultimately, Sallie decided that this was too good an opportunity for Tom to pass up so she accepted the dinner invitation despite Tom's reservations. She reassured him that she would work it out with Liz.

When she first heard of the change in plans Liz was disappointed and angry. She told Sallie that she felt she should go to the concert anyway. "It's not fair," she said. "We've been planning this for over a month and I don't know if I can find anyone to use your ticket on such short notice! Can't they do this another night?" But Sallie held her ground, saying, "Tom and I talked about it and they can't. This is a chance that hasn't come his way before and he can't be sure when, if ever, it will again. I'm really sorry, but Tom needs me to do this with him. I know it's not fair, but he's got to come first this time." Sallie went on to describe the conversation she had with Tom and how he was worried about hurting Liz. She recounted how they talked about carefully weighing how important this was against how Liz might feel about it. She asked Liz to try to understand that this was an important opportunity for Tom and that Liz wanted to be supportive of him.

During the session in which Liz described this interaction, she revealed what went through her mind at that point. "I suddenly realized that the two of them had really given this some thought. They had considered my feelings—Sallie wasn't being callous. I was disappointed and frustrated, but I didn't feel invisible. I realized I had to compromise. Tom is more important to her right now, and the way things were going with them, he'd probably hold that position forever. I realized that I'd better get used to it if I wanted to stay friends with Sallie. She was being sensitive to my needs, she just couldn't give me what I wanted this time. Things can't be the way they were exactly, but what we have now I really value." Their conversation ended with Liz telling Sallie that although it was disappointing, she did understand. She asked Sallie to wish Tom good luck.

Because Liz had *expected to compromise* on what she wanted from her friend, she was not thrown off when Sallie told her that Tom had to come first right now. By focusing on what was there to be had in their friendship rather than on that which could not be had, Liz ended this conversation feeling valued by her friend. Because she realistically evaluated what Sallie had to give and stopped taking the new distance in their friendship so personally, Liz was able to mourn the old friendship and embrace the new one. Moreover, she was able to help her friend not succumb to the common pitfall of ignoring the needs of single loved ones whenever you start a new relationship.

When Your Needs Don't Count As Much

Liz's experience with her friend Sallie is one of the more obvious scenarios in which single people become invisible to coupled loved ones. But many subtle interactions between coupled and single people that result in invisibility experiences are even more common. Here are six of the worst things that coupled friends and family do to make their single loved ones feel invisible.

1. *Rarely go to your place.* When you look around your living room, it's hard to imagine what your loved one(s) would look like sitting on your sofa because whenever you get together it's always on their turf. If you suggest having dinner at your home, or just meeting there before going out, the answer is almost always negative. The implied, if not explicit, message is "Our place feels like more of a home than yours does and besides, it's easier for you to come to us than the other way around."

2. *Make unilateral decisions.* They consult each other, but not you, when deciding what you will do together when you see them and when it will happen. The date and time are almost always dictated by the couple's schedule and not yours, the implication be-

ing that their lives are busier and less flexible than yours is. From their perspective, their needs outweigh yours so they assume you won't mind if they make the decision without consulting you.

3. *Change plans with you easily.* Your coupled friend or relative cancels plans with you at the last minute because her partner has become free and she'd rather see him. Or the couple you are close to changes plans with you because another couple they are friends with can only see them during the same time they had planned with you. Once again, the implication here is that there are fewer demands on your time and your needs don't matter as much.

4. *Make love to each other in front of you.* They make love to each other, in the 1940s sense of the phrase, in your presence. She sits on his lap, they kiss deeply, or simply sing each other's praises incessantly when you are together.

5. *Split the check as if you are two.* When sharing the check with one or more couples, your share is equal to that of two people. This is a particularly good example of how difficult it can be for coupled people to understand the experience of someone single.

6. *Assume they know how you will feel.* You are not invited to dinner with your loved ones because they decided you would feel out of place as the only single person with two other couples. Or they invite someone over for you to meet even though you asked them not to. Although they are clearly attempting to be responsive to your feelings, they miss the point because they never asked you how you would feel.

Whenever you are single, you are in danger of becoming invisible to loved ones in the ways just described. It's not that your friends and family don't love you, it's that they're wearing blinders provided by the cultural mandate to marry. Adam, whom you will read about next, experienced nearly every one of the things on this list, yet was able to get himself seen by his friends once he realized what was happening.

Adam

P rior to his divorce, Adam and his ex-wife had spent every New
Year's Eve for several years with two couples they were close to.
He described the first New Year's after the breakup as "a nightmare."
Adam and his ex-wife had always invited their friends to a cabin they
rented every December in the mountains. The three couples would
spend several days together skiing, staying up late talking, and making dinners together. Adam had decided to continue the tradition, so
he invited Jack, his wife Cathy, and Dara and her husband Leo to
spend a week with him as they had done before. The two couples had
maintained their friendships with Adam after the divorce and were
delighted at the invitation. They agreed to split the cost for the rental
that weekend as they always had before.

Adam had gone skiing every weekend prior to the New Year's
gathering, and although it raised some painful memories, he was glad
that he had decided to rent the cabin again and keep the New Year's
Eve tradition alive. When the holiday weekend came he was the last
to arrive at the cabin because he could not leave work as early as his
friends.

What was normally a two-hour drive had turned into a nail-biting
four hours because it was snowing heavily. But as he turned into the
driveway, his headlights illuminated a heartwarming winter scene
that put a satisfied smile on his face. Snow was swirling around them
as Jack and Leo shoveled the steps leading up to the cabin, and, inside, the fire in the fireplace cast red and yellow ribbons of light that
glowed through the frosted window pane. He could smell the
woodsmoke when he rolled down his window and shouted a greeting
to Jack and Leo. He was happy to be there and felt he was where he
belonged.

They helped him unload his car and walked him in before return-
ing to their chore. Inside, there were hugs, kisses, and excited greet-
ings between Adam, Cathy, and Dara. While giving Cathy a hug
hello he saw that his clothing, which he had left in the master bedroom the previous weekend, was now stacked neatly in a corner of
the living room. In past years Adam and his wife had shared the master bedroom, with one couple in the guest room, and the third in the
living room on the pull-out couch. Adam asked about his clothing
and Cathy revealed that she and Jack had arrived first and figured

that since Adam was alone, he wouldn't need his own bedroom and could sleep in the living room. This would give the two couples more privacy.

Adam felt terrible. He felt invisible and that his feelings and needs weren't considered simply because he was "alone." Pulling into the driveway he had felt happy and a sense of belonging. He felt anything but alone. But now he felt angry and as if he were a "third wheel." He was in danger of sliding back into the alienation stage of being single in a couples' world.

Fortunately for Adam and his friends, he was not one to fall easily into the cycle of blame. He knew very quickly what he was feeling and because he had an open and honest relationship with Jack and Cathy, he realized he could do something constructive with his feelings. The first thing he did was go back to his car to unpack his skis and calm down. When Jack came over to help, Adam took the opportunity to tell him what he had just learned from Jack's wife and how he was feeling about it.

"Cathy told me the two of you made sleeping arrangements and that I was assigned to the couch."

"Yeah, we didn't think you would mind since you're alone. Do you?"

"Actually I do mind. What's the deal, man? I walk in and my clothes have been moved out of my room without anyone talking to me about it? I can understand your perspective, and for that matter I might even agree with it, but it really makes me mad that you guys decided this without even talking to me. Do you have any idea how this makes me feel?"

"Not very good by the look of things. We didn't mean anything by it. I guess we just didn't think it through. I'm really sorry, I'll go talk to Cathy, and we'll put your stuff back in your room."

"Wait!" Adam answered, "You're doing it again!"

"Doing what?"

"You're deciding for me. You're assuming how I feel."

"I'm not assuming anything. You're obviously feeling hurt and pissed off," Jack shot back, getting a little angry himself.

"That's not what I meant. You're assuming what it is I want to do about the bedroom situation."

Jack closed his eyes and grimaced with embarrassment, saying, "I got it . . . I really do. I'm sorry, pal. What do you want to do?"

"Thanks . . . I don't know yet. Let me think about it for a few minutes, unpack the car, have a glass of wine, then let's decide together."

When they spoke, Cathy apologized upon learning how Adam felt about what she had done. She explained that she was just trying to be efficient and honestly didn't think that Adam would mind. In fact, although he would have preferred to stay in the master bedroom as he always had, she was correct in her assumption that Adam would be willing to give it up so his friends would feel more comfortable. But it was their assumption about how he would feel, making the decision unilaterally, and placing their needs above his that were hurtful. They didn't realize it at the time, but Cathy and Jack were unwitting disciples of the marriage mandate. Because their friend was now single, his needs were naturally less important than theirs. Fortunately for everyone involved, Adam helped them to not only see him, but also the cultural script's biases about singlehood that they had adopted.

In the end, Adam offered to sleep in the living room. Although he never said this to his friends, giving up "his bedroom," as he referred to it, was a much larger sacrifice than he let on. The divorce was recent and many of the wounds were still open. He was struggling with feeling like a failure and it felt as if he was being demoted from "master" of the house to a guest in his own home. But he thought it made sense to compromise in this instance. He understood how his friends felt about sleeping in the living room. The lack of privacy made it close to impossible to make love if they wanted to and it was New Year's Eve weekend after all. When Adam felt that his friends were being responsive to his real feelings, rather than the ones they imagined he had, compromise came easier.

We have to add that Adam must have done an exceptional job at getting seen. When the weekend ended, both couples approached Adam to say that they felt the financial split on the cabin was unfair to him. They had accepted his offer to split the costs three ways as they had in years past. It never occurred to them, until the conversation about the sleeping arrangements, that this too was not fair to Adam. The irony is that Adam didn't realize the inequity himself! They further surprised him by asking if he would accept a five way split, rather than simply handing him a check. In other words, they included him in the decision-making process. Adam happily agreed to the new arrangement. As Adam told us about how the weekend ended, he grinned and said, "You gotta love friends like that!"

Below, we provide specific advice for coupled people, like Jack and Cathy, who are close to someone single. If you are single, read about the advice we give here. It will help you to teach your coupled friends and family what they can do to avoid adding to single stigma and to improve their relationship with you.

ADVICE FOR COUPLED LOVED ONES

I f you have read this far, then you already know much of what we are about to say and we know that there is a single person in your life you care for deeply. If you didn't care, you wouldn't be going to the trouble to find a way to fine tune the love you give. And that is really all that is involved, minor adjustments to the ways in which you express your love. Here, we provide you with some do's and don'ts to help sensitize you to the needs of your single loved ones. As you read through the list of "don'ts" try to imagine what it would feel like to be in your loved one's shoes. But don't be tempted by the cycle of blame. You are not to blame for these culturally sanctioned insensitivities. However, you can take responsibility for whether or not you will continue to subscribe to them.

Do's and Don'ts for Couples

Do   Socialize in their home
         Include them in your decisions
         Honor their wishes
         Check in

The first item on our list refers to a tendency for coupled people and their single loved ones to socialize in the couple's home exclusively. Oftentimes, the single person doesn't even realize the extent to which this adds to the experience of alienation. But when you are single and your loved ones never come to your home, the implicit message is that your life is somehow less important. One single woman named Terri described it this way: "I always have to go to the mountain, but the mountain never comes to me!" The coupled person's side of this issue is illustrated in a quote from Terri's friend Jenny given at the start of this chapter: "I have a husband and a daughter to think about. They have to come first. Frankly, I am exhausted at the end of the day. I have a lot more going on than she does. I wish I had Terri's life! She's responsible to no one but herself. The bottom line is . . . if she doesn't come over to my place then we usually don't see each other." Jenny has a lot of demands on her life and it would be much easier for her if whenever she and Terri got together it was at Jenny's house. But by assuming that Terri doesn't also have demands on her life, Jenny is ignoring and belittling her friend's feelings. Try to spend some time in the home of your single loved one; it doesn't have to be a fifty-fifty split to make a big difference.

The next item on our list, "include them in your decisions," refers to the kind of experience Adam had with his friends Jack and Cathy. If you are making a decision that affects a single loved one, make sure she is part of the decision-making process. The third item, "honor their wishes," refers to a tendency for loved ones to assume they know better than their single friend or relative, especially when it comes to romance. If your single loved one told you he doesn't want to be fixed up, then don't fix him up! Honor his wishes. When you don't, you undermine his self-confidence and give the message that you know better than he what it is he needs. The final item on the list, "check in," refers to the now familiar empathy check. Find out what your loved one is actually feeling rather than what you think she might be feeling. Ask the question and listen to her response before you decide you know the answer.

DON'T   Always socialize on your turf
         Make decisions for them
         Assume you know better
         Project what you would feel

The meaning of the first three "don'ts" should be obvious following our elaboration on the list of "do's." However, the last item, "don't project," warrants a little further explanation and an illustration. For that, we return briefly to Sarah, the twenty-eight-year-old travel agent we told you about earlier. A telephone conversation with her mother, upon her return from France where she had traveled for two weeks on her own, or "all alone" as her mother referred to it, left her feeling completely invisible.

"Paris was one of the most romantic places I have ever been. Everything about it was beautiful—the art, the architecture, and the food. The French are really much friendlier than most people think. It was great!"

"I am sure it was," Sarah's mother answered, "but weren't you lonely? It must have been so hard for you to be all alone in such a romantic place."

"No, not really, Besides, I wasn't 'all alone' at all! I met some other Americans in Paris and we spent a lot of time together. In fact, we spent three days together traveling through the Chateau country in the south. Tasting wine, bicycling, and tasting more wine. It was wonderful."

"Oh, that's wonderful honey, why didn't you mention it in your postcard? So you met someone. . . . Does he live near you? What does he do?"

"Oh my God, Mom! Is that all you think about. I said I met some Americans, that's plural. I didn't say I met a man."

"I'm sorry, it's none of my business if you don't want to tell me. I'm just glad you had a good time."

"You still think I met someone don't you? It was a couple I met, and yes, I had a good time. They live near me and she's a nurse and he's an engineer. OK?"

"All right, all right, I'm sorry . . . I guess I wasn't listening closely enough. I just want you to be happy."

"I am happy. At least I was until we started having this conversation!" Sarah snapped back.

"I said I was sorry—you don't need to take that tone with me. I just want you to be . . . never mind, nothing I am going to say is right. I just thought it would have been hard on you to be there all alone."

Sarah's mother was so indoctrinated into the cultural marriage script that it was practically impossible for her to hear, much less believe, that Sarah truly had a good time in France. Although Sarah did have a few moments of thinking how nice it would have been to share the romance of Paris with someone special, she was on the whole very happy and fulfilled during her trip abroad. As Sarah put it, "Sometimes you are hungry for steak and when you can't get it at that moment it doesn't mean you can't eat other things and it also doesn't mean you can't have it in the future." She had been excited and pleased with the trip and wanted to share that experience with her mother. But her mother was too busy projecting what she thought Sarah was feeling, or more precisely, what she thought Sarah *should* feel, to see the truth. The best way to guard against projecting the culture's biases onto your loved one's experience is to ask questions and listen carefully to the answers.

Sarah persevered and ultimately helped her mother to see that she had made her feel invisible. One week later, her pictures from Paris were developed and she showed them to her mother. Sarah was pleasantly surprised when her mother focused on one picture in particular saying, "This must be the couple you told me about. They look like a lot of fun. What were you all laughing at?" Her genuine interest in this couple that Sarah had enjoyed immensely, sparked an animated conversation between the two of them that left Sarah feeling not only seen, but also loved.

If you follow these do's and don'ts, you will help your loved one to feel less alienated as a single person in a couple's world. You also will avoid the common mistakes friends and family make in their well-intentioned efforts to be supportive. But even more importantly, you will improve the quality of your relationship with your single loved one. It may be a couples' world, but learning to give your single loved one what she actually needs, rather than what you think she needs, is the key to making her feel loved and a part of the world in which she lives.

Afterword

If you have read this book and practiced the guidelines and if you gave it to a coupled loved one to read, then you have undoubtedly taken charge. Now that you are no longer blind to the ways in which the culture's marriage script abhors singlehood, you have put your situation into a more realistic perspective. You are not abnormal, a "loser," or "pathetic," and you are not going to end up all alone simply because you are currently single!

If your loved ones are still following the culture's script, then you have more work to do if you want to stay connected with them. If you don't deal with the misconceptions they have about your singlehood it will lead to tension and ultimately to your avoiding spending time together. Don't be afraid to speak up, to make yourself seen and understood. And don't slip into the blame game. Remember, our culture is continuing to evolve at a rapid pace, and it's nobody's fault that the old marriage scripts have not caught up with the reality that single people face today. But it is up to all of us to insure that they get updated.

In our personal lives and in our work with our patients, we have seen the tremendous freedom and power that will come when you uncover your personal marriage script. The best way to use the knowledge you gained about yourself in the preceding pages is to talk about it with someone you're close to. The more you talk about your ideas about marriage, your experience of your first intimate relationship in life, and of your parents' marriage, the more skilled you will become at keeping the script from ruling your life.

We have one final piece of advice. Stay open to the possibilities. It's no longer necessary to persist in the belief that there is only one lifestyle worth having. So many more options are available to single men and women today than our parents ever had or could even dream of. If you are willing to take the risk, you can create a lifestyle that fulfills your unique vision. And that is what this book has been about: understanding what your dream is and realizing it in the way that works for you. Whether your vision includes a spouse, a partner, or a community of friends, when you understand and accept yourself more fully you will be more open to connection with others. You will be happier and more open to love.